P9-BVM-345

EDUCATIONAL THEORY
AND THE
PREPARATION OF TEACHERS

Educational Theory and the Preparation of Teachers

John Wilson
Department of Educational Studies, Oxford University

NFER Publishing Company Ltd

CARNEGIE LIBRARY
LIVINGSTONE COLLEGE
SALISBURY, N. C. 28144

Published by the NFER Publishing Company Ltd.
Book Division, 2 Jennings Buildings, Thames Avenue
Windsor, Berks. SL4 1QS
Registered Office: the Mere, Upton Park, Slough, Berks. SL1 2DQ
First published in 1975
© John Wilson
ISBN 85633 080 9

Typeset by Jubal Multiwrite Ltd.,
66 Loampit Vale, Lewisham SE13 7SN
Printed in Great Britain by
King, Thorne and Stace Ltd., School Road, Hove, Sussex BN3 5JE
Distributed in the USA by Humanities Press Inc.,
Hilary House—Fernhill House, Atlantic Highlands,
New Jersey 07716 USA.

370.71
W749

Educ / COB

#12.81

847

3/23/83

Contents

PREFACE   7

INTRODUCTION: SOME INITIAL DIFFICULTIES   9

PART I   EDUCATIONAL THEORY   25

Chapter 1   THE SUBJECT OF EDUCATION   27

Chapter 2   ELEMENTS OF METHODOLOGY   46

Chapter 3   PRACTICAL REQUIREMENTS AND   72
              SERIOUSNESS

PART II   THE PREPARATION OF TEACHERS   95

Chapter 4   FIRST STEPS   97

Chapter 5   'THEORY'   115

Chapter 6   'PRACTICE'   130

Chapter 7   TAXONOMIC SKETCH AND   143
              CONCLUSIONS

A NOTE ON 'MAKING SENSE' AND 'DEFINING TERMS'   174

REFERENCES   181

115489

PREFACE

This book is a modest attempt to establish some firm ground in the morasses marked by 'the study of education' or 'educational theory', and 'teacher-training' or 'teacher-education': to gain some clarity where little or none, as I believe, now exists. These are serious topics: part of my case is that not many people take them seriously, though plenty of people may seem to do so.

It is addressed not only to those (professors, directors, delegates, administrators, etc.) who are in some sense 'in charge of' institutions which deal with these areas nor only to those (lecturers, tutors, etc.) who work within such institutions, but more generally to all those who feel that these morasses ought to be drained and cultivated. Of these, students of education and intending teachers are very much in my mind: they are obliged actually to tread this ground, and have a strong personal interest in improving it. Possibly for this reason I have found their comments particularly helpful, but I must also express my thanks to many colleagues and other critics too numerous to mention individually.

J.B.W.
Oxford, 1975.

Abbreviation

PER — WILSON, J. (1972) *Philosophy and Educational Research*. Slough: National Foundation for Educational Research.

Some Initial Difficulties

Where an academic discipline or field of study is well-established, properly organized and intellectually respectable, an author who wishes to contribute to it has some kind of academic framework or tradition within which to work. He can follow the usual canons of impersonality and scholarship, of taking the reader's knowledge of the subject's literature and authorities for granted, and so forth. But this is not, as I see it, true of those areas marked by 'educational theory' and 'the preparation (training, education) of teachers'.

This generates a number of difficulties, not the least of which is that any attempt on these areas at once runs into vested interests or predetermined attitudes towards them. These attitudes are very widespread, and it would be unrealistic to ignore them completely: particularly since any progress in this field of study may be more impeded by them (or whatever lies at the roots of them) than by anything one could describe as serious *intellectual* disagreement. So I will try to say a little about them here, even though these (necessarily brief) remarks cannot do them justice, and what I say is bound to seem superficial and at times brusque, it may at least help to clear the ground and explain what I am trying to do in this book.

1. On the one hand, these areas represent what one might call major industries in our own and many other societies. They are solidly (and expensively) institutionalized, and must presumably be thought by many people to be a sound investment. Academic study within them is often guarded by a strong set of traditions and conventions, apparently designed to convey at least the impression of scholarship and intellectual respectability. Thus if this book were presented as a post-graduate thesis in 'education' − the kind of thing I have currently to supervise in my present job at Oxford − I should be expected to

collate 'definitions of education', 'aims and objectives of teacher-education', and the views of 'leading educationalists'; to show full understanding of 'the literature' and 'the authorities'; and to generate enough footnotes, appendices and bibliographies to convey an impression of scholarship. But one might well believe that most of 'the literature' is, in fact, hopelessly muddled and often unintelligible, riddled with doubtful assumptions and jargon-defended theories; the product, it might appear, more of fashion and fantasy than of any real concern for truth. One might even believe that it was not clear whether there *were* any 'authorities', or at least that it was not clear *who* they were. That is, in fact, my own view, but it can hardly represent the attitude of those many people who man the industry — the professors of education, directors, principals, lecturers and so on — nor, one might naturally suppose, of those in government departments or elsewhere who are responsible for financing it.

It would be naive, however, to suppose that all or even many people in these positions *seriously believed* (as against acting as if they believed) that this whole apparatus was intellectually satisfactory as it stood. The attitude here described is more evident as an implication of practice than as any set of propositions, and for any individual it may fluctuate wildly depending on the particular context in which that individual is asked to give his opinion. For instance, in many Departments (Faculties, Colleges, etc.) of Education plenty of people can be found who will, in private, admit to the view that a great deal of educational theory is both intellectual rubbish and irrelevant to practical teaching, but who stand up for it in public and may even write books and articles which suggest their deference to it. More often, I guess (it would be interesting to *know*), they have simply accepted the existing traditions, if one may so call them, of educational theory: the three or four institutionalized 'disciplines of education' (philosophy, psychology, sociology, history), the 'names' and 'authorities', the supposed 'research findings', and so forth. By 'accepted' I do not mean that, knowing which side their bread is buttered, they are content to play along with the tradition; that, if pusillanimous, might at least be more clear-headed. Rather, I suspect, they accept it out of deference or inertia or lack of critical enthusiasm, just because it is there and it is not easy to think of what to do instead. This calls for sympathy, rather than contempt: it is indeed not easy, and such a posture is certainly less tiresome than that of various groups, whether of the 'left' or of the 'right', who abandon serious thinking in favour of advancing some semi-political movement.

There are other people again, who take the view that some or perhaps a lot of educational theory and teacher-training is sound, even if a lot or some is not; that some solid ground has been gained, even if much remains to be won. Such a view sounds comfortingly balanced or judicious, but (I am persuaded) is in fact more deeply rooted in error than almost any other. For the impression conveyed, or the background assumption, is that we already possess a satisfactory methodology for the study of education; all the more satisfactory and reputable, as it appears on this view, in that we can readily distinguish between 'solid ground' or 'certain knowledge gained' on the one hand and unknown territory on the other. I shall take the view that it is not so: that 'educationalists' are in the un-Socratic position of not even knowing their (our) own ignorance.

Naturally this does not imply that all educational theorists are stupid, or that they have not said a lot of sensible things, or that *some* knowledge (of whatever kind is appropriate to the subject of education) has not been gained; after all, a large number of people, including some of at least moderate intelligence, are in the business. It implies only that, because we are not clear how to operate in this area, we cannot be sure *which* theorists are to be listened to, or what things are really sensible, or what to count as knowledge rather than as just guesswork or muddle. A sort of parallel exists in the pre-scientific period of alchemy: amidst a vast quantity of fantasy and superstition, intelligent men were working and interesting things being done — but, for lack of a clear idea and tradition of doing science, they would then have been difficult or impossible to identify.

I cannot in this book undertake to show fully the degree and extent of our ignorance and confusion. I have tried to do this elsewhere[1] with particular reference to some aspects of educational research, and there is, I think, enough literature to raise these basic doubts in the mind of any intelligent and critical person. Anyone who has entered these waters (with or without philosophical help) can hardly have avoided noticing many fundamental disagreements. When, for instance, a leading and level-headed philosopher who is also well up in psychology and 'learning theory' is prepared to say, 'I do not see how it is possible to say anything both significant and general about human learning processes,'[2] it is surely time to worry. There are too many other examples of such doubts to dismiss;[3] and I shall take it for granted in this book (since there is not time or space to cover all the ground) that these doubts *may*, at least, be justified. If any reader is entrenched enough to write them off as 'irrelevant', or 'only interesting to philosophers' (or, worse, 'Oxford philosophers'), this book is not for him.

The same holds for the training (education, preparation, etc.) of teachers, which may obviously be connected (though it is not clear how) with educational theory. Indeed the prejudices and fantasies here are, if anything, still more apparent. Irrational reactions in this field, however, tend to be somewhat different: people are sometimes more specifically disenchanted with teacher-training than with educational theory, perhaps because the former has a more easily visible 'end product' — good or competent teachers — whereas it is not even clear in general terms what the 'end product' of educational theory is supposed to *be*. Generally speaking, the reaction (at the time of writing) is in favour of being more 'practical' and creating the impression of more down-to-earth activity: spending more time in schools, having 'work-shops' instead of seminars or lectures, rushing around on visits to places where 'lively' or 'stimulating' work is being done, and so on.

In some quarters this amounts to a virtual confession of intellectual bankruptcy; perhaps most evident in a tendency to move away from the whole idea of *examining* student-teachers, at least by traditional methods. A trivial example: I once heard a director of an institution for teacher-training, within a respectable university, press for the abolition of any written examination at the end of a one-year post-graduate course. It was unclear whether his reason was (a) that intending teachers did not need to know anything, or display any form of understanding, that could best be assessed in this way; or (b) that, although there might be such things, it would be too much like hard work to determine what they were — so that, since we were all in a muddle about it, the easiest thing would be simply not to have any examinations at all. Of these, (a) is clearly implausible, and (b) hardly to be taken seriously. It looks very much as if even the most capable and well-placed people are so alarmed by the difficulties of making intellectual sense of teacher-training, or so impatient of the labour involved, that they prefer to try and bypass the whole operation.

As with educational theory, the only honest attitude towards the preparation of teachers at present is something like, 'We're not clear what we ought to do, and we had better try to get clear'. Naturally some of this process may involve practical activity, in the sense of trial-and-error experiments of one kind or another, but clearly a lot of it will involve hard thinking, if only because we are not clear what *counts* as error, or what sorts of trials to make for what purposes. Nothing is easier than *doing* things in education; the difficulty is to know how to determine whether what is done is *correct*. There is perhaps a fantasy here that, if we only try enough experiments and make enough changes (based on some uncritically-accepted idea, such as 'less theory', or 'more practical experience'), we shall somehow light intuitively on the right answers. But what in fact we shall light on is what happens to suit our particular temperaments, or the political climate, or what is popular with students, or what seems to 'go well' in the general sense of everyone feeling vaguely that they have learned something, or 'participated', or been 'active' — very much, in fact, like what happens in many contemporary schools. There are 'right answers', or at least more clarity, to be gained for the preparation of teachers, but it will not be gained thus — if only because the 'end product' is by no means as clear as we sometimes think.

2. On the other hand, there are also a great many people — not only academics who profess a reputable and well-established discipline, but also men of ordinary common sense and critical ability — who take the view that what goes on under 'educational theory' is irredeemable rubbish. Only half of this view is correct: it is indeed (mostly) rubbish, but it is not irredeemable. A more or less similar group of people might hold that 'teacher-training' (or, if they have caught up with the latest terminology, 'teacher-education') is a waste of time; perhaps that one cannot really train teachers at all. Again, only half of this is right: most 'teacher-training' *is* a waste of time, but it does not have to be.

Here too it is difficult to know whether we are dealing with anything that could count as serious belief. If someone were to advance the view that there was some *a priori* reason why education could not be studied theoretically, or why teachers could not be effectively prepared, it would be hard to understand him; just as it is hard to know what could be meant by the sceptical question 'But is education a *subject*?' Whatever phenomena the word 'education' may demarcate, clearly these phenomena can be studied, and this (surely necessary) truth is sufficient for us to use 'education' either as referring to these phenomena — the *subiecta* or subject-matter of study — or as a title for the study itself, just as we use 'history' either to refer to the past deeds of men or to our study of such deeds. It may not consist of a single, logically *sui generis*, discipline, but then neither do subjects marked by, say, 'classics' or 'English'. Even if most actual or existing 'educational theory' is rather like astrology — largely fantasy-based — it would not follow that one could not reputably study education, any more than that one could not reputably study the stars.

One common variant or form of this attitude is that education is too 'practical' a thing to make an 'academic' subject out of;[4] it is seen, perhaps, as something one just *does*, not something to write books or run courses or have theories about. But in its own way this is equally hard to understand. Certainly the word suggests *some* things which remind one of a practical *techne* (art, science, enterprise) like cooking or swimming, but it also suggests *other* dimensions which one might, as a sighting shot, describe as 'theoretical'. One would need a lot of heavy argument before accepting the view that the kind of inquiry which (for instance) Plato pursues in much of the *Republic* was a waste of time, or misconceived, or not properly to be described as the study of education. Secondly, even if the term did mark a practical *techne*, why should it be thought that such *technai* could not be profitably studied in an academic way? Literary criticism may still be a respectable subject, even if we construe 'literature' or 'writing' as essentially practical, and history is not disqualified from its status as an academic discipline because it inquires into practical action.

Rather than chase these hares further, we may rest content with the view that there is no clear *a priori* case against the study of education. I suspect that, in practice, the most influential attitude is of a fairly general kind. The thought is perhaps 'Nothing very intelligent/ scholarly/interesting/academically reputable has been said so far. If and when it is, we might take it seriously, but until then, why should we?' Whether or not such an attitude is justified — and confronting *this* question seriously might pose individuals some quite complicated moral problems — the trouble with it is that it merely strengthens the vicious circle. As I shall argue more fully later, it is precisely at the first (methodological) stages that the subject of education needs to be taken seriously. To 'wait until something intelligent (scholarly, etc.) is done' amounts to abandoning it altogether. It is rather like saying that one will wait until a child does something intelligent, or at least asks for help in a coherent way, when one knows perfectly well that the child is too young and incoherent to make the first move. This is, I think, not a serious attitude.

Equally and perhaps more obviously non-serious is the idea that education is a free-for-all. Many people accept (often rather too quickly) the view that not much has been achieved in these areas to date, but seem content to draw the conclusion that, since little or nothing is definitely known or established, there is little or no homework to do. If one is often disappointed when reading the literature produced by the current orthodoxies and the 'professionals' in educational theory, it is certainly far more boring to read or listen to pronouncements 'about education' made by amateurs who, however eminent, have demonstrably failed to take the literature seriously at all. Almost every day some person — perhaps a vice-chancellor, a well-known professor in some other subject, a peer, a politician, an *éminence grise* or just a 'personality' popular with the mass media — is reported as making some such pronouncement; even reputable philosophers are, I fear, not totally immune.

The only use of such amateur pronouncements, as far as I can see, is that they make suitable passages for criticism to set to first-year students of education. Education, perhaps particularly nowadays, is of course a tempting arena for anybody to step into; rather as, for some reason, it is (or used to be) popular for elderly and eminent scientists to pronounce about ethics or society or religion or life or whatever. The point here is not that one wishes to preserve a trades union type of demarcation of disciplines: it is, as I have said, just that these people have not done their homework. For example, whatever may be thought of the work and writings of Richard Peters and Paul Hirst,[5] amongst others, they clearly have at least to be read, understood and (so to speak) *faced* by any genuine truth-seeker in this field. If somebody claimed to be a serious student but had taken no account of this work, I should not understand his claim. It is certainly the most sustained and intellectually coherent effort to make sense of the subject of education that we have seen over the last few decades.

As this example indeed shows, I am not of course denying that it is possible for serious scholars to contribute usefully; but it is, in practice, not easy for them to do so simply *ex vi ingenii* if they stand too far apart from these (admittedly chaotic) areas. There are two connected reasons for this. First, they are likely to underestimate the intellectual complexity of the areas, which is far greater than that of any single discipline, and hence requires a kind of methodological or conceptual competence very different from the competence implied by 'a first-rate historian (scientist, sociologist, etc.)'. Educational problems will yield neither to well-meaning 'educationalists' who possess little competence in any discipline, nor to the *ad hoc* performances of scholars or disciplinary experts however able; the position is far more complicated than this, and it is naive to suppose otherwise. Secondly, it is difficult or impossible even to *identify* problems as *educational* problems without some practical experience in schools or other educational institutions; there is a temptation to hive aspects of them off too quickly under some single discipline, which is methodologically disastrous. I shall have more to say about these difficulties later.[6]

3. The effect of the attitudes in 1 and 2 above, which may be (briefly if rather unfairly) summarized as (1) everything is more or less all right as it is, and (2) the whole thing is intellectually absurd, emerges very clearly in examinations set to students of education – including, of course, teachers. A few examples may help us to get the feel of the current situation. Here are some questions taken more or less at random from examinations set for master's degrees, one- and three-year courses, and so on:

(i)   What measures might be devised to test the efficiency of a school system?
(ii) How may one account for individual differences in creative talent?
(iii) Estimate the importance of Illich's view that society should be 'de-schooled'.

(iv) Distinguish curriculum evaluation from the assessment of pupils' progress.

(v) In what ways have school examinations been improved in the U.K. over the last fifteen years?

(vi) What is the value of Bloom's taxonomy of educational objectives?

Now there are, in effect, only two approaches one could adopt to such questions. The first (probably necessary if one actually wanted to *pass* the examination) would involve *taking for granted* a great deal that ought, strictly, not to be so taken. One would have to assume, for instance, that notions like 'efficiency', 'creative talent', 'curriculum evaluation', etc. were clear and intelligible, and then go on to display some adequate knowledge of the psychological and other work done in these areas. One would also have to assume that the work of the 'authorities' mentioned — here, Illich and Bloom, but one could add plenty of others (Bernstein, Piaget, Bruner, etc.) — was worth taking seriously; to answer with the single word 'None' for question (vi) would not get many marks. Here one might often wonder whether one was being asked, as a kind of sociological question, whether (for instance) Illich was 'important' in the sense of 'influential', or whether one was meant to talk about whether his views were right (or even coherent); and in fact one would have to try to forget about this distinction as far as possible.

The other approach would be more intellectually respectable, but would clearly involve starting from scratch. What are we to mean by 'the efficiency of a school system', 'creative talent', 'curriculum evaluation', and so on? What is to count as a *curriculum* anyway? What are 'school examinations' supposed to be *for*? What *kind* of thing could a 'taxonomy of educational objectives' be? These questions must, obviously, be satisfactorily answered first, and it is hard to see how one could both answer them and still have time to talk about what the examination clearly wants one to talk about — actual measures devised to test 'efficiency', psychological work on 'divergent thinking' (whatever that is), Illich, what is in fact done under the heading of 'curriculum evaluation', the practical changes in school examining over the last fifteen years, Bloom, and so on. Somebody who wanted to tackle the questions in a serious way might very well come to regard the whole thing as impossible.

It would, of course, be at least a step towards respectability if such questions were divided into two basic types. If we felt it essential for students to *know about* certain things — though I shall argue later that there are very few such things, and that it is not at all clear what they are — then we could, I suppose, ask questions of a straightforwardly factual (non-critical) kind, like 'Summarize Piaget's work on stages of development' or 'Trace the changes in the public examination system in the UK over the last fifteen years', followed by quite different questions like 'What sense does the notion of a "stage of development" make?' or 'Why do we need examinations?' To take a more plausible case, we might at least think that intending teachers should know something about what most UK schools were like today; so that, having given them lectures or reading lists about this, we could then ask them strictly factual questions. We could then *also* raise questions, which would have to be firmly distinguished from these, about whether schools *ought* to be 'comprehensive', or 'serve the local community', or whatever — very difficult questions, which would involve looking very hard at the concepts and arguments involved.

Even this is not done, because there is a tacit presumption that the subject is respectable. In a respectable subject like science, for instance, we can reasonably set questions like 'What is the importance of Einstein's theory of general relativity?', or in philosophy 'Estimate the validity of Kant's views on moral motivation', because we know what disciplines we are concerned with and know that Einstein and Kant are intellectually important exponents of them. Further, we are not called upon to discuss the 'influence' or social 'importance' of Einstein's and Kant's work, and we thereby avoid the pressure to reduce all questions to sociological ones — a pressure which is very evident in education, partly because there is no *other* clearly-demarcated disciplinary ground on which to stand. This is why the examinee is reduced, in effect, to trotting out his knowledge of the approved 'authorities' and the ongoing work in education which has miasmically established itself as 'important'; not, indeed, being forcibly prevented from criticising it, but being given no kind of lead or incentive for tackling the questions seriously, no adequate intellectual framework within which to operate.

This imparts a nightmarish quality to the whole proceeding, enhanced by the avidness with which educationalists (perhaps from a semi-conscious desire to gain respectability at all costs) are prepared to throw in any well-known theories or theorists that seem even tangentially relevant. Students are told to read, understand, and see the 'educational implications' not only of Piaget, Bruner and a few other more likely thinkers, but also (I again take some names at random from various lists) Kuhn, Popper, Chomsky, Durkheim, Gagné, Wittgenstein, Bernstein and many others, not to mention transient pseudo-sages like Illich. Even if all of these were readable, intelligible, and clearly relevant to education, it would be an enormous task to relate them to educational problems in an intellectually coherent and practically useful way; a task which, I shall argue, we have not even begun to accomplish.

All this clearly shows the bankrupt state of the subject. But this does not mean that we have no proper subject-matter to study or examine — that 'education' is an improper subject-title: it means only that we are not clear about what it is or how to do it. The point does not lie in detailed objections to particular aspects of courses or examinations, as if educationalists needed to 'sharpen up their thinking a bit' or 'set questions in a clearer form'. It is rather that they find themselves *landed*, so to speak, with the subject in its present intellectually intolerable (and pragmatically useless) state; and have not yet found the nerve, seriousness, time and encouragement to take the difficult and radical steps required to reflect on it and put it on a proper basis.

4. It is very important to be fully aware of our intellectual bankruptcy in these areas, if we are to have any hope of doing better; but I want also to stress the way in which these feeble-minded and uncritical attitudes affect our practical operations and day-to-day procedures. If one spends some time sitting in on practical contexts of discussion — a committee-meeting about some new research enterprise, a working-party about new courses in teacher-education, or whatever — one can pin down with slightly more precision various assumptions or implications which underlie most of the talk that goes on. Some of these are fairly predictable, though vague; they seem to add up to the ideas:

(1) That the enterprise's constituents and objectives (for instance, the researcher's interests) can fairly be described as *educational* — rather than, say, 'social', 'political', or whatever;
(2) That the work lies for the most part in areas described as 'psychology' and 'sociology';
(3) That the criteria both of (a) what is to count as an important or worthwhile enterprise, and of (b) what is to count as success (or improvement, or a proper solution), are to be taken from 'society', 'the needs of the age', 'a general consensus', 'what people (teachers) feel worried about', etc.;
(4) That we possess, or at least can clearly conceptualize, both (a) a satisfactory methodology and procedure for the enterprise, and (b) a satisfactory social working context in which to operate this procedure;
(5) That we can make sensible plans, and engage in the necessary politics and public relations, *before* reaching intellectual clarity and agreement about (1) — (4) above.

All these implications are, in my judgement, nearly always entirely and disastrously wrong. The last three are straightforwardly so: (3) assumes that 'society' or 'a consensus' is to set the standards for work in these fields, a position both intellectually absurd and practically dangerous; (4) assumes that we know how to do business, when clearly we do not; (5) assumes that we can sensibly plan a political or structural framework before we know what it is supposed to support. The other two assumptions are in practice nearly always false, since (1) a great deal done under the term 'education' does *not* merit that description, and (2) what currently passes under the headings 'psychology' and 'sociology' is very often *not* of central importance for this sort of work.

It will readily be seen that, in order to make good these brusquely stated points in this book, I shall need to make some severe and fundamental criticism of what goes on. Much of what I have to say will not, I fear, be popular in some circles. It is not (I think) so much that many people will positively disagree with the propositions advanced – that, indeed, might lead to a fruitful dialectic – but rather that many will see them as too 'philosophical', 'abstract', or 'general': perhaps as not sufficiently 'down to earth' or 'practical'. Underlying my whole case is the belief that we are in an appalling muddle about the whole business; and when I say this, I do *not* mean that it is 'philosophically' untidy, or that it would be nice to think about some very basic general questions on the side (as it were) while we 'got on with something useful', or that a good deal of educational study 'needs new directions', or that 'it is good for us to have some stiff philosophical criticism sometimes', or anything of that kind. I mean, as I have tried to suggest already, that we are really in a hopeless muddle or mess: a mess which it is our first duty to sort out for *practical* (not just 'philosophical') purposes, and which has to be sorted out *before* we can entertain much hope of doing anything sensible.

Some people have a curious picture, which acts as an effective defence-mechanism, whereby these 'abstract' ('basic', 'philosophical', 'general') questions can be put into a separate compartment and occasionally brought out and aired: 'After all, the philosopher has something to contribute', 'We really ought to spend *some* time discussing "basic issues" ', and so on. On this view we are to carry on, more or less as before though perhaps with some new ideas or 'initiatives' or other *ad hoc* excitements, as if we already knew what we were doing – or at least, knew enough about what we were doing to know that it is sensible. The idea is that we should spend most of our time and effort carrying on in this way, sometimes taking a look at the 'philosophy' or 'methodology' of what we are doing *pari passu* with doing it, but not needing to get properly clear before we start.[7]

It is this general idea, I think, which permits people to make the five assumptions mentioned above. There are of course certain situations to which this is appropriate; and it may be that there is an unconscious assimilation of these educational enterprises to such situations. For instance, if (a) we are already clear about the objectives and 'goods' that define our field, as on the whole we are clear about medicine and its correlative 'good' of health, then we may not need to put in much conceptual work on what counts as success: but 'education' is not in this position — it is more like 'mental health' or 'social welfare', where we are not at all clear about what is to count as success under these headings. If (b) we have already established a satisfactory methodology, as perhaps with those inquiries which we broadly entitle 'science' or 'history', for instance, then again what 'philosophers of science (history)' have to say can usually be safely compartmentalized while the actual scientists and historians carry on; but, again, the subject of education is not in this fortunate position. Finally, if (c) we are engaged in a strictly practical enterprise which more or less *has* to be carried on, like the Queen's government, then of course we cannot wait until we have successfully concluded some second-order enquiry (perhaps 'political theory'): we have to go on governing somehow. But the enterprises relevant to this book are not of that kind. We do not *have* to engage in research and development projects, countless working parties and conferences, courses in educational theory, or even in 'teacher-education', in the way that we do have, in practice, to educate our children somehow.

Of course there is a sense in which we are obliged to *try* to put these exercises on a proper basis, as I shall be trying to do in this book. Similarly of course it is true that, if one finds oneself in a position of responsibility in some organization (institution, exercise) concerned with educational theory or teacher-education or whatever, one has to do *something* in this position. But my point is precisely that the most practically useful thing to do is to try to make sense of the exercise, rather than just 'carry on'. This involves an immense amount of sheer hard thinking and arguing — a quite different matter from creating the impression of activity and progress by committee meetings, new courses, and so forth.

What is lacking here is a certain intellectual and moral seriousness; a notion which in a way runs throughout this book, and which I shall describe in more detail later.[8] It is not that we are insufficiently earnest, or hard-working, or active, or intelligent; it is rather that we do not take the rational basis of what we are doing, or trying to do, seriously enough. Yet we know quite well, in our saner moments, that other kinds of activity (however desirable) cannot by themselves deliver the goods we need. For instance, some suppose that the study of education will flourish if we can persuade a number of well-known scholars in other disciplines, or senior academics in general, to take an interest in it and lend their names to it; yet we also know that part-time injections of this kind of ichor cannot be an effective substitute for full-time and properly-coordinated engagement in an immensely complex field. Again, in some places professors, departments, research projects and other enterprises are multiplied *praeter* any plausible *necessitatem*; but the results of this over the last few decades seem to have increased the jungle rather than cleared it.

The truth is that we do not possess a clear view, or an effective methodology (either theoretical or practical), in these areas, and it is no good trying to pretend otherwise. We have thus to face the probability that much of what we now do is either time-wasting or positively bad, and that what we may (after inadequate reflection) feel inclined to do by way of change might be no better; indeed, might be more likely to echo fashion or political advantage rather than perceived truth. It is certainly arguable, and in my judgement likely to be true, that until then we would do better to follow our noses, and our common sense, than to delude ourselves and our students with pseudo-exercises of this kind. If someone were to advance the view that these exercises, as conducted over the last few decades, have in fact left parents, teachers, pupils and practical education in general no better off than they were before, I think it would be hard to disprove. To go back to what I said earlier: we have to take seriously the view that most of what we do is, at least, more like alchemy, or astrology, or some other form of fantasy and superstition than we like to believe.

5. In such a situation, the only sensible thing to do is to go back to the beginning and see if we can establish and agree on at least some solid ground. In Part 1, we shall look first at what it is to study or otherwise engage academically in *education* (Chapter 1); then at the muddle commonly termed 'educational theory', to see if we can get at least the glimmerings of a sensible methodology (Chapter 2); and then at the practical or operational moves needed to make such a methodology viable in practice (Chapter 3). The force of whatever points I succeed in establishing in Part 1 should carry over, obviously enough, into Part 2 — the area I have called 'the preparation of teachers' (more usually referred to as 'teacher-training' of 'teacher-education', but finding proper descriptions is one of the many problems here). For it is not very daring to suggest that teachers should be prepared with a view to their purveying education. In this Part, after clearing the ground in a few first steps (Chapter 4), we shall be concerned with the aspects of teacher-preparation normally called 'theory' and 'practice' (Chapters 5 and 6), and end by attempting some kind of taxonomy or set of categories intended to put the preparation of teachers on a firmer logical basis, together with some practical suggestions.

All this is appallingly difficult, and at the risk of being tedious I shall try to go cautiously, hanging on to what is clear even if unexciting. So far as possible, I want to avoid complex philosophical questions; if we have to have a name for the whole business, 'methodology' is perhaps less misleading than most. If there is one point which I want to get across rather than any other, it is that the study of education and teacher-training is *extremely difficult*. It raises problems not only in a very large number of disciplines, but also in areas which no discipline has even looked at seriously. Behind these problems lies the central difficulty of setting up a context of communicaion or work which is both logically and empirically adequate; I shall have a good deal to say about this later,[9] because without it there is (I believe) not much hope of progress.

There could be a temptation here to attempt some massive work calling for adjectives like 'definitive' or 'comprehensive' — as if one could somehow settle the hash of these topics in detail. But such adjectives operate in a dimension inappropriate to the prevailing chaos. In the present state of the subject, what we need is more initial clarity and agreement; not works of giant pseudo-scholarship. It is not even clear what a 'definitive' work would look like; certainly it would involve, for instance, a full understanding of the logic and relevance of studies now labelled 'psychology' and 'sociology'; also of 'curriculum theory', 'training in social skills', 'the philosophy of education', and a large number of other matters: some of which are still very hot potatoes in the philosophy of mind and other areas, and others of which have not yet even attracted the attention of serious philosophers. I would have said that only a megalomaniac could try to produce a book which was both scholarly and comprehensive in this area, were it not that this has actually been attempted by authors whose sanity I have (otherwise) no reason to doubt.

It is, indeed, pretty bold to think that one has something useful to say about all this: in fact it is dangerous and absurd, in the present state of our knowledge, to suppose that we are any further advanced than we actually are. Almost nothing is *known* about education, however much is claimed; and though I feel tolerably confident about the truth of the claims I shall be making here,I feel much more confident in maintaining that this is the level at which much more work needs to be done. If educators spent far more of their time in hard and sustained arguments at this level, instead of wasting it on enterprises which look more 'practical' or 'down-to-earth' but are in fact largely based on fashion or fantasy, I should be quite happy even though my particular judgements were thereby shown to be false. This sort of work (as I shall argue)[10] is suitable not only for experienced 'educationalists' but also for beginners; professors of education and first-year students are in the same boat, and I should welcome the use of this book as an introduction to the study of education for students of all kinds.

Finally, a word about style. It is, on my view, no accident that many academic writers on education adopt a style which appears highly 'professional' or 'scholarly' — extreme impersonality, a mass of technical and jargon terms, quantities of footnotes and references, and so forth. This acts as a kind of autistic defence against serious consideration of the possibility that *the whole thing* may suffer from unnoticed but quite devastating weaknesses right at the foundations; the possibility, in other words, that we have as yet nothing to be 'professional' or 'scholarly' *about*. If this is so, the reader will forgive me for not following suit. Insofar as the concept marked by 'scholarship' is applicable at all to such a situation, it should chiefly include such notions as clarity, intolerance of nonsense and confusion, and some attempt to make progress of a reasonably solid kind. Such aims, and such a conception of the subject, are no less bold than those which seem to pervade most 'professional' educational literature, but they are, I think, at least more appropriate.

Notes

1 PER, *passim.*

2 Hamlyn in Peters (1973), p. 186.

3 Among the earliest are Peters (1958) and Winch (1958); see also Mischel (1971), (1974), Hirst (1967), Harré and Secord (1972), and many others.

4 Mary Warnock, for instance, says flatly (Peters (1973), p. 112) that 'in this particular field there is no such thing as proof . . . The whole subject of education is practical'. I am sure there are clear and important things to be said along these lines, but as they stand these remarks seem wholly mysterious. (I mean, if someone said that one couldn't *prove* that some ways of teaching French were better than others, or that trying to get philosophically clear about what it meant to be 'educated in morality' was a *practical* matter, or that these issues were not part of the study of *education*, I think we should say that such a person did not know what these words meant.)

5 See references.

6 Chapters 2 and 3.

7 Most people in the education business are to some degree afflicted with these ideas; or at least have an insecure grasp of the nature of the conceptual inquiry or 'philosophising' (if we must call it that) which is necessary. Of course this is not their fault, in any simple sense; and philosophers have not perhaps done as much as they could to explain its nature and necessity. But without at least some willingness

to understand and take it seriously, progress is virtually impossible. For this reason I have added a Note (p. 174 ff.) which some readers may find it useful to consult at this stage.

   8 p. 86 ff.
   9 Chapter 3.
  10 p. 123 ff.

Part One

Educational Theory

Chapter One

The Subject of Education

It seems entirely obvious, and indeed rather boring, to say that we ought to start by considering what phenomena we are going to demarcate by 'education' before we sit down and study it or have 'theories' of it. Considerably less boring, however, if more depressing, is the realization of how people in the business actually stand in relation to any such procedure. This forms a striking example, indeed almost a model case, of what has in practice to be contended with if we wish to achieve any sort of respectability for 'education' as a subject.

On the one hand, we have an enormous quantity of literature from Plato onwards which is (roughly speaking) 'about education' in general. The bulk of this uses the substantive mode, in which authors try to penetrate the 'true nature' of education or — more usually — to advance some particular educational ideas of their own, often connected with some more general philosophical position or 'doctrine of man'. More recently there has been a lot of work in the formal or linguistic mode, by way of 'analysing the concept of' (or, worse, 'the word') 'education'. Whatever the merits or demerits of particular pieces of work along either of these lines, it seems pretty clear that they have not to date succeeded in winning any publicly-accepted answer to the question 'What ground are we going to allow "education" to cover, at least for the purposes of studying it, or having theories of it, or appointing professors of it'?

It could be argued that this lack of success is due either to the incompetence of those doing the work, or to the inattention and stupidity of the audience; that is, either they have not given a proper answer or it has not been listened to. A bit more subtly, it might be argued that the task is impossible, since any answer would be 'contestable', 'culture-bound', 'relative', 'value-dependent' or in some way up for grabs (an argument which I shall try to show later to be misguided). But it is, I think, at least possible to claim that it is not *this* (fairly practical) question which authors have usually addressed. They have characteristically talked of 'the aims', 'the nature', 'the purpose' or 'the concept' of education, and arguably this sort of talk is, in widely different styles, too high-minded to get the kind of working agreement we need.

On the other hand, we find the vast bulk of educational researchers (professors, lecturers, tutors, etc.) carrying on as if the question did not have to be answered at all, or as if only 'philosophers' needed to be interested in the answer. This is true not only in the general case – that is, how we are to specify 'education' – but also, as I have pointed out at length elsewhere,[1] in almost all particular cases, e.g. an almost total lack of interest among empirical workers as to what is to *count as* 'intelligence', 'altruism', 'prejudice', 'learning English', and so on.

It will be worth our while exemplifying this, in order to see what happens when the required strategy is neglected. Perhaps the best-known contemporary work about the study of education,[2] which stands as parent-volume to the best-known series, contains contributions from six of the most reputable professors of education in the UK. Of these, the editor[3] and the author of the first article (on 'Educational Theory')[4] make no attempt to say what they mean by 'education' at all; the philosopher devotes two or three pages to what he chooses to describe as 'the' concept of education;[5] the historian is content to say only that 'Education is a social function';[6] the psychologist has a few remarks on 'the nature of educational thought when it assumes the form of the personal'[7] ('The study of education is concerned with the ways in which we come to be constituted by, and come to constitute ourselves through, our relations with others'); the sociologist has a lot to tell us about what 'sociologists of education are interested in',[8] but about education says only that 'the focus of all educational efforts is the acquisition of knowledge, skills, and ways of behaving by individuals'.[9]

Unsurprisingly, the book hardly hangs together. A critical reader, faced with such a title – *The Study of Education* – will first of all want to know just *what* these writers purport to be studying. Of course this comes to the surface as each writer tells us what he, or his discipline, is in fact interested in. But in this sense what each is interested in seems to be very different: it is palpably *not* the case that they are all concerned with the same ('educational') problems, and 'bring different disciplines to bear' on them in any coherent manner. Quite obviously we are presented, whether deliberately or not, with a picture which reflects a certain institutionalized set-up, in which 'sociologists of education' do so-and-so, 'historians of education' such-and-such, and so on. This in itself is not without interest, and does not prevent several of the articles from doing rather more than this: I am not trying to say that it is a 'bad book'. But it leaves our basic problem quite unscathed.

Pursuing this a bit further, we can see that at least some of the difficulties of dealing with the problem are in an important sense wholly *practical*. It is not to be believed that these authors are unaware of this incoherence, or think it totally unimportant; certainly this cannot be true of the philosophical contributors, since they have more than compensated elsewhere by working out a particular concept of education on which, one supposes, the study of education ought in their view to be based.[10] But consider the practical difficulties of obtaining coherence. Not only should we first have to get, presumably from philosophers, some clear idea of what ground 'education' should cover; we should then have to ensure that other contributors understood this and agreed to it; and these contributors would then have to tailor their contributions to fit this ground. All this presupposes a degree of communication, goodwill and methodological sophistication which is hard to get.[11] I shall have a good deal more to say about these difficulties later.

We find what we should expect in such a situation: that those engaged in the study of education simply carry on doing whatever their own interests or the demands of their disciplines (or of 'society') suggest to them. Changes of direction come from changes in these interests and demands, not from any determined attempt to study education as such (whatever we are going to mean by this). One result of this, or at least a correlative of it, is a very general notion of education which is permissive to the point of lunacy. Thus one historian of education quotes Durkheim's description of education as simply 'the influence exercised by adult generations on those that are not yet ready for social life', and adds that 'this is in some respects *more* limiting than the views held by some present-day historians of education.[12] Examples would be boring to multiply; the line is that more or less anything that happens to children, perhaps even to people in general, can count as education (or even, nowadays, as part of 'the curriculum'). Now of course all of us (even sociologists) know perfectly well that we should *not* use 'educate' or 'education' of any and every 'influence' on children. But this is conveniently forgotten, for all sorts of conscious and unconscious reasons, among which, it is tempting to say, may figure the thought that if we *did* take the problem seriously we should be involved in a great deal of hard work and a long struggle towards clarity.

It is not clear that many professional 'educationalists' fully understand or accept that the business of defining an area ('education') is one in which philosophers have, at least, the right to be taken seriously; not, of course, the right to dictate, but perhaps the right to be seen as having some kind of expertise. This has to be said, simply because little progress can in practice be made in this business unless those who take it seriously are listened to. Of course it does not much matter whether such people are *called* 'philosophers' or not; what matters is the desire for clarity and precision, respect for language, and seriousness about saying what one means. Some contemporary philosophers — notably Richard Peters — have, in fact, made many of the points that need making here, and much of what I have to say owes a considerable debt to them. Nevertheless, there are reasons why this ground has to be covered in a different way.

One such reason is (so to speak) strategic. The concept of education advanced by these philosophers is fairly complex and highly specialized; whatever its merits, it is clear that many people 'in education' either do not understand it or do not accept it. For our particular purposes, it may be better to try for a more general agreement at a lower level of conceptual sophistication. Secondly, and more importantly, I think that serious doubts can be raised about this concept, or at least about its presentation in most of the current philosophical literature.[13] To investigate these here would be far too long a job: it would involve, amongst other things, a very close inspection of the *kinds* of arguments used.[14] Sometimes these appear as 'linguistic', 'conceptual', or 'transcendental' arguments — whatever such terms may mean; sometimes authors admit to being 'conscious that a definite moral point of view is implicit in their approach',[15] though this is not explained or justified. On the other hand, I doubt whether there is much use (or even perhaps much sense) in claiming 'the' concept of education as 'essentially contestable', or that nothing of philosophical or methodological value can be said about education except as flowing from some 'doctrine of man'.[16] It ought, surely, to be possible to reach some rough agreement without the benefit of these particular exercises.

To stipulate a definition of 'education', as some philosophers do,[17] is to miss the point here: philosophers may stipulate what they like, but why should anyone else follow suit? Equally it seems that linguistic considerations *alone*, or accounts of how contemporary English-speakers use the word, may be insufficient; for one thing, many 'educationalists' (to judge from their writing) use it to cover almost any ground they are interested in — it has become an almost totally plastic term of art, rather like the words 'social' and 'society' in many contemporary discussions. It seems better to try a line recently exemplified by one moral philosopher,[18] and consider what the object of education might be.

Even the word 'object' (much more 'point', 'purpose' or 'aim') has its dangers: before we know where we are, we may start thinking about some ulterior or extrinsic 'object' and be driven back to discussions about 'ultimate values', 'doctrines of man', or whatever. We have to steer a middle course between this and the opposite temptation of over-specifying the notion of education, by asking broader questions which nevertheless have, if not 'right' answers, at least adequate or sensible ones. What *sort* of thing does one try to do when one educates? What is education *about*? What is its *species boni*, what kind of 'good' is it concerned with? Well, there is surely one thing we can say here, which is both extremely obvious and extremely important. Briefly, it is that education is about *people learning things*. Whatever other objects or benefits we may wish to connect with it, we can hardly disconnect such objects or benefits as gaining more knowledge, or more under-standing.

How much further one wants to press this is, I think, to *some* degree arbitrary or context-dependent. It is clear that we do not nowadays talk of educating trees, worms, or even cats; and this seems to have something to do with the idea that it is only fully or potentially rational creatures who can in a full sense be educated. Equally it is clear that we deny the term to 'influences' or other phenomena which do not, in a fairly direct and straightforward way, help to develop knowledge and understanding, or at least to many of these; nobody would describe poisoning a child, or giving him money, or hugging him, as 'education' *per se* — though, of course, they might be brought under this description if they were seen or devised as part of some process of learning. On the other hand, we may (and no doubt should) argue at great length about when we are going to use 'education' as against 'training', 'indoctrination', 'socialization', 'upbringing', and so forth; and also about a great many other matters, as for instance the nature of the 'worth-while activities' into which we should 'initiate' pupils [19], whether our 'most fundamental objectives of all are those of a cognitive kind' [20], and similar topics notorious in the current literature.

But these waters need not be entered here. It is enough to say that 'education' marks a set of phenomena or gives us a description under which to view any phenomena, specifically connected with human learning. By 'specifically', I mean that if this marker or description is to be of any use it must *exclude* certain things or aspects of things; and since almost anything might be thought of as having *some* connection with human learning, we have to insist on this connection being rather specific or 'direct' if anything is to be excluded. Thus clearly a child cannot learn effectively if he is ill or mad or hungry, but we consider these deficiencies under the headings of medicine, psychotherapy, and nutrition rather than 'education', because they have no sufficiently direct or specific connection either with the particular benefit of having knowledge and understanding or with the particular process of acquiring them. Clearly we need this concept, and if 'education' comes to be used to cover wider terrain we shall either have to use another term or remain conceptually impoverished.

All this may seem extremely obvious, but it produces conclusions which, if also obvious, are certainly not realized in practice. A parallel, naturally not exact, may give us some hope of objectivity here. If asked what medicine was for, we should say something about the cure and prevention of illness or the increase of health. The processes of medicine, perhaps describable as 'curing' or 'treatment', would be concerned with this object. It would follow from this that some such phrase as 'the study of medicine', or 'medical studies', would be most naturally taken as centrally concerned with this object and process: one purpose of such study, presumably, being to determine how the process could be improved or the object more effectively attained.

What do we now say about historians of medicine, medical administrators, drug manufacturers, research scientists, and Civil Service officials who take decisions about a national health service? Well, first of all, some of these are not *studying* medicine at all, but engaged in some practical activity — the administrators or civil servants, for instance. About some of the others we should at least feel tempted to say that they were not studying *medicine* but rather something else — the history of medicine or the economics of medicine or whatever. We should feel that in a sense such people took the process of medicine — the curing and the treating — for granted, and were concerned with various dimensions logically external to this process: its past history, or how much it cost, or whether it was to be found going on in certain types of societies, or whether it was staffed by middle-class people — and so on.

Note, however, that there are two things which we should *not* naturally want to say: (1) We should not want to say that what these people were doing was in any general sense necessarily less *important* than what doctors or professors of physiology or anatomy were doing, nor even that they were less important *for medicine*. Suppose a country is very poor, and cannot afford to have much medicine going on at all; then what a clever economist may do to make the country rich may be both more generally important and, however indirectly, more important for medicine. (2) We should not insist that there should be *more* people engaged in cure and treatment, or the direct study of these, than are engaged in these other things. For it might be that the front-line workers and researchers (so to call them) needed a great deal of support in terms of logistics and man-power, just as large numbers of technicians, administrators, etc. may be needed to keep one fighter pilot in the air.

Nevertheless, we could hardly avoid entertaining some such picture as that just presented. We have to ask what the whole apparatus is *for*; and once we ask and answer this, we have to see some parts of the apparatus as 'central', and other parts of it as 'peripheral'. There is a clear sense in which the people and apparatus concerned with, say, ensuring that school buildings stand up and are adequately heated are peripheral to education, though their importance is obvious. A rough distinction between two sorts of peripheral apparatus might be made by the words 'enabling' and 'supportive'; someone has to see that the process of education is possible, that the basic preconditions (money, buildings, a supply of teachers, fed and healthy children) are there; somewhat different, if only in degree, is the task of ensuring that the front-line workers are supported — for instance, by the provision of enough textbooks and visual aids. A similar distinction might be drawn by the terms 'preconditions' and 'aids'.

Let us now try to apply this to 'the study of education'. *Prima facie* this will be naturally understood as the study of teaching and learning, the processes for which 'education' stands. Supposing somebody now wants to study the effect that different types of school have on social class and mobility, or the cost of schools, or the history of Parliamentary edicts about the educational system or, to add an extreme case, the average height of teachers in different schools. In these examples, we could well say that the first person is really interested in the sociology of educational *institutions* — that is, institutions which (from his point of view) just *happen* to be overtly concerned with teaching and learning, but which also have important social effects; the second is interested in the economics of such institutions; the third in Parliamentary history in a certain area; and the last, perhaps, in the relationship between what jobs people do and how tall they are. This does not imply that what these people find out may not be of great *importance for* education, even in the last case (height may be correlated with 'social class', whatever that is, and if too many teachers are underprivileged midgets no doubt this has some relevance to teaching and learning). But it seems reasonable to say that such concerns are not *central to* the study of education.

The same point can be made by introducing two largely unclear terms, the 'psychology of education' and the 'sociology of education'. Suppose that the former were concerned with the study of learning and the development of understanding, and that the latter were concerned with, *inter alia*, the effects of segregated secondary education on social class mobility, or the economic advantages in later life of going to a private school. Then, we could say that the 'of education' in each phrase bears a different sense. The first phrase means something like 'the psychological factors inherent *in* learning'; the second 'the sociological effects generated *by* a certain institutional system (for learning)'. Now, to get this quite clear, suppose this is not so: suppose that the 'psychology of education' were chiefly concerned with, say, the left-wing or right-wing attitudes of educational administrators, or the degree of mental health possessed by Ministers of Education, and suppose that the 'sociology of education' were concerned with the social aspects of learning — that is, social factors within the school itself which were directly relevant to the acquisition of knowledge and understanding. In that case the positions would be reversed.

One standard objection might be raised to this kind of argument, an objection to the kind of Platonic purism from which it derives. It might be said: 'By the over-remorseless pressing of a particular concept marked by 'education', you have made it seem as if there was a 'central' area of greater importance than the 'peripheral' area. Yet you admit that, in practice, phenomena and studies in the peripheral area may actually be of greater importance. What, then, is gained — other than a certain linguistic or conceptual purity — by this sort of demarcation? In particular, how can it possibly be used (as you obviously want to use it) to produce any substantive conclusions about practical methodology or procedure? Briefly: what is the *point* of making this distinction, however naturally we may be led to make it when we reflect on what we should say about certain cases?'

The quick answer to this is that 'education' marks an intentional activity, conducted by human beings in relation to other human beings; so that we need to be clear what *sort* of benefits we hope to produce by it. This is not to say that it marks a very specific *techne* (as, say, 'sheep-shearing') with a very specific end-product built into the term. But neither are the sorts of benefits *completely* contestable, as they might be thought to be with terms like 'personal relationships', or 'town planning', or 'business', or 'government' — though even in these cases some very broad specifications seem applicable: not just *anything* counts as 'governing well' or 'the results of good government', and sometimes we would want to make Plato's move and say 'I don't call that governing, I call it exploiting people'.[21]

Classification in terms of types of benefit is essential, for the quite practical reason that we need to be clear about what we are trying to do. If a man spends some effort on his land in trying to grow crops or raise cattle, and some in trying to make it look attractive by landscaping, and some in so arranging things that he pays less income tax, then it may not matter much whether he can, with linguistic propriety, call himself 'a farmer' but it matters a great deal that he should not muddle up his aims and types of benefit, otherwise he is likely to fail in some or all of them (he may find himself with thin, ugly and taxable cattle. Further, whatever may be linguistically acceptable in particular contexts, we should in general stop saying that he was farming, or had a farm, unless the centrality of growing crops and raising cattle was preserved: we should begin to say that he had an estate, or a park, or a piece of land to off-set against taxes.

There are, as a grammarian might put it, something like internal accusatives attached to these notions: one can only farm land (to raise produce), or educate people (to give them knowledge and understanding). Or we can say that the terms have built-in direct and indirect objects: 'educating a person in (some kind of) knowledge or understanding' is not all that far away from 'teaching Smith mathematics'. Just as farmers may not always farm, and governments may not always govern, so of course people 'in education' may not always educate. But the central connections remain: if they did not, there would be practical as well as linguistic chaos.

It is important not to confuse this general specification with questions about *why* we should develop knowledge and understanding. Politicians and sociologists may wish to use education to fit people for their social roles; religious believers, to fit them for salvation in the next world; communists, to fit them for 'maintaining the cultural revolution' in this one. Liberal-minded philosophers, unsurprisingly, will want to deny that education should be primarily viewed as something to be extrinsically justified at all: knowledge and understanding are goods in themselves. None of this is relevant here: my point is the much simpler one that education is connected to the development of understanding much as medicine is connected to health. We could raise questions about why people should be healthy (a good thing in itself, so that they can fight for their country, to avoid over-crowding the hospitals, and so on), or how we are to weigh health against other goods. But we can still be clear, without answering these questions, that someone who is interested in medicine must be interested in health. Similarly to study education is, at least centrally, to study the development of knowledge and understanding in people. For whatever reasons, we have a common interest in this type of 'good', which in our language is marked by the word 'education'.

I am not, of course, claiming that if the word 'education' is not used within this specification it must therefore be used improperly. Thus the term might with propriety be used to mean something like 'the education industry' (the 'ed. biz.'): a man could perhaps say that he was 'in education' if he were an educational administrator or civil servant, as a man could say he was 'in oil' meaning that an oil company paid his salary (or just that his money was invested in the company). There are limits, not at all clear, even to this use: he could hardly say he was 'in education' if his job was, say, the repair of school buildings or the cooking of school food. We retain the idea that education is centrally concerned with educat*ing*: that is, of education as a characteristically intentional activity conducted by human beings on other human beings, involving a certain kind of process and having a certain kind of point.

This connection is hard to sever even in 'normal usage'; and there is also the point that what might be described as the 'sociological' use of 'education', to mean roughly 'the educational system', is parasitic upon this central use. We could not *identify* institutions or systems as 'educational' unless they were already so in the central sense; if they ceased to be so in this sense, nothing could be meant by saying that one was studying *educational* institutions — rather than, say, holiday camps or indoctrination centres. In the same sort of way, it is not just a piece of Platonic purism which makes us distinguish the study of religion from the study of the Church of England, the Baptist Church, and other religious institutions: or even distinguish it from the study of various specific religions. For religions and religious institutions are properly so called only if they measure up to *some* criteria which define what religion is or is about. Both in this case and in the case of education, this process of identification is itself often difficult, and involves a lot of hard work: some schools are, or at least have been, not totally unlike holiday camps or indoctrination centres, just as some institutions commonly *called* 'religious' may have often functioned in quite other ways.

Some may find this acceptable, indeed obvious. But I suspect that many may still want to make some protest about the whole procedure, perhaps somewhat along the lines of Thrasymachus' protest against the idea of governing as a *techne* with a subject-matter and standards of its own.[22] 'This "philosophical analysis" may be all very well in an ideal world. But in fact, as things actually are, education is not like this at all. In *fact*, whatever may be said about *words* or *concepts*, we can describe education in all sorts of ways which are much more to the point: as a major industry, as a tool for economic survival, as a way of 'gentling the masses', as the vehicle for cultural transmission, and so forth. These and other things are what actually goes on, and what we ought to attend to. If you are talking about what education *is*, then this is the kind of talk that is relevant: if you are talking about what the word "education" might or might not mean, why should we bother to listen?'

This is why it is essential to hang on tightly to the notion of different kinds of 'goods' or benefits which men try to achieve by different *technai*. For only such a notion gives us any chance of *identifying* and fairly *judging* or evaluating 'what goes on'. Suppose that, as Thrasymachus claimed, most government was in fact a largely self-gratifying enterprise of the ruling classes or that, as Marx thought, religion was used as opium for the people. We should still think that there were, or at least could be, human enterprises, not improperly called 'governing' or 'practising a religion', which were supposed to attain certain benefits, and we should need to investigate these further and get clearer about these benefits, if only in order to describe much of what actually went on as 'abuses' or 'distortions' of the enterprises. In the same way, whatever various governments or societies may do, we have to preserve some culture-free and time-free notion of education against which to measure what they do. This necessity emerges clearly in the extreme cases, as when one might say of Nazi indoctrination camps (for instance) 'I don't call that *educating*'.

There is, naturally, such a thing as bad education, just as there is bad government; we do not have to make the additional Platonic move of saying that education, or government, or medicine, or any other intentional enterprise, cannot count as such unless it is done properly. But at least there must be some fairly close connection with specific goods. Either, as is characteristically the case, the goods are intentionally pursued and, to some degree, realized or they may, perhaps, be realized in some accidental or unconscious way. But without any such connection there is no coherent concept. Not just anything a tyrant or a doctor may do counts as governing or practising medicine; and not just anything a person or an institution does to a child, even by way of upbringing (a much wider concept), counts as educating.

Of course this leaves it open for somebody to say 'Very well, but I am not concerned with education in that sense at all. I am concerned with (for instance) what goes on under the heading "education" in the UK or the USA or Nazi Germany — never mind whether it is properly so entitled, or whether it "measures up" to your notion of education'. But this is to take as given, or for granted, the criteria applied (semi-consciously) by various societies or power-groups — Ministries of Education, for example; it is, in effect, simply to *avoid facing* what must be the first question for any serious study of education, namely 'Just what *ought* we to be studying under this heading?' It would be like trying to set up the serious study of religion, whilst uncritically accepting that 'religion' was what the Pope, or the Mormons, or the local witch doctor said it was. I am not saying such study is either impossible or unimportant — but it could, I think, only be a study of very heterogeneous social and political phenomena. In the same way, it would be difficult (and perhaps dangerous) to set up study in 'mental health' without some attempt to determine, in the first place, what should *count as* 'mentally healthy' — rather than accept the criteria of totalitarian psychiatrists who classify political opponents as mad, or of primitive tribes who classify mad people as divinely inspired.

Our specification in terms of 'people learning things' may seem so wide as to be entirely harmless (or useless). But the kind of arguments we have been advancing encourage us, I think, to tighten it up in a number of ways which may give it more teeth. First of all, it can be said that the study of education is necessarily normative in roughly the same way as 'medicine', 'mental health' or 'social welfare' are normative. This necessity can be seen as conceptual: that is, 'education' may with some plausibility be so defined as to entail the notion of *improvement* in a person's state of mind.[23] But this move need not be made *a priori*: nor need we specify *a priori* a contestable end-product, 'the educated man' (any more than we need to specify 'the ideally healthy man' for medicine). The point is rather that, as soon as we get down to explicating the conceptual trappings involved in the vacuous-sounding phrase 'people learning things', we begin to see more clearly into the kind of 'goods' with which education is (necessarily) concerned. This is perhaps most obvious in relation to *learning*.

If we study human beings learning things or increasing their knowledge and rationality (and the same goes for notions like 'development' and 'growth'), we cannot conceivably do so without the use of criteria which determine what is to *count as* 'having learned X', 'knowing Y', 'being more rational in respect of Z', and so on. We have to form some idea of *what it is* to gain more understanding of (say) the world of nature or of symbolic systems, or of works of art; a point that becomes obvious when we use disciplinary titles to stand for such studies — 'science', 'mathematics', 'musical appreciation', Briefly, we cannot study education without bringing in the ideas of success and failure in learning, making progress and making mistakes, developing rationality and remaining in a state of prejudice or ignorance.

It might seem as if such study could take certain norms or criteria for granted, without (as empirical researchers are fond of saying) 'making value judgements'. In some sense, and some cases, this is true: we could, for instance, study the learning of chess, taking the rules of chess and the — pretty clear — criteria of what counts as a good chess-player for granted. But this is because the criteria *are* pretty clear or, insofar as they are not, we should not know whether to say that one pupil had learned more chess than another. In very many (I think, most) other cases, we are not at all clear. What *is it* to have 'learned more science', or to have 'a better appreciation of art', or to be more 'morally educated'? Of course there are answers to these questions; my point is that it is not possible to study learning in these areas unless and until the answers are satisfactory.

Nor will it do to take the criteria or norms as 'given' by someone else — for instance, by the society in which the learning is going on. The point here is not only that the society or other authority may 'have the wrong values'; it is also that what is thus 'given' may not be coherent or intelligible as it stands at all. Suppose a student is interested in 'education in science' in the early Middle Ages, or in areas marked by 'moral education' or 'religious knowledge' today. He will come across a great many studies and practices which seem to fit into these general areas, and which the society (or its representatives) may *call* 'learning science', 'religious education', and so on; and he may even be handed lists of aims and objectives to work from. But much that actually goes on may not in fact be *learning* at all: it might rather be, for instance, the transmission of a set of institutionalized fantasies and superstitions, to which terms like 'knowledge', 'rationality' and 'understanding' would not apply.

If the student did not enter this arena, satisfying himself both that genuine learning and understanding was going on and about the criteria of such learning, he could only view these studies and practices under the description of general social or individual behaviour; and even here he would often have problems in determining just what sort of behaviour it was (what it *meant*), problems of a kind familiar in contemporary philosophical literature.[24] But for our purposes the point to note is that such a student could not be said to be studying *education*. The point is perhaps clearest in the case of 'religious education': one can study such practices as the compulsory morning assembly in British schools, Bible readings, discussions about 'ultimate reality' and so forth, and of course there is a sense in which we would say that this was 'studying religious education'. But there is a certain permissiveness about the use of 'education' here. Suppose we thought that what now passes under this heading was not much different from, say, the superstitions of voodoo and astrology; then we might doubt whether anything was being learned at all (because there might not be anything *to* learn), or at least would have to get clear about *what* was learned and what counted as learning it well or badly.

We can say all this without having to deny, what is obvious, that there is still plenty of room for dispute about what *particular* benefits or goods we wish pupils to gain in or from learning. This may take the form of arguing about what they are to learn, or how much of it they are to learn or how they are to learn it; and in many cases the question is likely to be more open than it is, for instance, in the case of medicine. Clearly this is because we are agreed, and have good reason to be agreed, about what counts as health; 'the healthy man' is less contestable than 'the educated man'. Parallels of such contestability might be found in 'mental health' and, perhaps more clearly, 'social welfare'.

But even this suggests a limitation on what can fairly count as 'the study of education'. For — again without the need for overt linguistic fiat — we incline to think that education should be serious or at least non-trivial. If someone were to study little bits of casual, fragmentary and trivial learning (for instance, learning that somebody's grandmother is called Flossie, or that cigarettes have just gone up in price), this would not be sufficient for saying that he was studying education. It does not matter much here whether this is because the *content* of the learning is not thought to be sufficiently worthwhile, or because the learning process itself is too fragmentary and uncoordinated (unsurprisingly, these two in practice tend to be linked). The point remains that when we say that education is about human learning, we do not have just *any* learning in mind — or if we do, our study of it is inextricably bound up with our views about its importance.

Further, it seems that this importance has to be viewed in *some* degree *sub specie aeternitatis*: that is, freed from particular social, economic or other pressures which we may not wish to endorse. Thus when the UK was at war in 1939, it was clearly very important that certain people should learn certain things — how to make armaments, how to use ration books, how to fly Spitfires, and so on. But we did not say that this learning was part of their education: we said, rather, that their education had been (in some cases) interrupted by the war. We have a vague but insistent idea, though of course the content of the idea varies from one thinker to another, that the learning involved in education should be important to people *qua* people, not just important for particular purposes or *ad hoc*. If, like the Spartans, we lived in a society which was more or less constantly at war or at least under direct threat of war, the importance of military learning might no longer be *ad hoc*: it might pervade our notion of what a properly-educated person was.

Even in a Spartan-type situation, however, we should need to be on our guard about what we were or were not prepared to endorse. Suppose we were conquered by Martians, whose occupying potentates threatened to kill our children unless they learned certain things. Then plainly it would be important that the children should learn these things, and learn them well. We might come to call this their 'education', and even appoint professors 'of education' to make sure that the job was done properly, and the situation might last long enough to make the description *ad hoc*, in *one* sense, no longer applicable. Nevertheless, if this usage became firmly established and universal — if we were prepared to describe our star pupils under this system as 'well-educated', without question or irony — this would mean that we had endorsed the Martian view about what was worth learning. We should have come to think, not just that (things being what they were) it was expedient for our children to learn all this, but rather that it was truly desirable for them to do so. Of course we might argue about whether it was 'truly desirable', but this would be argument about what we might call either the *content* of education or the proper practical application of the concept: it would not be argument about the concept itself.

These additions to our specification, when combined with what we said earlier about the need to demarcate a certain kind of 'goods' or set of reasons, yield quite powerful conclusions. What we have said amounts to this: that, in order to make any sense of our deliberations or decisions about children (or schools, or society, or whatever), we have to demarcate and classify different kinds of 'goods', or sets of reasons: that one such kind or set, fairly marked by 'educational', is concerned not just with 'people or rational beings learning things', but (a) with their learning things in a reasonably coherent or serious manner, and (b) with their learning things which are of importance to them as people in some comparatively time-free and perhaps culture-free way, or at least not just *ad hoc*. Some such specification seems to me incontestable, or if not that, something which ought to be accepted by any sensible person, since it would not improve our clarity in thought or action to contest it.

But if we do accept it, we must face the clear consequence that it *excludes* a good deal that now passes or seems to pass under 'the study of education'. Thus the study of sub-rational behaviour — the behaviour of animals or of children insofar as they behave sub-rationally — is not the study of education. Nor is the vast amount of work done in areas which we might fairly term 'background studies' to education, for instance, the poverty of certain pupils' homes, or the pupils' physical health. Nor, again, will we count under this heading all the work of sociologists which is concerned with non-educational interests, such as social class; we appreciate the distinction, to pick one case out of many, between a (non-educational) interest in whether comprehensive schools increase social mobility and a genuinely educational interest in whether their pupils actually *learn* more than pupils at other schools. Nor, finally, can we be quite so light-hearted or uncritical in accepting as 'education' various things that may be done in schools and elsewhere for what I have described as *ad hoc* reasons, rather than for reasons connected with what it is desirable for people to learn *per se*.

Another consequence, also to be pursued in later chapters, is that there will be much less room for disputes about what is educationally desirable. I do not say that there will not still be a good deal of room nor that such disputes will be less in number, but that they will take place within an agreed and (however roughly) circumscribed area. Once we are clear about what is to be *meant* by 'educationally desirable', certain things of a more specific kind — for instance, that pupils should be literate or well-disciplined, or that teachers should have sufficient powers actually to conduct the enterprise of education — may turn out to be conceptually necessary or obvious to common sense. At least we shall not, as Bruner does, 'take it as self-evident *[sic]* that each generation must define afresh the nature, direction, and aims of education . . .'.[25]

These consequences clearly have serious methodological and practical implications, but before passing on to consider these in the next two chapters, I want to make it quite clear that the specification does not down-grade or denigrate the importance of the (non-educational) studies which it excludes: rather, it sharpens our perception of different kinds of goods. To take a fairly topical example, suppose we are interested in some area initially marked by the term 'discipline': and, to make this at least a *prima facie* candidate for the study of education, let us say 'discipline in schools'. Now suppose we construe our interest as an attempt to find ways by which the violence of some pupils can be abated, or more generally by which pupils in schools can be rendered trouble-free or properly controlled. We may now find that an efficient way of doing this is to give them tranquillisers or electric shocks or some form of hypnosis. But it would be grotesque to say that we were *educating* pupils if we did this, and equally grotesque to say that if we studied the process we were studying *education*. There is a way to study discipline as an educational topic, which incidentally does more justice to a proper concept of discipline: roughly, to notice that discipline is or can be about the *obedience of rational creatures* to certain rules for certain *reasons*, a notion that our previous study wholly omitted. We could then proceed to investigate what rules and reasons were proper for education, and how in practice to give pupils instruction in and experience of them: not as a culture-bound, *ad hoc* enterprise (how to keep certain types of pupils in British schools 'trouble-free' for the next few years), but as an *educationally* necessary enterprise, inasmuch as it is important for people (pupils) of any society or historical period to grasp and put to use certain concepts to do with 'authority', 'rules', 'obedience' and so forth.

Such a study would, as I think anyone who has ploughed through books with titles like *Discipline and Control in Education* might agree, look significantly different from a great deal of what is currently done. One reason why educational theory seems not only confused but barren is that a great deal of possible study, which could be useful and significant, is never even planned or thought of, and this is because the stage is at present held by other actors. It is not just that these actors are engaged in plays which could not seriously be described as 'education' at all: it is also that they prevent the entrance of people waiting in the wings who may, if given a chance, be interested in plays that could be so described.

Consider this example, however, from the point of view of those whose business it is to look after 'the educational system' — for instance, local educational authorities, or perhaps people in government departments, or Ministers of Education. They might say: 'All this is well enough, but in practice we have the job of making life possible for teachers, cutting down violence in schools, keeping the kids off the streets, keeping the parents happy, and so on. We are interested in "discipline" from another point of view — a "political" rather than an "educational" point of view, if you like. And not only that: there are all sorts of demands which society can fairly make on the educational system — we want there to be enough technologists to keep our economy going, we want as small a number of unemployed people as possible, perhaps we even want to use the educational system to change the class-structure of society, and so on. Your narrow definition of "education" excludes these (surely legitimate) interests'.

This is entirely acceptable, but it is crucially important to distinguish these (heterogeneous) interests as clearly as possible — both in theory and practice — from *educational* interests. There may, indeed, sometimes or often be conflicts between the two: thus the quickest or easiest way of getting children to be 'disciplined' in the sense of 'trouble-free' (if that *is* a sense of 'disciplined', which I doubt) might be to use methods — say, tranquillisers or chloroform — which would militate against the educational aim of getting them to be 'well-disciplined' or to learn about 'discipline' in the more plausible sense of rational obedience. Partly because of these conflicts and partly because we cannot make clear decisions without clear distinctions, we have to distinguish these 'other interests' — however legitimate — from the particular interests or 'goods' we have marked by 'education'.

It is, surely, entirely clear that much that goes on in connection with the word 'education' — what is done not only in government and schools, but also in universities and other institutions — is, in fact, of this kind: that is, it subserves social or economic ends, not educational ones. How these classes or ends or 'goods' are to be weighed against each other and who is to do the weighing are difficult questions but here irrelevant: what we have to keep hold of is the difference. It has to be as clear as possible how much of a pupil's or teacher's time, or how much of our money, or how many professors 'of education', are supposed to be concerned with the one as against the other. In particular it has to be clear, in any context of discussion (conference, commission, committee, etc.), whether we are, at any one time, seeking for what is educationally desirable or what is desirable on other grounds — and the fact that we might want both, if we can get them, only makes it more important to keep the distinction clear in the first place. Effective compromises can only be made if we know what we are compromising between.

When we fail to distinguish in this way, both types of ends are badly served. Certainly one thing, perhaps the most obvious thing, that can go wrong is for the political (utilitarian, social) ends to take over or submerge the educational ones: truth, rationality and understanding give way to political or economic convenience. But it is also possible for those unspurred by the prick of utilitarian necessity to engage in something which they may call 'education' or 'research', but which has little or no connection with serious learning or the development of understanding. If I may be allowed an empirical judgement, my guess would be that in many 'liberal' or 'democratic' societies today we succeed neither in turning out an economically efficient and politically trouble-free citizenry, nor in producing educated people; neither — to take a more specific description — in generating non-violent and law-abiding adults, nor in generating adults who are properly educated in morality. And for similar reasons much that is called 'educational research' may not be either of practical use or academically respectable.

In practice, it is a question of *how one views* (in any particular context) a child. One may view him as an employee, a citizen, a defender of the state, or some other kind of social unit; or, again, one may view him as a (physical or mental) patient, as rich or poor, handsome or ugly, black or white, and so on. To be interested in education is to view him primarily as a *learner*: to have in mind the process and benefits of learning and understanding and knowledge themselves, rather than other goods — whether or not some of these other goods may be, indirectly, achieved by learning, and to view him under other descriptions only insofar as these descriptions are importantly relevant to him as a learner. Unless we keep this view, this type of goods, and this description clear in our minds it seems to me impossible to engage seriously in 'educational theory' (because we should not know what sort of 'theory' we were engaging *in*), and virtually imposible to make sensible decisions in educational practice (because we should not have a clear picture of *one* type of goods, at least, which must be central to any practice to be seriously described as 'educational').

Notes

1 PER, Part 2.
2 *The Study of Education* (ed. J.W. Tibble, Routledge, 1966).
3 J.W. Tibble.
4 Paul Hirst.
5 Richard Peters.
6 Brian Simon, p. 91.
7 Ben Morris, p. 153.
8 William Taylor, p. 182.

9 p. 184.

10 See Peters (1966), (1973); Hirst and Peters (1970); Dearden (1972). Cf. Downie (1974).

11 Even, apparently, for a parent-volume of such importance. But this book is not, of course, the only example. Compare for instance the first number of the well-advertised *Oxford Review of Education* (Vol. 1, No. 1, 1975), devoted to the theme of 'equality'. The contributors include some very well-known 'names' in education (Bruner, Eysenck, Jensen, Halsey, Mary Warnock and so on), and quite a lot of what they say is interesting; but the contributions do not cohere with or relate to each other, partly because the authors have quite different notions of 'equality' and 'education'. As Bullock says in the foreword to this volume, '. . . the problem is *how* to involve the others — from philosophers to medical scientists — whom everyone would like to see taking part in the discussion of educational issues'.

12 Seaborne (1971), p. 50 (my italics).

13 Readers may pursue the arguments from Peters (1966) via Hirst and Peters (1970) and Dearden (1972) down to Peters (1973). Cf. also Downie (1974).

14 See Downie (1974), Chs. 2—5.

15 Hirst and Peters (1970), p. 41.

16 These remarks are commonly made in reviews of the current literature, and in philosophical discussions generally. See also Peters (1966), p. 232 ff.

17 For a clear stipulation of this kind, see Downie (1974), Ch. 2 and p. 173.

18 Warnock (1971). But the basic idea here is Platonic: see, e.g., *Republic* Bk. 1.

19 This is the orthodox line in philosophy of education; see Peters (1966) and elsewhere.

20 Hirst and Peters (1970), p. 62.

21 *Republic*, Book I, 340 ff

22 *Republic, loc. cit.*

23 Cf. Peters (1973), p. 11 ff.; PER p. 1 ff.

24 Winch (1958) and Ryan (1973) are good guides.

25 Bruner (1966), p. 22.

Chapter Two

Elements of Methodology

To use the phrase 'educational theory' at all jumps a number of guns; and though these are, I think, loaded only with blanks, it is important to establish a few points at the beginning. Those concerned to go more deeply into various concepts marked by 'theory' will find plenty of literature elsewhere.[1]

If we accept some such specification of 'education' as 'the development of serious understanding (knowledge, rationality, etc.) by rational beings', then it is already clear that almost any proper investigation, study or inquiry in this field will necessarily involve a number of different types of understanding — if you like, different 'disciplines' or sorts of knowledge. Even in the simplest, one might say paradigmatic, cases of education — for instance, Smith learning Latin — we shall need to know something about what the person is learning, and about the person who is learning, and probably about the person who is teaching him; perhaps more besides. It is difficult to know what could be meant by someone saying that he was studying education *only* as a philosopher or a psychologist or whatever; or at least one might see what such a person meant, but it would be hard to see how his study could, in isolation, count as the study of education. A may work out the conceptual complexities of Latin, B may tell us something about Smith as a person, but unless these (and other) inquiries are in some way put together, we should not call them inquiries into education as such.

But what could be the point of 'putting them together' (whatever this may mean) unless we wanted to get some general picture of whether things were going well or badly? Indeed, as I argued in the last chapter,[2] to get any correct or adequate picture of what goes on itself entails some attention to the norms or rules inherent in what is being learned: we could not properly describe what happens when Smith learns Latin unless we know what counts as successful learning in this case. Even the most 'factual', 'descriptive' or 'non-normative' studies commit themselves, however obliquely, to marking success and failure in this way — and hence, again perhaps obliquely or under disguise, must point in principle to possibilities of practical improvement. I am not, of course, saying that the only 'point' (justification or motive) in studying such enterprises as education must be the immediate promotion of practical programmes in schools and elsewhere; still less that those who study them should have such promotion in mind when they study. What I am saying is that the idea of 'studying education' in a way that has no direct or indirect relevance to possibilities of improvement is an incoherent idea: when people try to do this, the study turns out not to be the study of education at all, but rather the study of historial or sociological or psychological or some other kind of phenomena disconnected, in this case, from our specification of 'education'.

Whatever the dangers of the term 'educational theory', its merit is that we are less likely to overlook this point. 'Theory' here will mean something pretty general, like 'more sophisticated understanding' or 'a higher-level awareness': it will not, of course, refer to particular *theories of* education (Plato's, Rousseau's, etc.) nor to particular *theories in* the study of education (e.g., various 'theories of learning' advanced by psychologists), though both of these may have something to contribute. We have also to avoid any presupposition that 'educational theory' must consist of, or issue in, some one particular *kind* of understanding (for instance, 'scientific'), or — worse — some *one* 'theory' or set of 'theories' in a more specific sense of the word. Given these rubrics, we can accept 'educational theory' as a reasonably non-misleading title, and one which retains a desirable connection with the practical improvement of education. The best and best-known exponent of the logic of educational theory is Hirst,[3] whose main thesis seems plainly correct for reasons already given.[4] However, within this thesis there still remain a number of general notions which, I shall maintain, stand in the way of the development of a practically effective methodology. I stress 'practically effective', because it is easy to say that the theory 'draws on all the knowledge within the various forms [*sc.* forms of thought, or disciplines] that is relevant to educational pursuits but proceeds from there in grappling with practical problems,[5] or that it is 'a rational structure where knowledge from the forms provides the basis of justification for a series of educational principles'.[6] But what we want to know is how all this is supposed to *work*. What 'forms' (disciplines) are relevant? How do they fit together? What sort of contribution does each of them make? In a word, what would this operation *look like*?

Hirst seems to suggest that some at least of these questions have no answers:

'. . . it might be thought that educational principles must somehow follow from a theoretical synthesis of all the contributory elements, that unless some harmony is brought to the relevant philosophy, psychology, history, etc., the principles will lack adequate justification. Not only would this be a task for educational theory that is quite impossible practically, for no one could have mastered all the relevant specialist knowledge, it would be asking for something that might well be logically impossible. It is not at all clear what is meant by synthesizing knowledge achieved through the use of logically quite different conceptual schemes. But such a synthesis is in fact quite unnecessary for the formation of practical principles'.[7]

But one would hardly be inclined to take this passage at face value: there are obviously senses in which we not only can but do 'synthesize knowledge achieved through the use of logically quite different conceptual schemes', and bring 'some harmony' to the 'relevant' disciplines. For instance, the geographer makes use of mathematics and history; the historian uses radio carbon dating, seismology, palaeo-botany, and so forth; and they put the knowledge thus gained together in order to say something about (for example) Anglo-Saxon settlement patterns or Mycenean history. More relevantly to our present inquiry, the moral agent may make use of many different types of fact or even different disciplines (e.g. psychology) in order to decide what he ought to do. If someone said that these were not cases of 'synthesizing knowledge', or that in these cases 'synthesis is in fact quite unneces-sary', one might be forgiven for failing to understand what he meant. At the very least, it is odd to say that we do not need 'some harmony' to be brought to the disciplines; a requirement that might be interpreted along quite practical lines, just as geographers and historians might consider how far, and when, their interests involved the need to understand mathematics or mediaeval Latin or the styles of Mycenean pottery.

Hirst is perhaps over-anxious to make the point[8] that there is no logically *sui generis* 'form of thought' or kind of knowledge to be labelled 'educational', on all fours with other kinds labelled 'philo-sophical', 'historical', 'psychological' and so on. We need not deny this (though there are plenty of complications about what criteria we are to use for a *genus* here); but it should not prevent us from considering whether there are any general methodological principles for educational theory. For clearly, since not just *anything* counts as 'educational theory' or 'educational knowledge', there may well be certain charac-teristic features or peculiarities of it: even though these may not include a 'conceptual structure unique in its logical features' or 'unique tests for validity' — though, again, before granting even this one would want to look much harder at what to *count as* 'logical features' or 'validity'. I shall argue, anyway, that there are certain features of a general or procedural kind; whether one should describe these as 'logical' is perhaps here not of the first importance.

We are trying now to get behind the idea that 'the disciplines of education' (whatever these may be) are *methodologically on a par* with each other; an idea which seems to be institutionalized in the setting up of equal but separated 'departments' of educational theory (philosophy of education, psychology of education, etc.) and which Hirst certainly does not attack. He does, however, flirt with the idea of 'characterizing' educational and other practical theories 'under moral knowledge', on the grounds that 'What is distinctive about them is that they issue in practical principles for a particular range of activities'.[9] But although educational theory 'formulates principles of a distinctly moral kind', 'the principles formulated are not high level statements about what is good or what ought to be done in general'. Hence 'even when a practical theory centrally involves moral questions, its restricted focus limits the level and character of these moral considerations . . . In these theories too by no means all the questions are essentially moral. Educational theory has to deal with many questions . . . which are purely technical.'[10]

There is a certain oddity in the idea that *moral* issues are involved *in* the study of education at all — except, possibly, in moral education itself, where we should have to be clear about what morality was in order to educate at all. Various moves may be made about what we are going to do with the word 'moral';[11] but the oddity would only vanish if we took it to refer to almost *any* situation in which we had to decide what we ought to do; and then various distinctions, like Hirst's distinction between 'essentially moral' and 'purely technical', are called into question. We should be taking simply about the formulation of 'practical principles'. Suppose we are studying medicine: then in this study we shall not be concerned with what is morally valuable, but with what is valuable for *health*. If there is some conflict between the two — if, say, some supposedly health-promoting practice in the general area of contraception or abortion is also thought by some to be morally objectionable — no doubt we must study this conflict, but this will not be *part of* the study of medicine. 'The morality of medicine' might be a fair title for it, and 'the morality of education' might be a fair title, if a vague one, for studies concerned with cases where educational 'goods' might come into conflict with 'moral' ones — however these latter are to be characterized.

In the same sort of way, when Hirst says that 'whatever one may think of the truth claims of metaphysical beliefs' they 'enter into the formation of educational principles and judgements',[12] or when other writers maintain that educational theory and practice must flow from some 'doctrine of man', 'ultimate beliefs', 'overall commitment' or whatever, it is not easy to see what *sense* this could make — always providing we keep firmly in mind the notion of education as a fairly specific *techne* devoted to a fairly specific range of 'goods'. Certainly in other cases we should not know what to make of phrases like 'Epicurean medicine', 'Communist mathematics' or 'engineering based on neo-Thomist principles': and 'Christian science' entitles not a particular way of pursuing science but a particular religion.

It will at once be said, as indeed we noted earlier[13] and Hirst also notes,[14] that the range of goods is greater in education than in, say, medicine or engineering, and that therefore there is more free play for the operation of 'value judgements'. I do not so much want to deny this as to put it in some kind of methodologically useful perspective: in particular to demolish the idea that one could, as it were, set up a sort of 'value-judgement' department in educational theory (to include 'metaphysical beliefs' or 'doctrines of man'), which could be practically or even logically disconnected from other departments which dealt with 'the facts' or 'purely technical' questions. This is a very powerful idea (and one which, I should add, Hirst in his later writing[15] is evidently as much opposed to as I am) which parallels a good deal of modern moral philosophy, as an echo of it, or a cause, or perhaps both.

As an illustration of this, consider some of the remarks made in a recent book on educational theory which is extremely lucid, commendably brief, and (I think) in this respect entirely typical.[16] Moore says that 'A general theory of education must, logically, begin with an aim, an assumption of value',[17] and has a lot to say about various kinds of 'assumptions' made by past educational theorists. Among these are 'that human behaviour is to some extent plastic'[18], 'that children are naturally good'[19], 'that knowledge is possible',[20] that education should produce 'the just man',[21] that 'Education peut tout',[22] and so on. It seems odd to call these 'assumptions', but in any case we could not get very far with them without spending quite a lot of time trying to find out what they *meant*. *Prima facie* some seem necessarily true, others necessarily false, others again conceptually incoherent. Would a world be imaginable in which knowledge was *not* possible, or human behaviour not to *some* extent 'plastic'? Will anyone stand up and say that education should *not* help to make people just, or that 'education' (even in France) can add a cubit to everyone's stature? Whatever we are dealing with here, these are not straightforward empirical assumptions nor is it anything but misleading to claim the necessity of 'assumptions of value', as if we were bound to consider anything that came under 'aims of education' as specific and debatable in the way that, for example, one might discuss the specific and debatable case of sex before marriage or the merits of voting for this or that political party.

Moore maintains a commonly held, indeed fashionable, picture of various theories (one might say, 'philosophies') of education based on 'fundamental principles'.[23] "To be adequate an overall educational aim must not only be clear and unambiguous, but must rest on normative principles recognized for what they are, deliberate decisions about what is to count as valuable. Such decisions are always open to challenge *and it may well be that ultimate positions of value are not capable of rational support.'*[24] At this point the reader might reasonably feel that we cannot really do business at all in this field; perhaps we are condemned to a shop-window tour of various 'ideals', 'assumptions', 'doctrines of man' or whatever.

We are presented here — and, I would guess, in the vast majority of educational literature — with a sort of deductive system which starts from some 'basis' or 'ultimate position of value'. You have your 'ideal' of man and/or 'society', and from this you draw your 'aims of education', and from these (with suitable help from various 'assumptions' and, in a more pedestrian way, from empirical facts) you generate educational recommendations. The general tone of these pictures is then labelled 'authoritarian', 'élitist', 'democratic', 'liberating' and so forth. I do not of course deny that a good deal of what has gone on under the heading of 'educational theory' has been of this kind, nor that it may often be interesting and important. Most of us, perhaps all of us, are consciously or (more usually) unconsciously dominated by some picture of this sort, and it is clearly desirable that such pictures should be made explicit, compared with others both past and present, and criticized; if only — a more important business than one might think — to get clear about how our fantasies infect our educational thinking. Further, there are of course crucially important points which are raised and, as it were, thickened out or made 'real' by various writers — not only 'philosophers': sometimes substantive points about human nature, sometimes conceptual truths, sometimes observations of a very general kind which seem to fall half-way between the two. It is plainly a task for philosophy that these points should be clarified and, so to speak, 'fed into' the more restricted area of 'educational theory'. But there are, I think, reasons for supposing that educational theory does not *have* to proceed in accordance with this sort of strategy, and may be best advised not to do so where it can be avoided.

Part of the trouble here, I suspect, is a standard temptation for philosophers and others to talk too much about 'education' *in general*, rather than considering particular cases. Thus, if we are reasonably content with a rough specification of education in terms of 'people learning things', it is natural and proper to go on quite quickly to consider the different kinds of things that can be learned; and we could

CARNEGIE LIBRARY
LIVINGSTONE COLLEGE
SALISBURY, N. C. 28144

perhaps agree, without the need for lengthy 'confrontations' or 'value-judgements', that (for example) it would be desirable for some pupils (never mind which) to learn some science and mathematics (never mind how much). When we get to this point, the 'values' come from the subjects themselves, *not* from any 'ideal' or 'fundamental assumption of value'. To do science, or mathematics, or any other subject seriously just does involve a person in certain principles and procedures; if someone said that our insistence that budding scientists should observe and experiment, or that budding mathematicians should understand various kinds of notations and proofs, resulted from some 'value' — 'the importance of science to our society', or 'because philosopher-kings need to know geometry', or whatever — we should justly criticize him for obfuscation.

Even in moral education, as I have tried to show elsewhere,[25] there is plainly some sort of distinction to be made between particular moral beliefs or 'values' and whatever principles, procedures and virtues constitute rationality (understanding, sanity, 'being educated', etc.) in this field. Suppose we were to include in this list such things as facing the facts, paying attention to language and not contradicting oneself, having the determination to act up to one's own decisions, being aware of what one felt, recognizing that there were other people in the world beside oneself, and so on. If somebody now said that these represented particular 'values' (flowing from some 'doctrine of man'), which were 'assumptions' that could in some basic way be 'challenged' (rather than clarified and inspected), I should find this rather hard to understand; and if such a person said that these items were particular *moral* 'values', I should not understand him at all — any more than I should understand someone who maintained that the acceptance of (say) the method of observation and experiment, or of some Popperian notion of falsification, was the acceptance of a particular *scientific* belief.

In any case, I do not think we need go that far in order to see at least the possibility of an alternative procedure. My chief interest in this book is not to take up the kinds of 'fundamental issue of value' which seem to dominate most educational discussion, but rather to attempt the more pedestrian task of sketching out a working basis for educational theory. Let us try another tack, and consider a fairly down-to-earth educational enterprise, the teaching of children to talk or to read. If somebody were to question whether children ought to be taught these things, or said that as educational theorists we were 'making a value-judgement' about it, we should find this hard to grasp: not, of course, because any suggestion that children should not be taught them is logically incoherent, nor because reasons might not be given for not teaching them — maybe they will die unless all their spare time is spent in collecting food. The point is rather that the notion of educating people, and hence the notion of educational theory itself, is too closely bound up with the idea of people who can use language in these ways to admit of much question. I do not say that education is logically impossible for illiterate mutes, but it is hard to think of any seriously-held educational ideal — that is, here, any set of views about what ought to be learned — to which talking and reading could not, at least in principle, be an asset. Of course, one might hold some 'doctrine of man' according to which children should be allowed or encouraged to be very like animals, or one might think that language brought more dangers than benefits, and hence should be eschewed. But then one would not be interested in education or educational theory at all.

Just how many of such truths would emerge from a close study of the defining characteristics of educational theory as such, and how much necessity they would be seen to have, is of course an immense question not to be tackled here. But it is possible to see, I think, that they might be far more in number and far wider in application than is commonly supposed. The notion of 'human learning', of people learning things important to them *qua* people, seems *prima facie* to carry a good many conceptual trappings with it. Best documented in the philosophical literature are (a) necessary characteristics of being a *person*, and (b) necessary characteristics of there being a *society* (itself necessary for the existence of people); we think here of things like language-use, a norm of truth-telling, the existence of social rules and authorities, and so on.[26] Still more might be gained by examining the notion of an (any) *educational context*: would not certain features — for instance, a minimum of seriousness, a certain type of discipline, the ability to relate to other people in certain roles or ways — be demonstrably required for us to talk of 'education' at all? It might even be that educational theory should be chiefly concerned with the development of these universally necessary features; and if that were so, any area involving 'value-judgements' might appear negligible.

To continue with our example: having seen the virtual necessity of teaching children to read, we might then get down to determining the best 'means' to this 'end'.[27] What is the value of this method as against that? Here, if anywhere, it seems intelligible to talk of 'value-judgements'; though, in existing quasi-philosophical jargon, it is just here that most people refrain from using the term. This is, I think, because there is a powerful idea that if there are *reasons* or an adequate methodology for making judgements in any area, they are *eo ipso* not 'value-judgements'. Whether anybody *really* believes that decisions about what to do, in education or other matters, are arbitrary — that is, outside the scope of reason — it is difficult to say: people sometimes write, more often talk or behave, as if they believed this, but that they should seriously do so seems to me incredible.[28] I think there would

even be difficulties in coherently maintaining that the relevant reasons
were not connected with notions with which we are already fairly
familiar, for instance, with happiness or satisfaction. Thus if somebody
argued that children should learn X rather than Y, but claimed that this
had absolutely *no* connection with their own or anyone else's happiness
or satisfaction, it would be difficult to see such a person as *reasoning* at
all, rather than, say, expressing a feeling or trying to share a fantasy.

Whilst therefore there are plainly *some* areas, free from any kind of *a
priori* necessity, which call for decisions in educational theory about
what we ought to do, it is not at all clear just where these are to be
located: they may appear as much in the 'method' as in the 'objectives',
and certainly 'the facts' in any area are going to operate as reasons for
'the values' — if we must use this misleading terminology. What is much
more important, and totally omitted not only in Hirst's account but in
that of almost every other writer, is the *methodological point at which*
these issues ought to come up for discussion. This is, so to speak, the
important practical question for educational theory: one disastrously
overlooked or else wrongly answered by the picture of a 'value-
judgement' department.

Our example will serve here too. A competent educational theorist
will in some sense take it for granted that children ought to learn to
read. But he will *not* then charge blithely ahead to look at various
'methods'; for it is by no means clear just what ought to be *meant by*
such phrases as 'able to read', 'literate', etc. For instance, we are talking
of the child's ability to read, or also of his willingness — would we be
satisfied if as an adult he could (at the point of a gun) read, but in fact
never read anything (including his income tax demands)? What is to
count as 'reading' anyway? Not, presumably, just facing a text and
emitting appropriate sounds. If we insist on some amount of 'compre-
hension', then what amount? What *sort* of texts must he be able to
comprehend? Are we to count it as 'reading' if a person can interpret
(a) coloured signals, (b) hieroglyphics, (c) mathematical symbols,
(d) Chinese or Cyrillic scripts (the sort of questions one would want to
raise in trying to understand what was meant by 'dyslexia')?

It seems to me entirely clear that this is the crucial point[29] for the
methodology of educational theory, as we can see by contrasting such
procedure with the severance of 'value-judgement' and 'fact-finding'
('empirical') departments. For, in this case of reading, how could one
either make sensible judgements about what and how one ought to
teach children *or* 'determine the facts about reading', except by some
process of asking questions and marrying up concepts with observables
similar to that described above? It also seems clear that the vast
majority of topics in educational theory are of this kind. What *is it to
be*, or what are we going to *count as*, well-disciplined, a serious student

of science, a sound judge of art, educated in morality, 'autonomous', 'creative', and so on? Of course one can collect 'brute' facts about children and schools and the educational system: sometimes these may be so 'brute' as to be non-controversially factual, and sometimes they may even be closely related to human learning. But they will rarely be facts which are central to 'education' as we have described it.

I have given some examples and further reasons relating to this point elsewhere.[30] Here it is, I think, worth noting that the current practice of educational theory reinforces the point precisely by its failure to attend to it directly. Clearly *behind* contemporary controversies and fashions about, say, 'the teaching of classics' (English, mathematics, or any other subject) lies the question 'What is it to be educated in classics (English, etc.)?' Similarly, different views about 'discipline', or 'integration', or (even more obviously) 'religious education' cry out for a clarification or mapping out of what we are talking about. The point here is not just (not even chiefly) that we must be clear what we are talking about 'before we get down to the facts' or 'before we launch research projects'; it is rather that, *in* trying to get clear what we are talking about, 'the facts' themselves become clearer, and it then becomes clearer also what sort of other 'facts' we need to know.

This last point is perhaps the most crucial. If one actually examines a particular area of educational study — 'discipline', for instance — it is impossible to avoid the conclusion that most of all of the empirical work done is based on a false, or at least a questionable, picture of the topic. Grant, for instance, as we outlined earlier,[31] that 'discipline' is not or not necessarily about just keeping children 'in order', or 'trouble-free', or 'controlled', but about children being able and willing to recognize legitimate authorities and obey rules *qua* legitimate rules (not, for instance, because they emanate from a popular teacher). On this supposition, it is at the time of writing correct to say that practically *no work at all* of a serious empirical kind has been done on discipline. Further — and this is our present point — it would be impossible to see what sort of work is required without adjusting one's picture (of what discipline is) in the first place; for, obviously, the *kind* of facts or observations required will follow from the picture.

Now how are we to describe this sort of work? To call it 'philosophical' may lead people in either of two false directions: they may suppose that the philosopher's work in educational theory is to produce over-arching 'aims' involving 'value-judgements' (or perhaps even 'metaphysical beliefs'), or that he is simply concerned to 'make us define our terms more clearly' or 'sharpen up our concepts'. 'Phenomenological' is obscure and probably equally misleading. It might be possible to describe it under the heading 'psychology', but we are clearly not talking about behaviouristic or so-called 'experimental' psychology: the more person-oriented and hence theoretically relevant apparatus of 'depth psychology', 'psychoanalysis' and so on is usually firmly wedded to clinical or medical procedures, and the logically much more soundly-based social psychology of which Harré has been the most scholarly advocate[32] is concerned primarily with people as social agents, and hence fails to cover all the relevant ground.

These (absurdly brief) remarks on 'psychology' show us the tip of an iceberg, which we have either to break up or steer round if we want to develop anything in the nature of a serious and workable methodology. Our position is that we have some sort of overall idea of the *kind of work* that has to be done here, an idea which could be made fuller and perhaps clearer by the use of more examples and particular cases, but when we try to marry this up with existing disciplines, or at least with the titles of such disciplines, we confront immense difficulties. Consider first the institutionalized titles, 'philosophy', 'sociology' and 'history'. Then add various branches of these, or cognate studies, or whatever it may be appropriate to say, for instance, 'moral philosophy', 'philosophy of mind', 'philosophical psychology', 'clinical psychology', 'social psychology', 'cognitive psychology', 'sociometry', 'social history' and many others. Next, add some titles which seem *prima facie* to stand for studies especially concerned with the understanding of *people*, and therefore perhaps highly relevant to educational theory — 'anthropology', 'literature', 'psychiatry'. Finally, add in those which (for a heterogeneous variety of reasons) may be, if only tangentially, relevant to particular educational problems: 'statistics', 'economics', and various branches of 'medicine'.

Now there are various things we can sensibly say, if called upon to answer the question of 'which disciplines are relevant'. Of these, the most important is that the studies concerned with people *qua* learners are clearly central. Here a good deal of what *in practice* is done under 'psychology', and even more of what is done under 'sociology' and 'history', would sink without trace. For it is wholly obvious that much of this is either not concerned directly with people (as rational beings) at all, or else concerned with them under some particular description which has no special connection with learning — for instance, as occupying a particular social class or fulfilling social roles, or as related to particular social institutions. From this point of view, we should naturally want at least to challenge the three institutionalized empirical disciplines ('psychology', and 'history'), since off-hand it looks as if more person-oriented studies are better candidates. Thus if we want to know, for instance, how to understand the mental processes of teenage gangs, or of pupils in a boarding school, 'anthropology' seems a better bet than 'sociology' or 'history', and similarly, if our interest lies in the conscious and unconscious thoughts of individual pupils, we should naturally be drawn more to 'literature' or 'psychiatry' than to 'experimental psychology'.

We could then, I suppose, plunge into a discussion of whether some of the institutionalized disciplines could be re-oriented so as to be more relevant. Could not sociology, for example, concentrate less on the wider society and more on the internal social relationships of schools? And could it not, with a big effort, do this with its eye firmly fixed on the connection between these relationships and *learning* (or education)? Might it not even drop, modify, or at least inspect the technical terminology which it now uses but which might not be suitable for these new interests? Of course moves in this direction might be made (some have been);[33] are we then to argue about whether what is now done should count as *sociology* rather than, say, social psychology or anthropology?

That such discussions need to take place is clear from the quite remarkable statements made by some of those who represent these disciplines. Thus, to use (purely for convenience) the book mentioned earlier, Professor Simon kicks off his contribution with 'There is no need to make out a case for the study of the history of education as an essential aspect of the course offered to intending teachers. It has long been accepted as such in most colleges and universities and is almost universally taught, in its own right [?], as part of the education course.'[34] On the same page we have the blunt 'Education is a social function'; and on the next it is presented to us as a conclusion that 'It is with the study of education as a social function, then, that historical study should be primarily concerned'. Similarly from Professor Taylor we have 'Sociologists of education are interested, first of all, in the way in which schools, colleges and universities are related to other institutions and structural features of the societies in which they exist', together with a good deal of talk about 'the demands of industry', 'the pressures of employers and the labour market', 'a multi-dimensional relationship with other aspects of social structure', 'the system of class and status stratification', and so forth.[35]

Remarks of this kind almost tempt one to think that representatives of the empirical disciplines have deliberately removed themselves from a concern with *education* as such by a non-act of inertia, if not by an act of will, but at least they will serve to show how urgent the need for proper discussion is. But this immediately returns us to a point adumbrated earlier,[36] more important for our purposes than anything that might be said about the 'relevance' of various 'disciplines'. The point is quite simply that *this question itself* − or rather, the immense variety of questions that arise when we consider the nature and relevance of various studies − could not conceivably be answered except in a certain context of communication, by people properly qualified to answer it. The problems here are like, though perhaps even more sophisticated than, those that arise in educational theory itself: they face the same, or even graver, difficulties as we noted when describing the kind of work that educational problems require.

I shall try to unscramble this vicious and apparently infinite regress in the next chapter: I mention it here because it gives us one reason for setting a limit on what can sensibly be said about the application of educational disciplines to educational problems in general — I think, the most important reason for such limitation. But there are also two other reasons. First, within the frontiers imposed by the concept of education itself, educational problems may still be very heterogeneous: for some, we may need a certain mixture of disciplines, for others, a quite different mixture. Some (as I have suggested elsewhere)[37] may lend themselves to a kind of treatment in stages, whereby the problem is first inspected by a philosopher and then passed to empirical workers, but this model is certainly not cast-iron. Clearly much will depend on what is allowed to count as 'a problem (topic) in educational theory', as opposed to a sub-section or branch of a problem. Secondly, a lot will turn on what or who the 'educational theory' is *for*; different 'practical principles' will be required for, say, teachers, head teachers, curriculum designers, local education authorities and others; and the notion that each of these would just be tailor-made cuttings from some total or overall 'educational theory' may not be a coherent one.

Nevertheless, I think there are some things of a general nature which can profitably be said. The first is that, even though much is still uncertain, we do nevertheless now have some kind of picture or model of the process of 'educational theory': I mean, some idea of what the actual task of looking at an 'educational problem' so as to produce some 'practical principles' would look like. We begin, necessarily, with the notion of a person or people learning something, of certain pupils learning about discipline, or learning to read, or learning to appreciate music, or whatever. Our central or initial task is thus to answer questions of the form 'What *is it for* a person to learn X?' or 'What *happens when* a person learns X?' Here we obviously require (1) a very clear grasp of the structure of the subject-matter, X; and (2) a phenomenological understanding, at the most basic level, of what goes on when X is learned. In fact these two are barely separable; certainly it would be premature to think that (2) could be cashed out in terms of some highly-generalized 'learning theory' — almost everything may depend on *what* is learned. But in any case, we have to start here.

Moving outwards from this inner or central area, we should then want to know something about the learners which was of most *immediate* or *direct* relevance to their learning X: we might call this their 'individual psychology'. Here we are interested in an area marked, extremely vaguely, by terms like 'intelligence', 'motivation', 'attitude' and so on. How stupid/serious/recalcitrant/attentive are they? How do they see the business of learning X, particularly perhaps in reference to the person who teaches them or other sources from which they learn? In what ways are they successful or unsuccessful in the learning? There are clearly overlaps here with our inner area, but it is possible to see this task under the description of *personal understanding* (the 'form of thought' that Hirst calls 'personal knowledge',[38] and which the kind of construction that Morris puts on the term 'psychology' makes tolerably clear).[39] Some of the questions here will of course concern the learners as members of a group: so that besides the techniques of 'individual psychology' we shall need the sort of 'personal knowledge' perhaps to be found in anthropology, social psychology, history, literature and other such disciplines.

Moving still further outwards, we shall find ourselves driven towards finding out what more *general* facts about these learners and their context of learning may be relevant: facts, for instance, about their home background, their attitude to school, their social and economic expectations, their physical health, and so on. This remains relevant to educational theory *if* (only if) these 'background studies', as we may call them, are directly geared to the more central areas of study. As educational (rather than political, social or economic) theorists, we are interested in, say, the child's physical health or home life or poverty *only* insofar as this relates to his *learning*. Thus it is educationally relevant to know that a child's language use at home is such-and-such, if only because it enables us to judge the gap between that language use and whatever language use we think it educationally desirable for him to have; the correlations of this with social class, for instance, are not directly relevant.[40]

We need to remind ourselves again here that the study of education is normative, in the sense described earlier (p. 38 ff.). That is, we are concerned to produce certain results or states of affairs which we take to be desirable — often, I think, because they form part of some sensibly expanded concept of 'being educated', 'having the kinds of understanding men need to have', or whatever. The desiderata are encapsulated in phrases like 'knowing some science', 'possessing some moral understanding', 'being able to appreciate literature', and so forth. These are our goals: we are not concerned, or not directly or necessarily concerned, to achieve some general understanding of the human mind or the social behaviour of men. This sets a sharper criterion over 'the psychology (sociology, etc.) of education' than we have as yet fully brought out. For the means by which our goals may be achieved do not *necessarily* have much, or anything, to do with the general psychological and social background — not, at least, above the level of common sense.

Consider briefly the example of learning science, a goal which we may fairly suppose ourselves to be achieving more effectively now than in the Middle Ages. But it would be hard to claim that this is because we now know more psychology and sociology; the ground we have gained is different, and consists (putting it roughly) (1) of getting clear how to do science, or establishing a proper methodology for pupils to learn, and (2) of being willing and serious in pursuing this methodology (rather than continuing down the avenues of alchemy, astrology and superstition in general). Psychologists and sociologists may now chip in with various empirical facts which will help us to improve our teaching: they may even be able, retrodictively, to explain to us the psychosocial conditions which enabled science to be established in this way. But they can do this only because (1) and (2) are already the case; only because we have a firm grasp of the subject, a grasp which (under any normal conditions) itself allows us to go ahead and *teach* it without the benefit of psychology and sociology.

Now consider areas where we are less clear — 'being morally educated', 'appreciating art', 'being educated in religion' (and there are many other less dramatic cases). How could the social sciences help us with these, unless and until we were clear — since they would not know what to help us *about*? In this position, a very common one in education, what tends too often to happen is that some sort of clarity is assumed prematurely; the psychologists and sociologists then get to work, bringing some standard theories and orthodoxies (e.g. the Piagetian 'stages of development') to bear, when it is still not clear what they are supposed to bear *on*.[41]

This produces not only a good deal of muddle and potential irrelevancy, but also more positive impediments to progress. It *may* be the case — as with science, and (I would guess) almost any other sort of understanding about which we ourselves are conceptually and methodologically clear — that once we know properly that we are trying to do we can simply go ahead and do it. Or, perhaps, we can do part of it: there seems no reason, for instance, why some ('cognitive') elements in moral education should not be directly taught to children, even though other elements require different treatment. In this instance, as I have suggested elsewhere,[42] it is wholly unclear just how the 'psychological facts' about 'development' fit in, or indeed just what sort of 'facts' they are.

Chiefly because the social sciences have (incoherently) attempted a 'value-free' or purely 'descriptive' approach, they tend to offer information which may sidetrack rather than enlighten the educator — who is, of course, *ex hypothesi* committed to the increase of genuine (and serious) understanding and knowledge, not to the replacement of some 'values' or 'attitudes' by others. Consider, for instance, the use of such terms as 'inner-directed', 'autonomous' and 'liberal'. Psychologists and sociologists employ such terms descriptively, in contrast to 'other-directed', 'heteronomous' and (perhaps) 'authoritarian'. Now if these terms could be cashed out without any implications of 'value' — I mean here, without it being part of their *meaning* that the 'autonomous' ('liberal', etc.) man is more *reasonable* or understanding than his opposite — then the educator will see no reason to produce such people rather than their opposites. On the other hand, if they contain implications of greater rationality within them, they may fairly describe educational aims — but then they can no longer be used purely 'descriptively'. In fact, such terms tend to fluctuate between these two uses, though I suppose that, most of the time, the former usage prevails; plus, perhaps, a sort of tacit 'ideological' endorsement of autonomy, liberalism, and so on which is not clearly stated or argued for.

If we were to extract and clarify the implications of rationality (assuming them to exist) in these and other phrases, much of the interests of psychology and sociology might fall away or alter direction. Take two terms with more obvious rational or educational implications: 'unprejudiced' and 'sincere'. Then what (one might crudely ask) is the point of detailed analysis of current and particular social prejudices (race prejudice, for instance), or of the various ways in which people are insincere ('the games people play')?[43] As educators we want them to abandon prejudice *in general*, not simply to submerge one prejudice; we want them to stop playing games *at all* and be more sincere. The more clearly we define the educational aims, the more doubt is cast on the relevance of the (often fascinating) descriptive details which the social sciences offer us.

The natural answer to this question is 'But surely these facts at least enable us to identify the opposition. We need to know what prejudices people have, and how they come to have them: what games people play, and why they play them. Without some such factual background, how can the educator know enough to change them?' Of course there is a lot in this. But the *kind* of 'factual background' to be sought would, I think, look very different once we appreciate the educational aims: we cannot 'identify the opposition' unless we are clear about what it is opposition *to*. What are the *general* temptations to prejudice or 'games-playing?' We need to know this, rather than a multitude of empirical facts about the details.

Many of such details, in any case, can be seen pretty clearly as the constructions of some fantasy or emotions of which the person himself is largely unaware. Not much, surely, is gained by a very detailed account of a racially-prejudiced Nazi, or by the particularized study of various lunatic-fringe religions at an overt level; if we do this, we should do it in order to detect just what sort of irrationality lies at the roots of such aberrations — rather as a psychotherapist would attend to a patient's symptoms. It is, in fact, difficult to see how empirical work can help the educator unless the whole business of the unconscious mind is taken much more seriously than most 'educational theory' now takes it.

All this means, I think, that the picture whereby educational theory 'draws on all the knowledge within the various forms that is relevant to educational pursuits but proceeds from there in grappling with practical problems'[44] has, in practice, to be considerably modified. The point is not only that one might doubt whether there was, in fact, a solid corpus of 'knowledge' or body of theory in the disciplines of philosophy, psychology, sociology and so on, nor only that, even granted such a corpus, one might doubt how much of it was relevant to the goods specified by 'education'. It is rather that, in any actual instance of serious research or study, one finds that one has to adopt a quite different strategy. So far from first 'drawing on all the knowledge in the various forms' and then 'proceeding from there in grappling with practical problems', we have to *start* with clarifying some objective, consider the practical difficulties of achieving it, and pick up whatever empirical knowledge we find to be relevant on the way.

This is the kind of movement of thought, or general strategy, I have been trying to describe. Its force is perhaps not easy to see without the use of numerous and lengthy examples. But I hope to have shown the inadequacy of the orthodox picture whereby, for instance, we suppose a person must be 'properly grounded' in some 'relevant discipline' (usually psychology or sociology), so that he can then 'draw on' the relevant 'knowledge' in order to make sense of educational problems. To put this another way: 'psychology (sociology, etc.) of education', insofar as we need such phrases at all, will not look like a chunk or cross-section of orthodox psychology 'brought to bear' on educational problems, so much as a heterogeneous and often *ad hoc* collection of empirical facts seen to be relevant to an educational problem or objective. Indeed it may well be the case (I think it usually is) that we do not yet *know* the right sort of facts, and that we shall only come to discover them by starting with the problem and expanding outwards from there; that 'psychology (sociology, etc.) of education', if 'of education' is taken seriously, is at present a more or less *empty* heading.

'The relevant facts' (and in practical study, as in philosophy, we shall rapidly be driven towards a more sophisticated attitude to what is to count as 'a fact') have to be gained or viewed within the magnetic field, so to speak, of our initial educational interest. We have to keep the magnetism strong enough — the interest clear and passionate enough —

to draw in the facts we need. Here lies the danger of talking, even to the small extent that I have done, of 'the relevance' of various 'disciplines' (psychology, social psychology, anthropology, and so on), for this at once implies bodies of knowledge that may be taken to be 'relevant' *en bloc*. It will already be apparent — and we will develop this in the next chapter — that in such a situation the *practical* or operative methodology will be all-important. More plainly, almost everything will depend on having the right sort of people (clearly, people of very high *general* intelligence) in the right sort of working context (clearly, a context of very good general communication). This is going to cut more ice than any number of 'models' or blueprints about 'fitting in' the various disciplines.

In operating this general strategy or movement of thought, it is clear that the criterion of *relevance to learning X* will be our guide throughout, not only when X is some subject-title like mathematics or reading, but even more when we are talking about more general powers of the mind which can, to whatever extent, be acquired by learning — that is, by education; for instance, whatever may sensibly be marked by 'seriousness', 'autonomy', 'creativity', and so on. Here the central area, with its central question 'What is it to be "serious" ("autonomous", "creative", etc.)?', is even more important, for two reasons. First, the terms used are even more uncertain than ordinary subject-titles: we have some idea of what it is to learn mathematics, for instance, but would find it much easier to stray into nonsense or muddle with 'learning to be creative'. Secondly, and partly because of this uncertainty, we may also stray away from the notion of education in dealing with such terms. Some or many powers of the mind may not be primarily produced by *education* at all, and we shall be easily tempted into areas better dealt with under some other *techne*. Not, again, that these areas would be totally irrelevant to education, inasmuch as they might at least give us important information about the background against which, as educators, we were working. But it is an interesting and important question, for instance, how far one can *learn* to be (say) self-confident — as opposed to being *made* self-confident or *given* self-confidence, perhaps by being given money or hugs or tranquillisers. These complications do not so easily arise when we are considering subject-titles.

There is one difficulty (amongst many, but this one is worth speaking about generally) in applying this criterion, however, which is generated by the notion of producing 'practical principles'. If this is taken in a strong sense — that is, to refer to principles that a teacher, for instance, could actually *use* as soon as he grasps them — then clearly an enormous amount will depend on particular parameters. Such parameters are very various. Some may be straightforwardly political or quasi-political: for instance, that head teachers, or local authorities, or the law, will simply not allow certain things to be done, however desirable they might be educationally. Thus if even the occasional use of, say, 'corporal punishment' (whatever this may mean exactly) emerged as justified by educational theory, this could hardly count as a practical principle for teachers in an area where it was forbidden by law, or on pain of losing their jobs. Others might be more 'brute'; thus with the best political will in the world, we may not in the near future be able to turn out 100 per cent of pupils as fluent readers by the time they reach the secondary school, so that a 'practical principle' for secondary school teachers based on this assumption would not be practical. Plenty of other examples could be given.

This is of course a very general difficulty which applies to all *technai*. We have to decide somewhere in the range between, at one end, principles like 'Well, ideally, what we ought to do is so-and-so' and, at the other, principles like 'As things are, what we ought to do tomorrow is such-and-such'. In such a range, the content of the 'we' will differ: thus in the first remark it implies something like 'All educators, once we realize the desirability of doing it, should persuade the government and the parents, and so on'; in the second, 'Teachers in schools as they now are in the UK' (or wherever). I do not want to make too heavy weather of such an obvious point, but it raises a strategic or tactical question which confronts educational theorists at every turn, and to which they need to give very clear answers in each case.

A model example of this, in the UK today (and elsewhere), can be seen in the notion of religious education ('RE'). Suppose one believed (1) that proper or well-considered religious education should be of a certain kind (roughly, trying to give pupils more understanding and competence in the general area of religious thought and feeling); (2) that, nevertheless, particular local authorities or parents or even teachers either did not understand this or did not agree with it; (3) that they might understand and agree with new educational practices which, while not really based on (1), nevertheless might be seen as 'moving towards' it — for instance, some minimal study of non-Christian religions, which did not too much threaten sectarian believers. What sort of 'practical principles' should the educational theorist issue in this situation? Or what, indeed, should be his starting-point for any practically effective 'educational theory' in the area of religious education?

Plainly, whether we like it or not, we are here in an area for which 'political' is a fair title — that is (as I shall use the term), in which we have to consider not or not only what 'we' as rational people ought collectively to do, but also what some more specific 'we', still rational but taking as given the irrational obstruction of others, will find it most effective to do. Since the answers to such questions will be heavily context-dependent, the most important thing is to *recognize* the difference and allow for it; in particular, to make it clear in each case to those who are going to operate the practical principles which as educational theorists we give them, in as honest a way as we can. This would involve saying to teachers something of the form: 'XY and Z are what you really ought to do, for reasons given here, but since tiresome politicians or parents or local authorities make it difficult or impossible, we suggest PQ and R as the nearest thing'.

The point here lies in the enormous importance of establishing educational theory as something which is as free from political and other irrational pressures as possible. If such freedom is not defended constantly, specifically educational goods become subservient to irrational interests, and educational theory turns into a machine for serving such interests — whether the interests are those of the Nazi Party, a consumer-oriented society, or the fantasies and prejudices in contemporary climates of opinion loosely attached to the business of education.[45] Such defence may sometimes cost us some practicality: there would not be many practical principles for *education* which had much hope of being carried out in, say, Nazi Germany in the 1940s. But then it is the duty of educational theorists to point this out, rather than to pretend to themselves and others. Without this, it is difficult to see that any proper educational theory could survive at all; indeed it is pretty clear how, in our own society for instance, such theory easily loses whatever identity it had and becomes a kind of applied sociology based on certain vague but obviously partisan doctrines.

In this connection, it is important that educational theory should face some very general and (as they say) 'abstract' questions; that is, questions not too tightly tied to particular local conditions. (We might, indeed, make out some sort of *a priori* case for this: if somebody was interested *solely* in what was learned by, say, pygmies or Oxford undergraduates, it would be odd to say that he was studying education. He could certainly be studying the education of pygmies and Oxonians, but that is importantly different. How many actual *generalizations* ('laws', 'theories') are possible or useful in another matter; I suspect, not many.) The practical need here is to resist the temptation to 'get things done', to be 'relevant', and create at least the impression of activity rather than 'mere theory'. But our present position is, quite obviously, that we actually *know* — or, it is better to say, are properly *clear about* — very little. Now there are no doubt many decisions in practical education to which *anything* that we could call theory would be only obliquely relevant. A teacher has to decide what to do with such-and-such children, from 10 to 11, on a rainy Tuesday, with only a blackboard, etc.; only he can decide, partly because there are so many particularities, and partly because only he is in a position to know what the children are like. What theory can, in principle, do is to equip teachers and others with useful understanding; I do not say 'general truths' or even 'knowledge', because it is an open question how far such understanding will take the form of specific (empirical) *truths* rather than a much less specific awareness or clear-headedness. But if theory is to do this, it must to some extent stand back from the particular; especially it must stand back from the temptation to *change* things without an adequate basis of knowledge for doing so.

I suspect that the passion for activity and change, very obvious in practical education over the last few decades (and not only in the UK), fills a vacuum caused by the absence of any serious and respectable educational theory. It is as if, lacking any proper scientific backing for medical treatment, not only doctors but professors of medicine were to spend their time desperately trying out this or that remedy; only our position is worse, in that it is even unclear what is to count as a 'remedy'. Educational theorists at present devote much time and energy to forwarding some particular cause; if not overtly of a semi-political or social nature, a cause which advocates 'a new curriculum' 'the reorganization of the secondary school', 'team teaching', 'the integrated day' and other wholly unproven suggestions. Those that do not want to, or cannot, go in for such causes tend (as we noted earlier) to fall back on their own disciplines, some of which at least suggest more solid and academically respectable ground.

However this may be, it seems essential that educational theory should face general questions. What can we sensibly say, and what can we prove, about discipline in relation to learning? What makes some pupils more serious than others? What sorts of things are there to be learned, and how are we to categorize them? We come back to questions of this sort, if only to see how little we know and how difficult the questions are, but the point about generality applies at many levels. What is it to learn to read? To learn to understand other people? To learn self-control? To care for art? More specific studies — how to develop art in the primary school, whether to use a look-and-say or a C-A-T teaching method, etc. — must wait on answers to these general questions. I do not say, of course, that all practical action should be held up until we have these answers, but it is not the role of educational theory to engage in practical action of this kind.

The muddle here emerges very clearly in the use of terms like 'research' and 'development' in education. Nowadays almost anything counts as 'research', and there are (otherwise) reputable public bodies, such as the Schools Council, who constantly promote 3-year and other short-term projects on major topics, projects whose point and status are wholly unclear. Consider, for example, a project set up for a 3-year period under the rubric 'moral education'[46]. What is this supposed to *be*? If it is fairly to be called 'research', what questions is it supposed to answer and by what disciplines? If not — for it would not be easy to believe that many truths of a general kind could be elucidated, in such a thorny and conceptually complex topic, within three years — , is it to 'develop' something? *What* established research-findings is it supposed to 'develop'? Or is it, as one might be driven eventually to believe, just the idea to have something generally 'going on' in the area of moral education: something to 'stir up teachers', 'provide new materials', and 'arouse concern'? The criteria of success here would, I suppose, be those appropriate to a successful advertising or public relations campaign; not *per se* contemptible, but why should anyone call it 'research' or 'development'?

This is the kind of muddle we get into for lack of any proper concern with establishing *truth*. Inevitably we start grinding particular axes, being concerned for the success of our own particular 'projects' or 'programmes' — and 'success' here will mean little more than 'popularity'. A special (and, of course, defensively unclear) terminology has been developed to cover this confusion, including phrases like 'operational research', 'action research', 'illuminative evaluation', and so on. The actors in this ritual drama are sustained by research grants or funds given for highly specific and 'practical' purposes ('the curriculum' is a fashionable one, because it looks like something down-to-earth and 'relevant'), and by pressure from teachers and others on researchers to produce something 'concretely useful'. Politicians chip in with specific social demands, such as the reduction of racial tension, or football hooliganism, or the need to 'break down class barriers' or learn French for the Common Market, or whatever it may be. It is not surprising that educational theory reels beneath these blows.

Such phenomena suggest that we are in fact operating in the *least* 'practical' way possible. Any effective practical 'development' or application must follow from an effective educational theory; unless and until we can set up such theory, the rest is mere fashion or policics or ritual. Moreover, it should already be clear that the connection between the theory or research and the practical development must be extremely close: the 'developers' must *understand* enough of the theory to develop it effectively — and the nature of such theory implies that this will be a great deal. It is not like producing pills which the teacher or pupil can just take, without understanding but to good effect; competent theory produces a better understanding, and understanding is not something that can simply be swallowed.

Somewhere on the outskirts of the circles of our educational theory, . then, we need studies and mechanisms which it may be harmless to describe under the heading of 'development' or 'application', though the nature of these will clearly vary, depending on both *what* is being 'developed' and *whose* benefit it is being 'developed' *for*. Much of this, if we are right about the nature of the central area of educational theory, will necessarily take the form of what may be called *translation*, that is, casting the acquired insights and clarity ('truths', if you like) into a readily-assimilable shape for the benefit of teachers, curriculum advisers, administrators and so on. In other words, 'development' will often be in the form 'Understand the following' rather than 'Do this'.

We are now, I suppose, in a position to do something beloved by educational writers: that is, to make a picture or diagram representing the operation of educational theory, which I have done on the opposite page. The notes beneath will, I hope, clarify it sufficiently; and it may help to reinforce some of the points made in this chapter. But these points have, of necessity, been discursive and heterogeneous. However important they may be, this in itself should stress the much greater importance of what may be called the *social mechanism* required to get educational theory or the study of education off the ground. Who are the 'properly qualified' people? What setting is needed for the 'kind of work' that has to be done? How, in practice, would we get it started? What political or other obstacles are there? What would it *look like*? These were the questions with which we began this chapter, and though I hope to have said something relevant to answering them, they have certainly not yet been answered. We shall address them further in the next chapter.

Notes

1 See O'Connor (1972), Moore (1974), and references.

2 p. 38 ff.

3 'Educational Theory', in Tibble (1966). See also a later discussion with O'Connor in Hirst (1972).

4 I mean, that 'educational theory' is not a single 'discipline' or 'form of thought': this can be granted here, I think, without too close an inquiry into the criteria of application for such terms.

5 Tibble (1966) p. 48.

6 p. 49.

7 p. 54.

8 p. 42 ff.

9 p. 52.

10 p. 53.

11 Wilson (1971), p. 251 ff.

12 p. 41.

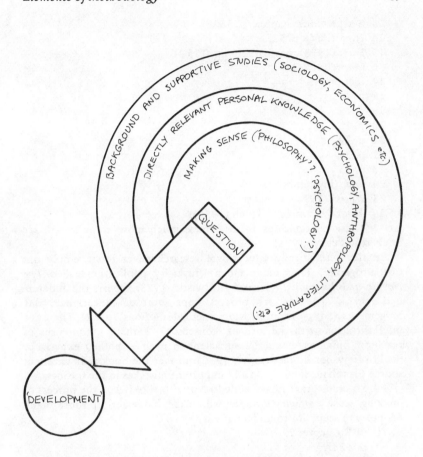

This diagram merely encapsulates the points that any, or almost any, question in educational theory (1) must at least begin with the 'central area' of philosophical/psychological work ('phenomenological'?), which I have here called just 'making sense'; (2) then moves us outward, keeping whatever clarity we have gained in mind, and selecting only 'the facts' thus perceived as relevant, (a) through the more immediately relevant area of 'personal knowledge' and then (b) through the 'background and supportive studies'.

This broad arrow of work thus cuts a swathe, the size and nature of which is determined by the way in which we 'make sense' (in the central area) of the question and which results in some kind of 'practical principles' leading to 'development'.

Some readers may find that this diagram clarifies what I am trying to say; others that it obfuscates it. I apologise here to the latter.

13 See previous chapter, p. 35.

14 Hirst (*ibid*.) p. 52.

15 Hirst (1972), particularly pp. 115-16.

16 Moore (1974).

17 *ibid*., p. 86.

18 p. 18.

19 p. 18.

20 p. 19.

21 p. 29.

22 p. 35.

23 p. 53.

24 *ibid*. (my italics).

25 Wilson (1971), Chapter 6.

26 A good example is Winch (1959).

27 These relationships are of course much more complicated: see Sockett in Peters (1973).

28 Characteristically educational researchers, at least, simply opt out altogether. Thus in an Open University publication called *The Nature of Educational Research* (Entwistle, 1973) appears the undefended remark 'The research process stops short of educational value judgements and so cannot provide practical solutions' (p. 12). There is a mild flirtation with the idea of 'consensus': 'Perhaps a consensus of teachers' opinions would be sufficient in itself — pooled experience could surely not be far wrong?' (p. 8); in fact the book is an excellent source for the most common and important mistakes in the business.

29 So crucial that I have added a Note (p. 174 ff.) on the process of 'making sense', which (I hope) will make it clearer to those many people who seem not to understand it.

30 PER Chapter 2.

31 p. 42 ff.

32 Harré and Secord (1972). Much of Harré's work in particular seems to me of great importance *for* education. But I should hesitate to describe it as work *in* the field (study) of education, since he is not very much concerned with how pupils *ought* to behave or what they *ought* to learn.

33 Among many other examples one might mention Lambert (1968) and Sugarman (1973). These are interesting books; though even here one feels that it is just when and insofar as they doggedly rely upon traditional sociological concepts and procedures that they become heavy-handed or distort.

34 Tibble (1966), p. 92.

35 pp. 182-83.

36 p. 29.

37 PER p. 118 ff.

38 See Hirst and Peters (1970), p. 63.

39 Morris in Tibble (1966).

40 An obvious consideration in reference to, for instance, Bernstein's work, which is highly important for education but clogged with such irrelevancy.

41 A clear case of this is Goldman's work on religious education: see, e.g. Goldman (1964); cf. Wilson (1971), p. 3.

42 Wilson (1973) p. 14 ff.

43 Berne (1966).

44 Hirst in Tibble (1966), p. 48.

45 Bruner (1960) echoes some of the most common: ' . . . a curriculum ought to be built around the great issues, principles and values that society deems worthy . . . ' (p. 53). Behind this lie the high-minded 'democratic' ideas (1) that it must be 'great' matters that go into the curriculum (as against, e.g., the three Rs, or a basic grasp of the main forms of knowledge); (2) that 'society' is the proper judge of these; and (3) that what you should start with is 'issues, principles and values' (as against, say, certain basic concepts or facts or skills). Of course there might be some intelligible thesis underlying these ideas: e.g. that if you start with some 'great' or burning social 'issue' (race prejudice, or survival, or pollution, or whatever) then the pupils' interest will be kindled, so that they will learn more than if you just taught them mathematics and science and so in in a traditional way. But such theses have to be (a) thoroughly clarified and (b) properly proved.

46 The 'Moral Education Curriculum Project': see McPhail (1972). I should add that (1) the project was given a two-year extension; (2) some of the practical materials it produced are, in my view, quite useful for moral education. But the example is nevertheless a good one: see Peters' review in *The Journal of Moral Education*, Vol. 3, no. 1 (1973).

Chapter Three

Practical Requirements and Seriousness

In this chapter I want to outline the practical requirements for any serious and successful study of education. As I see it, these requirements follow — with something like a conceptual or *a priori* necessity — from what we have noticed earlier. It needs to be emphasized at the outset, however, that such necessity does not depend by any means on the whole series of elaborate, if highly generalized, points made in the last two chapters. In effect, the reader is required to accept only (1) that the study of education, or 'educational theory', is methodologically very difficult; (2) that it does not fit snugly into one or more disciplines, as these are at present institutionalized; and (3) that it necessitates *some* prior or continuing concern with what I have called the 'central area', as explained in the last chapter.

Even these modest demands, in fact, may be overstated. In a way, all that is required is the belief that the nature and procedures of educational theory are at least *debatable*, in a fairly radical sense. For if this were seriously believed — and I shall want to put a lot of weight on the notion of 'seriousness' later on — then, presumably, it would be thought that they should in fact be properly debated, and that such debates should be brought to bear on current practice. To put this another way: what matters is not that I should have succeeded in showing educational theory to be methodologically confused or chaotic in certain specific ways, but rather that I should have shown it possible to think this. There are, in fact, plenty of philosophers and others (some of whom I have quoted earlier) who hold roughly similar views, whether or not they would agree with my particular points; this in itself is surely sufficient for my purpose. For if there is serious methodological or procedural doubt, or even if there is a serious possibility of such doubt, then we have to clear this up before we go further, and it is precisely the nature of this 'clearing up' that forms the core of our 'practical requirements'.

Educational theory is here in the worse possible position. On the one hand, there are subjects or disciplines in which the merit of the *work* is comparatively easy to verify: predictions are confirmed or not confirmed, equations solved or unsolved, and something like 'proof' (in a strong sense of the term) is possible. On the other hand, failing such easy verification of performance, there are fields where it is possible to identify 'properly qualified people' by means of some existing tradition or club (as one might call it) of *people* who can pronounce on aspirants. In such fields as literary criticism, psychotherapy and perhaps philosophy this happens often; and, despite its apparent incestuousness, has a validity of its own. Highly intelligent people who have immersed themselves in these fields can, in fact, make reasonable judgements about the qualifications of others; for their immersion, over a period of time, has resulted in a tradition of work which provides criteria (however difficult to define) for such judgements. But education comes into neither category: there is neither easy verification nor a well-established tradition. The question arises, then, of how we can sensibly *start* the business of making educational theory respectable.

Looking first at what actually happens, we can see clearly that *one* way of doing this makes no sense. Characteristically structures and contexts of study, in those areas whose logic is not yet properly established, are organized by a variety of people in the relevant administrative or political positions to do so. Such people may be commissars, civil servants, presidents or vice-chancellors of universities, administrators, and so on. In the UK such people are particularly hard to define: there is perhaps a sort of institutionalized amateurism, as with the occupation of parliamentary Ministries, whereby decisions are entrusted to committees of non-professionals known or believed to be men of standing, intelligence, sound reputation and some interest in the matter. These are, not without good reason, often preferred to 'educationalists', though they normally include or take advice from professional educators and teachers. Much the same picture, though with some important political differences, prevails in the organization of practical education (as against the organization of its theoretical study): members of Government commissions, for instance, are often chosen for their general (it would be wrong to say, 'intellectual') capacities and competence rather than their profound knowledge of the topic under consideration. This is to be contrasted, to a greater or lesser degree, with areas more professionally established: one would hardly talk of 'taking evidence' from nuclear physicists about the internal design of atomic laboratories or even power stations, except where administrative or other issues outside the realm of physics were involved. In these cases we should have little hesitation in saying that the physicists knew best.

To say that this way of organizing the study (or the practice) of education 'makes no sense' is not, of course, to say that it is not understandable, or that — at least in the past — it may not have been the wisest procedure. Given the logical chaos about educational theory, with no identifiable experts, what else could a government or other authoritative body do? There is, however, something to be said even in answer to this last question. We (they) could at least appreciate that the most urgent need is to *make sense of*, or develop an adequate working methodology for, 'educational theory'. If we cling to this simple truth, it is not likely that we should want just *any* person of high general competence on the job, and still less likely that this sort of job (kind of work) could be thought capable of being done in committee or even in a 'working party'.

Two requirements would surely be entirely clear: first, that we should need people of very high *methodological* or *philosophical* competence; and second, that we should need some context of communication much more like a sustained and intense *seminar*. From this might, with luck, result some set of general principles or practices which put the study of education on a logically secure footing; after which, of course, we should have to bring in administrators, politicians and others to help us with the organizational arrangements. In other words, we can at least be clear about *some* of the criteria governing the phrases 'properly qualified' and 'the right sort of context', though others remain to be discussed.

Before explicating this further, let me make it abundantly clear what I am *not* saying. I am not saying (to put it briefly) that we should down tools and do nothing in the study of education or in teacher-training until we are all clearer about our methodology or procedures. There are at least two reasons why this would be absurd. First, there exist *some* things which can usefully be done in these fields without such clarity, or at least without the degree of clarity which we hope for. We know, for instance, that it is useful for intending teachers to have some experience in schools; or that some discussion of different aims and methods in, say, teaching mathematics or RE may be valuable — even though we may not know what sort of school experience is useful, or what sort of discussion to arrange. Secondly, the task of clarifying our methodology and procedures is clearly a never-ending one; to suggest that nothing should be done 'until we are clear' would be rather like suggesting that psychotherapy should not be carried on until we have solved *all* the questions in psychological theory.

Nevertheless, as this last example may imply, there is an opposite and equally dangerous attitude: that of assuming that what in fact goes on (what is institutionalized), particularly if it 'seems to work', is actually best — or, at least, is disaster-free. The attraction of this view, and of 'empirical' as against 'rational' or 'blue-print' approaches to social arrangements in general, is that the *kind* of dangers inherent in the latter is very obvious. In effect, they are the dangers of a monopoly based upon one or more major mistakes. When we contrast 'totalitarian' with notions marked by, perhaps, 'democratic', 'pluralistic', 'empirical', 'experimental', and so on, we have this kind of disaster in mind (amongst other things). We want a system elastic enough to recoup mistakes, and pragmatic ('empirical') enough to avoid becoming too tightly wedded to doctrinaire views.

This sort of approach may, in fact, work extremely well under appropriate conditions: British constitutional and legal procedures may be advantageously contrasted, for instance, over the last few hundred years with those of most other countries. Such appropriate conditions usually include (a) operation in a sphere where a high degree of formalization ('rationalization') or blue-print planning may, for conceptual or empirical reasons, be inappropriate: arguably government is such a sphere (another possible and interesting candidate is town planning): (b) the existence of a strong if unspecified tradition or set of tacit norms which in fact bears the main load, and may give real content to such notions as 'the reasonable man', what is 'done' or 'not done', a 'consensus', 'common sense', and so forth. But in the sphere of educational theory this does not apply. Making sense of it is, demonstrably, a matter of great *intellectual* (not empirical, administrative or political) difficulty, and there is no existing tradition to rely on. To claim that the present system 'seems to work', as one might claim this of a political system that is free from civil war or economic disaster, would be merely to show one's ignorance.

I am not, then, proposing the revolutionary view that our existing mechanisms and institutions for the study of education should grind to a halt, but claiming only that we ought to feel deeply concerned about them on the grounds that they rest upon an inadequate intellectual base. There is, in fact, widespread support for some such claim, but this usually leads to another type of operation which I am also not endorsing here. Very roughly, what tends to happen is that people in these institutions — for a wide variety of motives — become dissatisfied with current procedures and the 'authorities' (both intellectual and institutional) in the field; they then engage in a massive and continuous operation designed to question the purposes and functioning of the institutions. 'What are we really trying to do with these students?', 'Can we make the philosophy of education more "practical"?', 'What sort of school experience should the students have, and how much, and when?', 'Should there be such things as "education departments"?',

'Can't we "integrate" the "educational disciplines" more effectively?',
'What about running new courses on "language" or "cross-cultural
cognitive studies"?' — these and a thousand other questions are raised
and discussed in staff meetings, committees, working parties and other
such contexts.

Much of this arises from a possibly laudable if clearly naive desire to
make such institutions more 'democratic', 'self-critical' or 'flexible', and
to encourage 'participation' or 'an open-ended approach'. With the
social or psychological advantages and disadvantages of this I am not
concerned, but as an intellectual exercise it is likely to fail — not
because the questions are not real and important ones, but because they
are far too difficult to be dealt with in this sort of way. To take any of
the questions seriously would involve a much more organized,
controlled and intense operation. We should naturally think of
something like a seminar, dealing with a limited area, with limited
numbers of people who had done a good deal of background reading,
were highly capable, and were anxious to spend a long time thrashing
out these complicated issues. That this does not happen (not, at least,
as often as it should) is partly because the problem is primarily an
intellectual one, and we do not see it as such.

We require, then, some kind of working group or groups which will
have more credibility than any current approach. So far as this book is
concerned, we are interested in only one type of group — namely, a
group that will be able to achieve solid results in the study of education
or educational theory; though it is already clear, I think, that we shall
have to look later at the criteria for other groups with different if
overlapping functions (for instance, the organization of teacher training
or the general organization of institutions concerned with all these
matters).

The criteria for our working group follow necessarily from our
argument hitherto, and may be set out in rough form under two
headings:

A. Individual qualifications

The immense difficulties of educational theory require that members
of the group should be, first and foremost: (1) people of very high
general intelligence and ability. It is worse than useless to have
second-raters. Because much of the work is centrally to do with what I
have called 'making sense' of whatever topic is on hand, the central or
leading members (2) must be particularly competent at this task, and
there will be at least a large overlap here with competence in
'philosophy', 'methodology', 'conceptual questions', 'phenomenology',
or whatever fairly identifies the required abilities.

Such people are, of course, to be found within the confines of the 'purer' and more well-established disciplines, but it is equally important (3) that they should feel a strong desire, and a lasting one, to bring their abilities to bear *on educational theory*. This criterion may be as difficult to satisfy as (1) and (2) above — after all, why should a person with these talents be particularly concerned with education? It would be easy to find people who are prepared for a time to bring their abilities to bear on education — philosophers, psychologists, etc. who are willing to have 'of education' tacked on to their disciplinary titles, and it would be even easier to find academics in areas peripheral or irrelevant to a proper concept of education willing to do this — economists, historians, sociologists and so forth. But this is very far from meeting the requirements. We need people who are specifically anxious (it might not be too strong to say 'morally committed') to *make sense* of educational theory.

Because of the practical nature of educational theory, an additional criterion (4) might be some practical experience of education. People (like myself) who have spent a lot of time in schools are apt to stress the importance of this: in fact I regard it as rather a weak criterion. Certainly the *ability* to be a successful teacher does not correlate conceptually with the more specifically intellectual talent and interests required for our working group, though some (successful or unsuccessful) experience of practical teaching may obviously help. The relevance of such experience fits in most naturally at the level of 'development' rather than here. Insofar as the criterion has weight at all, I suspect it lies rather in a correlation with a commitment to education (as against the 'ivory tower' pursuit of an academic discipline).

Much clearer is the requirement (5) that the person should be both able and anxious to *communicate* with other members of the group. This might be seen as part of (3) above, but is important enough to need highlighting. Anyone who is serious about wanting to 'make sense' of educational theory must of necessity be serious about thrashing out a large number of basic questions in the company of other people. Other members of the group will almost certainly have received a different training and education from himself, and perhaps represent a different 'discipline'. 'Making sense' will be impossible without an immense amount of hard argument, sustained debate, and tough-minded cross-questioning, as well as individual reflection. Not everyone has the desire and the capacity for this: plainly it will depend partly on personal or psychological characteristics, perhaps best summed up under the term 'seriousness', about which I shall say more later on.[1]

B. Conditions of work

First of all, it is entirely clear (1) that the group must work as a team, and with the minimum of hierarchical structure. We have at all

costs to avoid the autistic quality which pervades so much work at
present, which results partly from excessive prestige or power being
held by some one person (a 'professor' or 'director') who is immune
from radical criticism. It is difficult to fix such a minimum: obviously
somebody must in *some* sense be 'in charge', if only for administrative
purposes; and I am not suggesting that there is a determinate solution
to this problem, which of course is a well-known one in academic and
other contexts. But I should be inclined to err on the side of
egalitarianism, chiefly because the most important aspect of the work
involves argument among equals, and not tasks which can be 'directed'
in the usual sense.

For this reason, another requirement is (2) that the conditions of
communication should be optimal. This is an enormous topic in itself,
belonging (I suppose) to social psychology, and raising the general
question 'What conditions enable people to trust each other, feel both
secure and enthusiastic, and in general produce good intellectual
results?' One naturally thinks here of the importance of informal
contact as well as formal discussion (indeed any sharp distinction
between the two would be a sign of failure); of constant and lengthy
interchanges (even weekly 'interdisciplinary seminars', for instance,
would be totally inadequate); and of more practical working conditions
— time, space, comfort, and independence from external pressures. We
are talking of something like an *enclave*, a 'research team' if you like,
whose members are to work in very close cooperation and proximity.
Plainly this brings its own problems, as well as advantages, with it, but
it is the only set-up that has much chance of success.

Following from this would be the requirement (3) that the group
should not be too large for good communication (perhaps eight or nine
would be a maximum), being able to do business together effectively
over coffee, as it were, rather than constantly having to send pieces of
paper to each other or engage in non-intellectual aspects of administration. Any administrative or other practical requirements must (4) be
under the control of the group (not vice versa) and, more importantly,
(5) the nature of the research should be largely defined by the group,
and not wished onto it by anyone outside. This is because much of the
most important aspects of the work *consists* precisely *in* working out
what it means to be (for example) 'morally educated', 'well-disciplined',
'able to read', 'good at English', or whatever topics may be chosen for
study or research. If, absurdly, the group were to take definitions of
these topics or aims from (say) a government department, a local
education authority, or some grant-bestowing body, half of its proper
function would be lost.

For similar reasons, the group must be (6) autonomous in the sense
that it is not working *for* anybody except in the widest possible

interpretation of that phrase. It may of course use advisers, and there would naturally be some control exercised — in the last resort — over expenditure. Fatal would be any arrangement whereby the group subserved the interests of a particular institution or committee, unless, as (one might hope) in the case of a university or independent college, these interests were so widely defined as not to be dangerous. A further consequence is (7) that the members of the group should have some kind of lengthy, perhaps permanent, tenure; that they should not be beholden to outside pressures, or worrying about their jobs or future jobs, or feel pressed for time and anxious to 'produce results'. A further reason here, of course, is the quite practical one that without tenure it would not be easy to attract people of the required calibre.

All this may be thought utopian: have we not described a small team of demi-gods working under Olympian or at least Elysian conditions? But different *kinds* of practical difficulty must be distinguished here. First, though our criteria for (A) individual qualifications are stringent, I believe there are quite a few people who would meet them; these people can be identified, provided that we use *these* criteria to identify them — rather than, say, whether they hold higher degrees, or have experience of educational research, or whatever *cursus honorum* may be currently in favour. Secondly, attracting and retaining such people is not, in my judgement, chiefly a matter of money. It is much more a matter of making it plain to them that they are trusted to do the required work under the sort of conditions outlined in (B.) — conditions which would produce, in effect, something more like a group of Research Fellows along Oxbridge lines than anything else (at least in the UK). Titles and other artificial aids to prestige and status can be added if necessary without much or any cost, but my guess is that the conditions themselves would achieve the required result. Further, it might not even be necessary to create a large number of expensive new jobs from scratch: it is more a matter of identifying people, already in various jobs, *as* researchers who can give good service, and being willing to listen to them.

This is possible because, thirdly, it is not at all clear that *time* is quite so crucial a factor here as is often supposed. If those selected have a strong desire, as well as the ability, to do such work, then I incline to believe that — at least if their existing jobs are specified along normal university lines — they will find or make the time. Clearly there are limits to this, but I should doubt whether, for instance, a teaching load of 12 or even 20 hours a week during a university term would prevent or even gravely handicap the research efforts of anybody seriously interested in the work — and anybody who was not seriously interested would not be suitable. This appears more plausible when we remember that much of the work will not consist of the traditional hard slogs of data collection, statistical analysis, and so forth, but will be much more a matter of 'making sense'; not that this latter cannot be time-consuming, but rather that it is a task which a suitably committed person is more likely to enjoy for its own sake.

Two important provisos here may dispel alarm: (1) Certainly there must be *some* sort of pressure on the team to produce results, but with judicious selection, and tactful handling, this can be achieved even though the team members have the sort of tenure and scope I have described. This happens, after all, with regard to ordinary and research fellowships at Oxbridge and elsewhere; such a system is not perfect, but has perhaps produced better results in most intellectual fields than any other. (2) More importantly, it is not suggested that any one team should monopolize a research area. There is no reason why two or more such teams should not tackle the same area, though obviously each would have to be closely in touch with what the other was doing. Given any sort of genuine competence, however, it seems likely that the teams would rapidly establish themselves as *the* authorities on various areas; and the recognition of this would save an endless amount of time in bad research, 'development', conferences, committees and working-parties elsewhere.

This is perhaps sufficient to give some idea of what we may call the internal context or set-up required by the study of education. Many readers will still, I suspect, have the feeling that all this is 'impractical', 'up in the air', 'unrealistic', or whatever; being perhaps inclined to ask some such question as 'But what will these teams actually do?' I shall say a little more about this in a minute, but want first to stress that we must not over-determine the answer. One of my main points through-out has been that such over-determination leads directly to the kind of failure evident in so much contemporary study of education, and in so much educational research. This precisely involves a *practical* as well as an intellectual failure: the *least* 'realistic' or 'sensible' procedures are those we now adopt (or if there are still more unrealistic or senseless ones, I find it hard to imagine them). The over-specification of topics for research workers; the multiplication of professors and departments of 'the sociology (psychology, philosophy, etc.) of education'; the uncritical acceptance of supposed 'authorities' and 'research findings' — these and many other moves may appear 'practical' when taken individually, but taken collectively have resulted in chaos and igno-rance.

This is at least the most important reason why 'educational theory' is often and rightly dismissed as 'irrelevant' (*sc.* I take it, to practising teachers and others). It is not that we have too many high-powered but 'impractical' academics who achieve scholarly but 'irrelevant' results; it is rather that we have no solid knowledge at all, whether 'relevant' or otherwise — whereas if we had such knowledge, its 'relevance' would soon become plain, as it clearly does in cases where we are not so methodologically incompetent, such as medicine or engineering (even when the knowledge may begin by appearing to be disconnected from practical medical treatment or bridge-building). For the same reasons, it is foolish to be stampeded into thinking that 'theorists' or researchers must 'get more into schools', 'communicate more with teachers', 'come down from their ivory towers', and so on; just what a theorist or researcher needs to do will depend on what he is working on, and nothing is to be gained by forcing some particular interpretation of 'relevance' on him. We do not need down-to-earth theorists, or theorists who will be certain to get their hands dirty, or theorists who are always in the classroom: what we need is *good* theorists. The fact is that we do not as yet *know* what a 'good theorist' would want to do: we simply have to get good theorists and let them decide.

These considerations (much too briefly sketched here) clarify the prime function of such teams: that is, to establish some solid idea of *authority* in the study of education by establishing themselves as authorities. The lack of any such real authority in the study of education is, of course, just one facet of the contemporary failure. It should clearly be possible, at any rate in respect of some topics, that a team of this kind should establish itself as *really knowing* as much as there is (at any time) to be known, and that it should rapidly come to be *seen* as being in this position by teachers, 'developers', administrators and all others concerned with the topic. This is a very different picture from what now happens: pseudo-authorities, semi-competent research teams, and other individuals and organizations do some kind of (usually intellectually disreputable) work and then compete for attention from the educational world in general. 'Names' are made, and rapidly forgotten, in topical fields; many semi-sages, who may or may not be doing serious work, are tossed about by the mass media with a turnover not much slower than that of pop stars.

The first answer to the question 'What will these teams do?', then, is that whatever they do, they will do it *properly*: and this will at least mean that the whole thing will not have to be done again. (This is, of course, one reason why short-term studies, in many areas, are simply non-starters). Thus it would clearly be possible, with such topics as (say) 'discipline', 'the teaching of science', or 'reading' to establish one or two teams which, given the conditions described in A. and B. above, could be trusted to achieve an authoritative position. Even in mistier areas, such as 'the curriculum' or 'religious education', the innumerable short-term and competing studies could with profit be replaced by more serious work of this kind: at any rate, if we do not, we shall be discussing and 'researching' into these topics endlessly, and are likely (as is now quite evidently the case) to be driven more by political and other climates than by scholarship.

The second answer to the question goes back to condition B5 above, that the team should largely define its own topic. By this I mean that, whilst of course we have to assemble the nucleus of a team round some topic-phrase — for instance, 'discipline', 'motivation', 'moral education', 'teaching science', or whatever — , the rest of it should be up to the members: both in expanding a proper meaning for such topic-phrases, and (what is clearly connected with this part of the work) in acquiring additional team-members. The general outlines of such procedures would follow from the notion, described earlier, of the centrality of 'making sense' ('phenomenology', 'philosophy', 'psychology', or whatever we call it): we should anticipate, for most topics, a nucleus of people competent in this field, who would further define their task and add to their numbers as they proceeded.

The third answer is that, as being authoritative in a particular topic, they should service and so far as possible control those outside the team who stand in need of their authority. We have already seen the necessity for 'development' agencies to be closely attached to such teams; but it is extremely important to see that their general function spreads far wider than the notion of 'research' leading to 'development'. One very important direction of spread, highly relevant to the second part of this book, is towards the preparation of teachers; insofar as — still an open question — teachers need to know about 'educational theory', or at least about the topics covered by the teams, they will be able to refer to the teams as the only representatives of solid and well-established knowledge. Other obvious directions are towards politicians, educational administrators, schools, broadcasts in the mass media, the writers of text-books and so forth. All this and more follows from the notion of a reliable authority.

To pursue this point into various other practical difficulties which will perhaps be in the reader's mind: in the study of education we have somehow to alter the mechanisms which militate against authority or power being wielded by those most intellectually fitted to deal with the subject. In some areas — the physical sciences may perhaps be an example — this matters less, because there is an established intellectual tradition which is authoritative in its own right, and which even the most feeble-minded or power-hungry administrators would find hard to destroy (unless, like the Nazis, they go completely mad). There is, as it were, something clear and valuable for the administrators to administrate; any even fairly competent and well-disposed administrator will want to facilitate the progress of, say, research into nuclear physics or the study of biology; and such a person can rely on existing authorities in these fields to say what they need for this — all he has to do (and very important it is too) is to create the appropriate conditions. But in spheres where this is not so, such a set-up is disastrous.

A brief look round this area will be worthwhile. Many respectable subjects or disciplines can be practised by isolated individuals — lecturers or fellows of colleges, for instance — without the need for much administration at all; though even here we have to be careful to ensure that the administration serves the disciplines rather than vice versa, which represents a strong argument in favour of an Oxbridge set-up in which the (academic) fellows hold the ultimate power and can hire and fire their own administration. Other respectable subjects require more organizational arrangements, as do the sciences, but here, as we have just seen, the established academic tradition of the subjects is a protection. Similar traditions, practical as well as academic, protect the semi-practical areas of medicine and engineering. Areas like education, social welfare, mental health and others are in the worst possible position: first, the criteria of success are not clear, and secondly, they need more organizational arrangements than (say) the study of English literature or Greek history.

A further difficulty is that these unclear areas require administrative organization not only for their intellectual aspects, but also for a vast number of practical tasks which (for whatever reasons) are now traditionally attached to them. In education, not a few intellectually able people in universities and elsewhere may find themselves spending a great deal of their time on committees dealing with semi-political rather than intellectual problems; problems about departmental arrangements, the reorganization of colleges, relationships with local and central authorities, and so forth. Insofar as they have time or inclination to engage in research or more academic pursuits, it will not be as a member of one of our teams; more likely it will be in isolation, when such a person may be able to write a book — which few people may have joined in criticizing before publication, and which after publication is not likely to be properly read by similar people who have as little time to spare as its author.

Worse, it may sometimes (perhaps even often) happen that the most generally influential posts in institutions engaged on the study of education may be held by people who are not intellectually or academically in the highest class. It is important to get clear here why this is disastrous. The point is not that administration, semi-political decisions, public relations and so on are in some way inferior or unimportant, requiring only second-rate talents: it is rather that (a) we need a very clear institutional distinction between this kind of work on the one hand, and the work of studying education on the other, and (b) many decisions in the former area should flow from, or at least be heavily influenced by, the study of education itself.

This is an extremely difficult situation to unscramble, even theoretically. But we might outline some such system as the following: we begin by establishing a competent team of people along the lines laid down earlier, and make it their business to consider the study of education in general, together with some overall consideration of tasks which a particular institution might perform that fall outside this description (for instance, the preparation of teachers). We then empower them to arrange things as they think best: they may appoint an overall administrator, or a number of people on whom these non-theoretical tasks will devolve to some extent, or whatever they like. They may think it right to pay some of these people more than they are paid themselves, or even to give them titles which they themselves may not have, such as 'Director' or 'Professor'. But they retain the ultimate control, and are given both financial independence and the power to hire and fire.

This is, again, much more like the Oxbridge college situation, in which fellows may elect a Master (President, etc.) who has no power over them but who will fulfil certain functions effectively in the outside world. The difference of course is that our study-of-education team, even if it includes a number of different disciplines, will be working *as* a team in the way that Oxbridge fellows within a college characteristically do not need to do. The contrast both with most universities' arrangements for the study of education, and with organizations outside the universities devoted to educational research (the NFER, for instance), is pretty sharp; and it is quite plain that — if this is on the right lines — a great deal of radical reorganization of existing institutions would be required.

Nevertheless, a great deal can be done without having to rebuild all existing institutions from scratch. In most university departments (faculties, institutes, etc.) of education it should not be impossible either to hire people of the kind required for such a team, or to identify them already existing in the institutions. That done, nothing seriously prevents the institution from setting up something approximating to the conditions of work described earlier (p. 77, under B). This would at least establish, in all such institutions, a small team — perhaps only of two or three people — which acted as a kind of monitoring unit for the institution concerned, and which would have some chance of getting clear about the study of education in general and as applicable to the particular institution.

It may be said that this already happens: that the most competent people in such institutions are already working as teams and pondering the initial methodological problems involved. But this seems to me demonstrably false. The staff of most institutions proceed on the assumption, usually tacit, that either what they are doing in their day-to-day business must be more or less all right, or else there is not much that can be done about it unless conditions are completely changed. I should maintain, on the contrary, that any such staff who were serious about what they did, and perceived the importance of methodological clarity, would necessarily be led to adopt some such measures as I have suggested. Both the difficulties and the necessity of close communication, sustained teamwork, and the other conditions mentioned earlier would soon become apparent.

It may also be said, and with some truth, that this is all very well, but for practical or political reasons difficult or impossible to do; that these lines of approach may, indeed, be more or less correct, but that there would have to be very sweeping changes in the power structure and general format of most of our academic institutions, of a kind not within the academics' control. We are, so to speak, lumbered with job specifications not of our own making. But whatever truth there is in this is many times magnified by academics permitting, or even encouraging, certain modes of activity to flourish unduly. It is well known, for instance, that committees and administrative apparatus in general tend to proliferate themselves; that in many universities there is a pressure to publish and to move up a ladder of degrees, neither of which necessarily represents any real contribution either to teaching or to knowledge; that, in general, a great deal of time and energy is consumed on activities which could by no stretch of imagination be described as *advancing the subject*. Equally, I suggest, it would be dishonest to claim that *all* these difficulties are imposed by external pressures, against the will and the tooth-and-nail opposition of the academics themselves.

As so often, we find ourselves in a system which is partly of our own making, even if the making has been largely unconscious. Individual academics will, indeed, show awareness of the current disadvantages of the system, and tell horror stories about demands for publications, mass lectures in which the notes of the professor pass into the notes of the student without going through the minds of either, and the impossibility of simply finding time (and a context) in which they can *argue* informally with their colleagues. All this is well known. The way out of it is admittedly not easy, and will naturally vary in detail from one institution to another. But it must at least begin by a clear grasp of the *demands of the subject itself*. Notoriously some subjects — philosophy is often and correctly quoted as an example — demand particular contexts which are too often not actually found in institutions which profess to study and teach them. The study of education is plainly in this category; indeed, it seems to me one of the clearest cases.

It is perhaps not too much to say that the sense of fantasy or unreality, of having stepped into a world of dream and nightmare, which besets us when we consider what is said and done about practical education, is duplicated in different terms when we consider its academic study, and also when we consider the second-order task of studying how such study should be organized. This dream-like quality varies, of course, from one institution to another, but in all cases it betokens a certain lack of seriousness. It is just this, I think, which tends to produce the vicious circle mentioned earlier; one has the depressing and alarming feeling of trying to wade through treacle or fight with ghosts. Arguably we should perhaps have started with a clearer and fuller idea of what it is to be serious about something; and though this is in itself a considerable topic, the practical importance of making the study of education respectable may justify a few brief remarks.

The phrase 'serious about X' carries two implications. The first is obvious: it is that the person who is supposed to be serious should be in earnest. He should not be just playing, or half-hearted, or 'going through the motions'. The second is less obvious: that he should be, not just serious or earnest, but serious or earnest *about X*. Thus somebody who says he is serious about music or the theatre may indeed have strong feelings about something, but if he really only goes to the opera because it is fashionable or to the theatre because he wants to appear well-informed about the latest play, we shall say that it is not music or the theatre *as such* that he is serious about. In other words, 'serious about X' means not only that you have to have strong feelings, but also that these feelings must be directed towards X as such.

When I say that we are not, on the whole, serious about the study of education I am not thinking primarily of the first of these two criteria. It seems quite clear that plenty of people have strong feelings which are in some way connected with the term 'education'; indeed education has become, in the last few decades, a sort of battleground for passionate feeling, and has attracted to itself a good deal of the idealism, fantasy and sectarian commitment that used to be characteristic of religion. But it seems also clear that these passions are not directed towards the study of education as such. Any serious *study* will, by definition, be primarily concerned with truth and the advancement of knowledge; not with partisan commitment or with any other passion than the desire to achieve as much clarity and certainty as is possible.

We know well enough, in general, how to verify whether a person is serious about studying or acquiring truth and knowledge. Our evidence is gained, not so much by asking whether his views are right or wrong, but by inspecting his behaviour or mental posture. Is he guided by evidence rather than by his own partisan attachments? Does he welcome criticism? Is he not only able but anxious to test out his views by engaging in hard and sustained discussion of them with other people? Is he keen on making sure that his views are clearly-expressed and unambiguous? Is he capable of questioning his own role, or identity, or 'vested interests' of any kind? Does he try as hard as he can to understand what other people are saying? The answers to these and similar questions define for us what it means to be 'reasonable' or 'serious'.

In the area for which 'education' stands, which is on any account a very difficult and uncertain area, we might reasonably single out certain tests in particular. Among these might be (1) whether the person is not only willing but anxious to ensure that the *foundations* of what he is doing are sound, as against involving himself in some respectable-seeming but in fact fantasy-based enterprise (like astrology or alchemy): we want him to be able to raise and face doubts of the form 'But perhaps this is muddled *right from the start*', or 'Wait a minute, perhaps we shouldn't be doing this sort of thing *at all*'; (2) whether the person retains a very clear distinction in his mind between (a) what is true or right *sub specie aeternitatis*, so to speak, and (b) what is politically feasible, or fashionable, or 'in line with modern thought', or for other reasons acceptable.

Equally, if a person passes the tests for 'serious study', he has yet to pass the tests for serious study *of education*. This raises complex questions about the 'disciplines of education', about which I have said something earlier, but at least it is clear that one may be a serious and competent philosopher, psychologist, sociologist, etc., and yet not be serious about education. Important tests for seriousness will arise in 'bringing the discipline to bear on education' (whatever this may mean). It is perfectly possible — indeed, it seems to me very common — for a person to be extremely serious about, say, empirical research under headings such as 'conditioning' or 'reinforcement', but hopelessly at sea in trying to fit this to anything reasonably to be described as 'educating'; indeed, like Skinner, he may not even seriously try. Here is another reason why a very large part of our difficulties will be, in a broad sense, methodological or philosophical.

These (extremely obvious) remarks may be seen as merely reiterating, in a more personal or *ad hominem* mode, some of the points about the study of education made in earlier chapters. But it is, I am persuaded, extremely important that we do sometimes consider things in this personal mode. For, even from this brief reminder of what it is to be serious about the study of education, it is perhaps clear (1) that there is very little of this seriousness around, and hence (2) that there may be certain very fundamental reasons for this which need discussion. I suppose that this is, strictly speaking, a task for empirical scholarship — perhaps for the social or the clinical psychologist, but I am not persuaded that those with the necessary psychological expertise are sufficiently clear about the conceptual requirements to have done much useful work here.

One might follow various scholars in speaking of worthwhile intellectual products as the offspring of two parents: on the one hand, some very strong (and largely unconscious) desire which forms the 'enthusiasm' or 'enjoyment' part of seriousness and on the other, an equally strong passion for rationality and correctness which makes it more than just undirected or fantasy-oriented enthusiasm. The importance of this kind of marriage is, of course, fairly obvious; many writers have given different descriptions of it, amongst whom Freud is perhaps not the least lucid and compelling. I want to consider briefly what particular additions or specifications of it may be relevant to the study of education.

Those interested or enthusiastic about education, as defined in Chapter 1, are often those interested or enthusiastic about teaching or explaining things to people. This has its roots in some kind of desire to share or communicate, to act as some kind of parent-figure distributing — in a fairly close and at least semi-personal relationship — the particular goods which are marked by 'education'. The rewards of the teacher are like those of the parent in certain obvious respects. This picture is clearly very different from that of someone who is passionately concerned with a particular subject or impersonal product: with research into ancient Greek history, for instance, or with trying to write a good symphony. There is a sense in which he too wishes to share, but (so to speak) at longer range. I here do no more than slightly enlarge or write round what might be conjured up by the words 'teacher' and 'scholar' respectively.

It is hence no surprise that people who are enthusiastic about education are, in general, not 'scholars', and that the *study* of education, while it shows plenty of enthusiasm, bears few signs of intense and well-directed rationality. Equally it is clear that the 'scholar' will not naturally be drawn to the apparently hopeless morass marked by 'educational theory'; amongst other reasons, he will doubt whether there could be any 'subject' or 'end product' *solid* enough to satisfy him — any such product would be *toto caelo* different from, say, definitively deciphering a fragmentary manuscript or determining the behaviour of meson particles. 'Education' offers little encouragement to Browning's Grammarian. It is possible, as I mentioned earlier, to find people who combine some sort of 'moral commitment' (whatever that means) to education with adequate scholarship; but we still need to know what *sort* of passion to look for.

The same consideration that drove us to the notion of 'teams' also, I think, drives us to the notion of a passion for *shared clarification*. This is different both from the 'teacher's' desire to teach, and the 'scholar's' desire to produce something intellectually worthwhile on his own, though it shares something of both. My guess is that — the state of the subject being what it is — the serious student of education will have to be animated by a passion for what I can only call 'sorting things out' with his peers. I do not, of course, mean that he cannot profit from instruction and from books, nor that he has to be extroverted and talkative in debate and discussion; rather, there are reasons why the subject requires a passion for 'mutual sorting' — reasons not adequately expressed by saying that the work is 'interdisciplinary' or 'teamwork'.

Very roughly, these reasons stem from the immense temptations to autism which beset this kind of study. Much of the work, as we have seen, will be a matter of imposing some kind of order on phenomena, often in the form of a taxonomy or set of categories, but obviously involving difficulties much greater and more subtle than in the case of, say, taxonomizing flora and fauna. It is *one's own perceptions* (prejudices, fantasies, partialities, etc.) that are crucial here, and these can, in principle, only be controlled and adjusted by the perceptions of others.[2] Of course this is true of any truth-seeking operation, but in this field such adjustment and control has to be very fine, constant, and immediate.

The most obvious examples here are from philosophy: one thinks immediately of the context of a Platonic dialogue or one of Austin's seminars. But there are other parallels. Notoriously in various kinds of psychotherapy ground is only gained in a very closely-knit context of talk, in which one person (the therapist) attempts to change another person's (the patient's) perceptions in the direction of rationality. The same sort of thing applies, though of course with different subject-matter and perhaps with different rules, in discussion of literary texts and works of art in general. The more subtle is the business of 'making sense' — that is, in part, the less governed by very clear and easily-applicable rules — the more important the context of communication is. One can play chess or conduct certain kinds of scientific debate by correspondence; in less well-defined fields the returns are more marginal, or even non-existent.

In practice we tacitly deny the force of this point for the study of education, and this is, I suspect, the basic reason why such study often seems unreal. It has something of the kind of unreality in trying to conduct a love affair or a therapeutic relationship by correspondence; in a sense one can do this, but it results in the mutual clashing or interchange of fantasies rather than any truth-oriented enterprise. A great deal of philosophy, to a lesser extent, has suffered and still suffers from this, with the social sciences the point is still more obvious. This is not, naturally, to deny that seriousness may operate in the form of an internalized dialogue by an isolated individual; indeed the difficulties of adequate communication are so great that a large part of the best work probably still springs from such sources. But for the study of education in particular, such a paradigm is dangerous: for there are obvious reasons why education — even more, perhaps, than philosophy and the social sciences — tempts us towards fantasies of perfection and other kinds of dreams and obsessive pictures.

Education, in the sense of the 'ed. biz.', covers so wide and so vague an area that it is unlikely, for this reason alone, to include many people of the ability and temperament required for this operation. Institutions concerned with the study of education and the preparation of teachers in fact contain a very heterogeneous selection of people. At their head, for the most part, are people whose expertise lies primarily in the realms of administration, politics and public relations. Other staff members may be animated by an interest in the teaching of a particular school subject, by some social or moral concern for the general needs of children, or by an interest in the institutional or political mechanisms of the educational system. Others again, probably a minority, are primarily committed to their own subject or 'discipline' — psychologists, sociologists, historians, etc. 'of education'. Not many of these, even in the last category, are likely to be first-class scholars, and still fewer are likely to combine this talent with a passion for 'making sense' of education as a subject.

Hence it is not surprising that reputations in this field — I mean, above the level of transient popularity or ephemeral 'sages' — are usually made by people working in various disciplines who are themselves unattached to institutions concerned specifically with education: usually, in fact, sociologists or psychologists. Of course there are outstanding counter-examples to this (Peters, Hirst, Bernstein and others), but a typical case is that of a scholar who has established himself in some discipline, has a particular interest in (and usually a particular ideal about) education, and then lends his weight to furthering that interest. (Dewey, Bruner, Skinner and others spring to mind here). The results of this may be good or bad, depending on the sophistication of the person concerned; and certainly this is a bit nearer what the subject demands than, say, the writings of Bertrand Russell, whose eminence as a philosopher did not save him from doctrinaire absurdities about education. But there is clearly the danger of autism even at this level. Anyone who has witnessed, for instance, attempted dialogues between Skinner and philosophers interested in psychology cannot but be struck by the immense gulfs in communication.

This (to repeat a point made earlier) is why some strong and, as one might say, full-time commitment to *education* is essential; rather than to some field of interest which might, indeed, bear on education but which the researcher pursues primarily for its own sake. Seriousness requires a stronger, or at least a more single-minded, commitment than this: the researcher must conceive of his work as having a practical effect on schools, teachers, children, parents and so on. Nothing is easier, and in general nothing less productive, than to assemble a number of part-time scholars in various fields and encourage them to 'take an interest in education'. They must be given, or formulate for themselves, a full-time and tolerably specific *job* to do — to make sense of (say) moral education, or learning science, or 'motivation', or 'pastoral care' in schools, in such a way that practical development can be seen to follow. We are not talking about a vaguely-structured 'think-tank' in education: enterprises of that kind display fantasies of their own.

Closely connected with the idea of seriousness, and perhaps of particular importance for education, is the idea of *trust*. We have noted the practical importance of setting up teams whose members trust each other in the task of 'making sense' or 'shared clarification'; of trusting the teams with more institutional (administrative, political) latitude than is common; and of enabling them thereby to establish themselves as trustworthy *authorities*. Granted that there may be very considerable difficulties of other kinds in this sort of enterprise, there remains one basic psychological difficulty, which we might describe as a general disposition not to trust people (in this sort of context) at all, or anyway not much. I think this disposition is detectable even in most 'liberal' or 'democratic' societies; and that it partly accounts for the tendency, noted earlier, to do business by setting up committees, working parties, government commissions and so on which attempt a 'general consensus'. It is as if the very idea of having established authorities — even 'intellectual' ones — in any such field as education was alarming: as if we preferred the competitive, open-market, *laissez-faire* mish-mash that education now is to anything more definitively connected with *truth* and *correctness*.

To dig out and confront this nebulous feeling is far from easy (certainly I can do little about it here). But I think it is not so much that there are seriously maintained views (of moral philosophers or sociologists, for instance) which would attempt totally to expel inexpellable notions marked by such terms as 'authority', 'right answers', 'culture-free values', 'correct judgements', etc.: rather it is that we hesitate to trust any *persons* to be the sponsors or guardians of various kinds of rationality. Here the business of trusting 'academic authorities' — one might say, of having the faith that there is something to be authoritative *about* — is mixed up with the business of trusting people as such; notions like 'autonomy', not nowadays usually matched with other required notions such as 'due obedience' or 'appropriate deference', are used to justify escapes into autism.

It is fair and perhaps useful, as I see it, to view seriousness and trust as connected. Both in the 'academic' business of 'making sense' of unclear subjects (or pursuing clearer ones), and in the field of ordinary personal relationships, a person has somehow to feel the importance of some enterprise *outside* himself. The enterprise — love, friendship, the pursuit of truth — has to be real to him: he has to be able to invest emotionally in it, to *put himself* into it. In making such a move the person shows both trust and seriousness. He has to be free and secure enough, as it were, to let himself go; a freedom and security required even to begin (let alone persist in) the hard work and hard knocks which the enterprise involves.[3]

On these topics, of course, many other writers (from Plato to Freud, at least) have discoursed with greater force and at much greater length than I can here. The points made above will inevitably appear both disconnected and sketchy. But something, I think, emerges from them, something both simple and important. Briefly, they suggest the naivety of trying to tackle the problem of 'practical requirements' at only one level. In discussions about the malaise of education as a subject, various solutions are often propounded: 'create more chairs in education', 'persuade really good scholars outside the subject to take an interest in it', 'find more money for research', 'make it all more practical', 'change the system', and so on. Some solvers put their money on social or institutional alterations, others on economic or political improvements, others again on 'purer scholarship'. What I have tried (far too briefly) to show is that the problem has many dimensions, and that we can only even begin to grasp it properly by considering something of the psychological aspects of seriousness; after which we can then go on to consider both how the lack of seriousness may emerge in existing arrangements, and what revised arrangements would facilitate it.

In this Part of the book we have been concerned with educational theory, or the study of education as a subject; and hence concentrated, in this chapter, on *one* kind of group and on the characteristics necessary for its task, which may roughly be described as an 'intellectual' one. But, of course, departments (colleges,, faculties, etc.) of education also operate in other modes: there are, for instance, administrative or 'policy' decisions to be taken, perhaps in general staff meetings or committees. Whilst the necessary characteristics for such groups will of course be different to some extent (because their tasks are different), the basic points about the importance of seriousness, trust, and so on remain equally relevant; and most of the failures in communication, and hence efficiency, can probably be traced to the same basic causes. I mention these points, in themselves perhaps obvious, in order to stress that we need to take a step backwards, as it were, and think about what conditions are required for these tasks also.

This is necessary, not just because we want these other groups to perform well for their own purposes (though that is important enough); but because, unless we become more generally conscious of the need to marry up particular tasks with suitable contexts and group characteristics, the special kind of groups required for the study of education may never see daylight. Most institutions operate at present on a few extremely naive ideas about the proper vehicles for different enterprises. We employ, for instance, the concept of a 'committee' or a 'working party', some vague idea about 'democracy' or 'participation' by the staff of the institution as a whole, and perhaps some acknowledgement (usually unfounded) of certain 'experts'. Into the interstices left by this vagueness creep the forces of bureaucratic administration, of undue domination by the strong-willed and verbally forceful, or of simple inertia; we are apt to do the easiest thing, to use contexts already traditional or able to be produced without much prior reflection, rather than work out what sorts of groups and contexts will best do the — very different — jobs which ought to be done.

It is easy to say this, but it is also easy to see that there is a great deal more work that needs to be done in this area; not, I hasten to add, only or even chiefly by more 'research' into it, but by sterner thinking and by the practical efforts of the members of staff themselves. We do, of course, need more information: some frank and detailed studies, for instance, of just what goes wrong with various projects, teams, staff meetings, committees, etc. would be most valuable. But the important thing, yet again, is not whether this or that 'solution' (including my own suggestions) gives us a complete blueprint for success, but that the problem itself should be taken seriously.

Notes

1 p. 86 ff.

2 Wilson (1971), p. 227 ff.

3 One of the more striking facts is that very few of us seem to be able to manage the combination of warmth (friendliness) and impersonality which is clearly demanded by any operation of this kind. (Warmth, because people very easily feel threatened or otherwise insecure; impersonality, because truth is impersonal.)

Part Two

The Preparation of Teachers

Chapter Four

First Steps

In considering the study of education, we had at least the word 'education' to use as common ground, uncertain though its frontiers may be. But in considering what I have called the 'preparation' of teachers we have nothing similar to rely on. There are indeed a number of phrases in common use, headings under which conferences are held, research conducted, government reports written and so on: for instance, 'teacher-training', 'teacher-education', 'the role of the teacher', and 'teaching skills'. These and other phrases carry with them the danger of disastrous confusion and question-begging, for an obvious reason: each of them tacitly presupposes a particular picture or description of our subject-matter, a description which is certainly partial, probably prejudicial, and sometimes just plain wrong.

We shall need to start much further back, and to spend quite a lot of time in seeing the particular ways in which such descriptions are prejudicial, and in which our whole approach to the topic is vitiated by a number of more or less orthodox fantasies and uncritical behaviour patterns. This emerges, indeed, in the difficulty of even finding a reasonable title for our topic. I have used 'the preparation of teachers', which is as safe a phrase as I can find, but even here it might perhaps be argued that there is some question-begging. Perhaps teachers should in certain respects *not* be 'prepared', but (in these respects) just jump in off the deep end, as it were. Or, again, might not teachers be *over*-prepared? Or yet again, might there not be aspects of their work for which 'preparation' was impossible, for either conceptual or deeply empirical reasons — rather as, perhaps, E.M. Forster thought it either impossible or undesirable to 'prepare' for personal relationships?[1] I shall not pursue these doubts here, raising them only to show how extremely difficult it is not to preempt a number of issues right at the start.

The major fantasy here, which needs inspection in some detail, is unsurprisingly similar to that which we have glanced at obliquely in considering the study of education. There is, first, the idea that some aspects of the preparation of teachers – the 'aims', perhaps – are a matter for individual 'value-judgements' or political decision. Typically the process is construed on the model of policy-making or decision-taking in a 'democratic' society where different interest groups pull different ways, the idea being to teach a 'general consensus'. Thus Taylor:

> '. . . it is essential that there should be a continuing dialogue between the individuals and groups that have power and influence . . . If the education and training of teachers is some-thing in relation to which government, the universities, local authorities, teachers and the training institutions themselves all have a legitimate interest and concern . . . then the first steps towards the evolution of a workable policy must be to expose the differences and misunderstandings, and to explore the possibilities that exist for agreement . . . there might one day hopefully emerge some strategy for action which enjoys a substantial measure of consensus'.[2]

Taylor writes here as a politician or chairman; the question is not to be what is right *sans phrase*, but what will satisfy various views round the table.

Other aspects are predictably connected with this, conveniently illustrated in the same book.[3] There is the bland assumption that research into teacher-training must necessarily follow the orthodox empirical lines; in a 40-page section on research no serious philosophical studies are quoted and discussed, and questions about basic aims are treated in a strictly sociological manner – e.g. 'The educational and social values of society impinge upon the education of teachers in a variety of ways. They are inputs to the system', etc.[4] The other side of the same coin emerges in contributions which either attempt to sell,[5] or to give some highly generalized and 'cultural' account of,[6] various 'values'. Most of the rest is in the area of institutional administration. This sort of treatment is not peculiar to this particular book, which indeed contains (in an accidental sort of way) more of interest than most of such books. But plainly it is basically unsatisfactory.

This is because the authors misdescribe, misunderstand, shy away from, or at any rate do not actually *tackle* (or even *raise*) the essential prior questions. These questions, as we saw earlier,[7] should not be construed in the general form 'What are our "values" in teacher-training?' This leads directly into a number of defensive attitudes: we take it as a sociological or political question, and try to achieve a 'consensus'; or we take it as an opportunity to display our own enthusiasm and preferences; or we conduct some sort of cultural survey of 'the values' of 'modern society', or 'education in a technological age', or something of the kind; or we give it up as a bad job, and relapse into a kind of behaviourism which induces us to list 'teaching skills' or analyse 'the teacher's role' (on which see below). There are times when one wishes the term 'values' were taboo: it offers too easy an excuse to avoid hard work. The general form of question we have first to ask — if we insist on a general form at all — will be something like 'What *is it to* "prepare" teachers in various ways? What *sorts* of things are there that teachers might be thought to need? How can we sensibly categorize these?'

To some this may seem mere linguistic pedantry. 'Surely this *is* the sort of question we are asking with terms like "teacher-education", "teaching skills", and so on. Why make a fuss about the mere words?' Of course it is not the *words* that we want to make a fuss about; it is the predetermining pictures that lie behind the words. This point is perhaps most clear if we imagine an argument or two about 'skills' and 'roles'. Having seen the lists of 'teaching skills' that are supposed to categorize the requirements of intending teachers, any philosopher — or anyone with a grasp of normal English — would immediately want to say 'But not everything the teacher needs can be called a *skill*: 'skill' has a much more circumscribed meaning in English, fairly tightly tied to notions like 'dexterity', 'clumsiness' and so on.' 'Very well, let's call some of them "abilities" or "aptitudes" or "competences", will that do?' 'But that still won't do for all we look for in a teacher; for instance, how about whether he is actually *fond of* the children, or *keen on* his subject?' 'All right, we'll include "attitudes" — surely that covers all the ground'. 'No, mightn't there be personal characteristics which aren't skills or abilities or attitudes? For instance, the teacher may have certain mannerisms, or a certain style, or present a certain "image", or it might be important how *tall* he is, or how pretty she is — all sorts of things'.

The point is not (only) the simple linguistic error in using 'skills' to cover illegitimate ground nor (only) the vague realization that the teacher may need lots of *different* things, but rather that until we have sorted out these 'things' ('characteristics' might also be a safe word) we shall remain in a muddle, and that any discussion which *starts* with some particular description of them — 'skills' or another — must necessarily fail to do the required work. The real work begins where the discussion sketched above ends: the realization that such a discussion should produce is the realization that some kind of mapping out, categorization, or taxonomy is required.

Or consider, again, the use of 'role' and 'roles', which figures so boldly in chapter headings ('The Teacher's Role', etc.). Clearly not all the 'things' a teacher needs to do can be described in these terms: 'role' in normal speech is still fairly close to its original meaning of a part played on the stage, a preordained script. I am not 'playing a role', nor do I in English even 'have a role', when I am chatting with my friends, or trying to cheer some pupil up, or discussing the curriculum with my colleagues. I have jobs, tasks, duties, and other 'things' of many different kinds. Now if (a) 'role' is a technical term of sociology or social psychology, with a clear but limited meaning, then it will certainly not serve as a general description for what teachers need to do; and if (b) it is extended to serve as such a description – to *mean* just 'what teachers need to do' – then it leaves the important questions untouched. For we want to know what *sorts* of things teachers need to do, how far they should (in the normal sense) be 'playing (filling, having) roles', and so on.

It is not too hard to see – at a superficial level, at least – why so much educational discussion and decision-making has been taken over by sociology and similar disciplines. Suppose we raise another question about 'role': are we talking, under this heading, about what teachers are *expected* (required, persuaded, obliged) to do by 'society' (politicians, parents, local educational authorities, etc.), or about what they *really ought* to do (what it would be *right* for them to do)? These are clearly different questions, even though there are connections between them, and anyone who reads the relevant literature would agree, I think, that the difference is (to say the least) blurred. It is often impossible to determine which of the two questions *is* being discussed. The result is an unperceived disaster: it is often simply taken for granted that answers to the first question will also serve as answers to the second; that the given, sociologically-described roles of the teacher are (so to speak) the *right* roles. This is, in effect, because we shy away from directly asking and trying to answer the second question, and the omission leaves us with nothing to turn to except the sociological descriptions.

Of course nobody *really* believes that what 'society' sets out for us is necessarily right, or that what is reached by way of a 'general consensus' is necessarily rational;[8] indeed there are plenty of people (including teachers) who both in thought and behaviour react in extremist ways against what is 'given' by these and other sources. The extremism itself indicates the almost total lack of an accepted working tradition, context, or methodology of discussion; it is as if people had to fly to revolutionary or 'liberationist' movements in order to escape from the mortmain of 'society'. This is one (only one) of the things that makes it appropriate to talk here of fantasy rather than genuine or evidenced belief. There is a clear sense in which we *know*, in our saner moments, that we have to get down to the necessary procedures of conceptual analysis, the making of clear and sensible categories, and the provision of adequate descriptions if we are to gain any solid ground. We know this, but the knowledge — for more reasons than I have here mentioned — gets submerged.

It is, in fact, extremely difficult to find safe ground as a starting point. To illustrate the difficulties, consider a recent (oral and tape-recorded but not published) discussion within an institution concerned with the preparation of teachers. This began by somebody trying to answer the question 'What makes a good teacher?', but the discussion soon became unmanageably high-minded and idealistic, so that the director of the institution — a man of sound common sense who wanted to arrive at some working agreement — said words to the effect of: 'Well, let's leave 'a good teacher' and see if we can't at least agree on what makes a *competent* teacher'. Some of those present took this to mean 'what *counts as* a competent teacher', others to mean 'what *causes* competence'; so that the subsequent discussion was divided between people trying to list criteria of competence, and other people advocating the efficacy of particular methods of teacher-preparation (more school practice, or less sociology, or whatever). Nothing clear emerged.

More goes wrong in such cases than might be thought. To ask 'What makes a good teacher?' seems safe enough, and indeed there would be something like a contradiction in denying that we wanted good teachers. Yet even here something is likely to be assumed: namely, that this question covers all the ground we need for the preparation of teachers. But this is not so: we want to prepare the teacher in *some* respects that will not make *him good* but will be good or useful *for him*; for instance, we might think it important to tell him about the comparative advantages of joining this or that teacher's union; and it is a real and important question how much time we want to spend on things that might benefit him rather than his pupils — a question we cannot even raise if we do not recognize the category in the first place. Then again, there is the temptation to be 'practical' and subsume everything under 'competetence', but this too is dangerous. The point here is not that one wants to say 'No, we may want *in*competent teachers', but rather that one wants to say 'Some of the most important characteristics may not be matters of *competence* at all. Maybe pupils learn most from teachers who are, say, enthusiastic or inspired or friendly — competence may not matter much.' And, finally, there is the usual muddle between the questions (1) 'What are we to mean by (what counts as) "X"?' and (2) 'What produces (generates, causes) X?'; sometimes compounded by a different question again (3) 'What *is* (the nature, structure, substance of) X?' — a question beloved by psychologists when dealing with terms which apparently represent things with natures or structures, such as 'intelligence', and which I have commented on elsewhere.[9]

These and other difficulties, as we noticed in the last chapter, arise from the failure to appreciate the need to 'make sense', in a conceptual or 'phenomenological' kind of way, of such problems at the very first stage of the operation. Clearly, as this and innumerable other oral and published discussions show, this cannot be done in such contexts as a general staff meeting, a conference, or even a loosely-structured 'working party' which meets occasionally. Something much more intense and thoroughgoing is required, more on the model of the teams suggested earlier. Until we have this sort of context, most of what is said and written about the preparation of teachers will continue to suffer from the same — boringly obvious but universally disastrous — defects.

It would be otiose, and perhaps slightly sadistic, to give further illustrations of these mistakes; I hope to have said enough to persuade the reader that we must start much further back. Actually, it would be premature at this stage even to attempt a taxonomy of 'what the teacher needs'; for this implies that we already have a clear idea of what counts as 'being a teacher' and of what, in a general sort of way, we want teachers to do. In fact, we have no such clear idea; and our first task will be to see if we can gain any clarity on these points.

Not much is gained by hammering the *word* 'teacher', but it will at least introduce our problems to point out, very obviously, that preparing *teachers* must differ in important respects from preparing (say) policemen, baby sitters, or social welfare workers. That is, we can identify a rough category of 'goods' or benefits which are supposed to be dispensed by teachers rather than by other functionaries; and we may follow linguistic arguments far enough, at least, to expect that these goods will be largely co-extensive with the notions of *learning* or of education, as we outlined these notions in Chapter 1. For reasons similar to those there given, we should expect 'being a teacher' to be centrally concerned with teaching, dispensing learning, and educating.

However, we cannot plausibly run this argument in so severe a form as in the case of 'the study of education'. In that case, we were concerned with marking out a determinate area for academic study, roughly by using the criterion of what was (a) logically homogeneous and (b) most sensibly attached to the term 'education'. But here we are concerned with people who are going to act in a particular capacity — who are going to *be teachers*, and this is not entirely the same thing as saying that they are going *to teach*. To put this another way: suppose that 'being a teacher', in certain situations at least, necessarily or rightly involved doing quite a lot of things that could not be described as 'teaching' or even 'educating' (as in fact is the case in many schools). Then, if we are interested in preparing people who are going to be teachers, we shall have to be interested in these other (non-teaching) activities.

But we are immediately **assailed** by various difficulties. First, we shall not want simply to take for granted that the teacher is 'necessarily or rightly' involved with these other activities. Suppose, for instance, that in some society a teacher had to act as an indoctrinator (because the society insisted on its children being turned into good little Nazis, or whatever), or that in another he had to act as an all-in wrestler (because the society provided insufficient sanctions for keeping order by less personal methods). Now, it might be that — as practical men engaged in preparing teachers — we would feel it necessary to instruct intending teachers in efficient methods of indoctrination, or all-in wrestling, but we should have doubts about whether this, in general or in principle, *ought* to be the ways in which teachers were prepared — and we might want to share these doubts with our student-teachers. Certainly we should not always wish to *endorse* the immediate social necessities, even though we might have to recognize them. We are thus caught between the desire to make our preparation practical and the necessity to preserve some clear grasp of what it is to prepare for being a *teacher* rather than an indoctrinator or an all-in wrestler.

Secondly, the teacher's non-teaching activities will vary enormously from one context and society to another. In time of war, for instance, a teacher may be rightly required to deal with children in all sorts of ways which have nothing to do with education; even in peacetime, if the context makes it difficult or undesirable to do much that could be called 'teaching', he will find it necessary to do a great many things of this kind — things varying according to the country he is living in, the age, sex, ability range, social class, etc. of his pupils, and so on. There is thus a difficulty about knowing *what* non-teaching activities to prepare him for. It is not in dispute that many or most of these might be at the time extremely important, perhaps more important than teaching; but it is hard to see how any preparation of teachers could cover all the possible ground.

Here it is extremely tempting to say something like 'Well, as things in fact are in our society and our schools, teachers will need to do XYZ, so it's only sensible to prepare them for XYZ'. I think this temptation has in principle to be resisted, and should certainly be resisted at this stage of our discussion. Some reasons for this are fairly obvious: it is very hard to predict what XYZ will in fact be, even in ten years' time; the variety of schools or teaching posts in this country and abroad is very considerable, so that whatever the content of XYZ we shall find it hard to prove that all or even most of our student-teachers *must* encounter these demands; and, as we noticed above, we do not necessarily want to spend a lot of time endorsing XYZ as things that teachers ought to do, even if a particular régime demands it. A more powerful reason, however, is methodological: it seems more sensible to *start*, at least, by considering (if we can work this out) what more or less any teacher must do under more or less any régime; after we are clear about that, we can add in whatever *ad hoc* requirements are demanded by particular régimes and contexts.

This seems to me the only intelligent way to proceed: that is, to try to mark out some common ground on which we can rely for at least the conceptual core (so to speak) of our preparation of teachers. Such ground will not be derived from the concept of teaching itself, but from conceptual considerations of a wider nature. These considerations are valid within certain minimal assumptions: basically, that there are going to be people (teachers) in organizations (schools) regularly or irregularly attended by other people (pupils), whose job it is to see that these other people learn something, or are educated. Such assumptions can, I think, be shown to derive logically from any serious educational theory or ideal; in any case, I do not suppose that many will want to challenge them at this point. Two conceptual features emerge from this:

1. The notion of 'seeing that people learn something' does not entail that the teacher should spend a lot, or even much, time in actually teaching them; this is why it is merely linguistic puritanism to insist that teachers must teach, and that this must necessarily be the centre of their activities. For instance, it is entirely clear that pupils can learn a great deal if the teacher simply 'motivates' them very strongly to learn for themselves — from books, videotapes, films, 'programmed learning', and other devices. A very great deal of teaching, at least in the sense of instruction and perhaps also explanation, might easily be taken over by technology. There remains, however, something at once more general and more personal, encapsulated in the phrase 'seeing that people learn'. The teacher — or *someone* working within the parameters described above, whatever we call him — will still be required to 'see that' the learning goes on. This would naturally include such activities as supervising, 'motivating', checking up to see that learning has in fact been done, and so on. To put this in a general way, the teacher will still have to 'cope with pupils'.

This remains true, I think — for conceptual rather than practical reasons — even if we add other functionaries to take over other tasks. It would, for instance, be in principle possible to provide each teacher with a sergeant-major to enforce discipline, and with a child-minder to ensure that the pupils did not damage themselves; just as we can and do provide teachers with technicians to operate the teaching machines or closed-circuit television. There would still remain the task of 'seeing that' the *learning* went on: organizing and directing particular pupils in particular programmes, coping with whatever personal or emotional difficulties arose in this context, and in general dealing with the pupils as *people*, with special reference to their functioning as learners.

2. There are also conceptual reasons for supposing that *some* things, and these perhaps not the least important, cannot be learned except from and in relation to a person: that is, a teacher (rather than a teaching machine or a book). Very roughly, these things fall into the area of what Hirst calls 'personal knowledge'[10] (knowledge of human intentions, purposes, motives, etc.); enough has been written about this elsewhere to make the necessary points.[11] I incline to think that other areas too fall within the scope of these points: areas where the emotions and the unconscious mind are necessarily involved (e.g. the appreciation of the arts), and areas where the responses and under-standing of the individual pupil are so complex and personalized that it would be difficult or impossible to imagine a non-personal teacher. (Think of the difficulties of constructing a teaching machine for teaching philosophy.)

These two points give us a rough understanding of what it is, centrally and necessarily, to 'be a teacher': (1) to 'see that people learn', which (2) in some areas has to involve actually teaching them. This needs some sharpening up, along the line taken in respect of 'education' in earlier chapters. There is a sense or senses in which parents, truancy officers and government departments 'see that people learn': that is, they do things which encourage, enable or facilitate learning. These senses get thinner, or may disappear altogether, the further away we get from (a) a *direct* 'seeing that', and (b) a *full-time* 'seeing that'. For instance, we might predicate the phrase of, say, an inspector of schools or a marker of examinations, or even of a person who writes school textbooks or services a videotape machine, but we do not call these people teachers, because their involvement with pupils learning is not sufficiently direct or immediate. Similarly, a parent or an elder brother might in a fairly direct and forceful way 'see that' a young child learned, by visiting the school and threatening him if he were lazy, but this would hardly be a full-time task.

'Being a teacher', then, is roughly to be demarcated on these lines, the importance of which may perhaps be more obvious if we contrast them with other non-central or non-necessary tasks. It is not concep-tually part of 'being a teacher' to improve pupils' social or economic chances nor to ensure that they are qualified in various ways to enter various jobs or institutions nor to alter their home background, physical condition, or relationship to 'society' nor to dispense particular 'social values' nor to ensure whatever supply of workers and technologists may be demanded by governmental or other economic pressures. Teachers may, of course, often be required to do such things, and sometimes may be justly required to do them, but they are not conceptually central to 'being a teacher', any more than that teachers should belong to a certain trades union, or be paid a particular salary, or have to write with chalk on a blackboard.

The practical force of these conceptual manoeuvres should be clear enough. We can achieve some safety and invulnerability thereby, being able to say in effect: 'Well, *this* area at least is something we can be sure about: as long as there are such things as teachers at all, they will need preparation in *these* respects. Governments may come and go, particular social pressures may increase or fade, blackboards may be replaced, and so on; but this at least stays put'. Indeed, it would be tempting (if premature) to suggest that, if as is likely, practical considerations give us all too short a time to prepare teachers in, we might do well to concentrate on what we know is needed, leaving whatever time remains (probably not much) for the non-central, *ad hoc* requirements.

Such a suggestions is premature, because (again, as with the notion of education itself) it may well be, in particular contexts, that the *ad hoc* requirements are more important in themselves: it may be more important, in a war, that the teacher is properly trained to keep flying glass away from his pupils than that he should actually teach them anything. Clearly, if there are standard and recognizable demands which we can both justify and regard as constant over a foreseeable future, teachers must be prepared to meet these. But this does not detract from the value of seeing the notion of 'being a teacher' as centrally concerned with what we have outlined above. In just the same way, doctors or parsons might often — or even regularly — have to do things which are not directly related to medicine or religion (for instance, filling in forms) but we would think poorly of any preparation for being a doctor or a parson which did not make the notions of medicine or religion central. It is not just that, without starting from some such central idea, we could not begin to make sense of different aspects of teacher-preparation: it is also that, if we lose sight of the idea, we thereby lost sight of there being any specific *point* in having teachers at all.

I now want to look at some of the problems surrounding phrases like 'the preparation of teachers', 'teacher-training' and 'teacher-education'. The first of these problems involves a simple ambiguity in (say) 'the education of teachers' — are we talking about the education of teachers *qua* teachers or about the (general) education of people who (it so happens) are going to be teachers? The fashionable move from 'teacher-training' to 'teacher-education' makes this ambiguity particularly important: it is less likely (though perhaps just linguistically possible) for someone to include under 'teacher-training' types of training that were not geared to the specific needs of teachers. But it is very likely, indeed it is the case, that 'teacher-education' might be used in this way.

I have said that this ambiguity is a simple one, but in fact it is extremely difficult when reading the literature to be sure when an author is talking about educating intending teachers *for* their job as teachers or about educating intending teachers with some other criteria in mind. Two factors, very different in kind, may encourage the second usc: (1) there is some linguistic pressure to say that one educates *people*, and that one does not educate them *for* anything; (2) for various quasi-political reasons, chiefly concerned with 'professional status', there is pressure to use grander or wider terms in higher education generally — hence 'educate' rather than 'train'. The result is considerable confusion because, of course, the criteria of selection for what we want to do with teachers will be different, according to which side of the ambiguity we come down on.

There is nothing much we can do, at this stage, except to *note* the ambiguity. Clearly some things we want to do might be selected by either criterion — that is, either by the criterion of what education is needed specifically by *teachers* or by the criterion of what education is needed generally by *people* (who happen to be going to be teachers). This second criterion could, of course, be modified in all sorts of ways: thus we could educate them not just *qua* teachers but also *qua* social workers, or school counsellors, or therapists, or 'community guides', or whatever — which would be substantially different from just educating them as teachers, but also different from educating them generally as people. Any competent categorization, such as we will attempt in a later chapter, will have to take this main distinction into account.

Secondly, there is the training-education distinction. Not just anything counts as 'training' nor as 'education'; when we know more clearly what we want to do with intending teachers, we shall be in a better position to see how each item may be justly entitled. At present we are not clear, which is why it would be absurdly premature to fix on either. But it is very important to note at this stage that a simple-minded view, roughly to the effect that 'education' will include everything we want to do under training' and a good deal more besides that sounds important and prestigious, does not stand up to examination. The criteria governing 'train' and 'educate' are more complex.

In general, 'train' carries two ideas with it. (1) There is the idea that one is trained for a particular job or task: we can train (people to be) gardeners or housemaids or radar operators, and we can train people to speak clearly, write on blackboards, and (perhaps) keep order in a classroom. We can train dogs, and even plants. (2) There is some restriction on the kind of operation we perform when we train, as is clear from the training of animals: if the operation or type of learning involves (putting it very roughly) some sophisticated kinds of under-standing, conceptual awareness or emotional response, 'train' becomes inappropriate — we do not *train* people to appreciate Bach, or to love their neighbours, or to become wise (even though certain types of training might be relevant to these ends). Here we would naturally use something like 'educate' or 'teach'; and conversely, as we have noticed, we do not *educate* people to type or write on blackboards or jump through paper hoops.

We can already see that there may be important things we want to do with teachers that come under 'training' and not 'education', and other important things which come under 'education' and not 'training'. Getting clear about these things is complicated by the fact that 'train' has to satisfy both of the criteria (1) and (2) above. If 'train' covered everything that the teacher needed for being a teacher, this complication would not arise, but it clearly does not. For instance, it is reasonable to claim that the teacher, *qua* teacher, needs enthusiasm for his subject and some concern for children. These items could fall under 'training' if only criterion (1) was involved, for they are both required by the job. But we (logically) cannot train people to be enthusiastic or concerned, so that by criterion (2) they fail.

Nor is this by any means the end of the matter. There are many things which it seems plausible to do in the preparation of teachers which seem to call for a more specific description than either 'education' or 'training'. For example, we might think it useful for intending teachers simply to 'get the feel' of being in a school (in a classroom, the teachers' common room, etc.), and do this simply by dumping them in various schools for various periods of time. Whether or not we *also* get them to view this 'experience' in some more theoretical way (i.e. educate them) or put them through some specific hoops in class management and 'social skills' in the common room (i.e. train them), we might feel this 'experience' to be valuable in itself. Of course we might call this, in a broad sense, part of their training or their education as teachers, but it is clearly a different *sort* of process or operation, perhaps meriting some title like 'initiation' or 'immersion' or 'acclimatization'.

Or again, it seems *prima facie* as if there are some simple facts which intending teachers ought to know which have little or nothing to do with their subject or their pupils: for instance, their legal rights, or what teachers' union to join. We can say happily that this part of their preparation for being a teacher, but can we say that it is part of their education or training as a teacher? Well, of course we can say this, and it may seem merely fussy to object, but the point remains that we have a different category here. These facts might be profitably separated off from the central tasks of the teacher, and perhaps simply mugged up from books or hand-outs or perhaps it would be enough merely to direct the intending teacher's attention to the relevant sources of reference. On any account, the sort of way we want the teacher to be prepared here looks significantly different from other things that might be called 'education' or 'training'.

Here I am only trying to reinforce the openness of the question 'What shall we do in the preparation of teachers?' One might select even stronger examples: for instance, it is perfectly possible that a person's effectiveness as a teacher might be severely reduced by (a) having such bad false teeth that he cannot articulate properly, (b) being so badly-dressed or wart-covered that he puts his pupils off, (c) being so physically weak that he cannot keep up with his pupils on a school outing. These examples, less frivolous than they may appear, show that the relevant remedies are not always to do with education or even training: (a) calls for better dentistry, (b) the removal of warts or a better wardrobe, and (c) perhaps a course of vitamins. These are things we simply *give* to intending teachers; and this is, in fact, an area of teacher-preparation which is both extremely important and (so far as I know) largely unconsidered.

We have, then, to take into account not only (i) the distinction between the education of intending teachers *qua* teachers, as against the education of them *qua* people, but also (ii) a great many different distinctions in the *kinds* of preparation we give them. Most of these — but, as I have just made clear, not all — will involve different kinds of *learning*, and the education-training distinction is only one (crude) sort of distinction at a fairly basic level. Nevertheless, without wishing to prejudge any taxonomic question or attribution of importance to particular categories, it may already be possible to see reason for concentrating not only on the categories of learning, but on that particular category which we normally mark by 'education' rather than 'training'. I shall try to show that this follows from what we have already noticed as conceptually or necessarily central to the notion of 'being a teacher'.

The importance of education (rather than just training) for teachers has been supported by a number of bad arguments, most of which are semi-political in nature, which we need to look at first. Thus even Richard Peters is prepared to argue that

Unless teachers are well versed in these sciences [*sc.* the disciplines of 'educational theory'] which are ancillary to their task there is little hope of their establishing for themselves a profession which can retain some kind of authority in the community:[12]

and the teacher has to defend

his opinions on psychological, sociological or historical matters . . . in an informed and intelligent way so that he can hold his own in public discussion. The simple truth, in other words, is that the teacher has to learn to think for himself about what he is doing. He can no longer rely on an established tradition.[13]

I accept the simple truth, but the implications are unacceptable (1) that it would be all right for the teacher *not* to 'think for himself' if he *could* 'rely on an established tradition'; (2) that learning to 'think for himself' must take the form of being 'well versed' in psychology, sociology and history; (3) that the proper reason for doing this is to 'retain some kind of authority in the community'.

Behind this, and much else in the current literature, float two main ideas: (a) that — perhaps particularly 'in a pluralistic and democratic society', or something of the kind — we must do *something* to improve the professional status and authority of teachers; (b) that this has to be done by educating them in a number of high-sounding subjects or disciplines that seem 'relevant' — 'philosophy of education', 'psychology of education', 'sociology of education' and so on — which, it is thought, must be both desirable in itself and happily kills two birds with one stone by also satisfying our desire in (a). Clearly all this is not only muddled but premature. There are other ways of equipping teachers with authority and status besides this one (indeed I hazard the sociological guess that this one is not efficient — increases in teachers' pay, power and scope are likely to be more so), and we do not as yet know *what* kind of education or study teachers actually need.

Elsewhere Peters is nearer the mark in adumbrating *one* sound conceptual reason why teachers must be educated:

If anything is to be regarded as a specific preparation for teaching, priority must be given to a thorough grounding in something to teach.[14]

In other words, he must know something, otherwise he cannot teach it. We have to take some care with this argument, for (as we noticed earlier) 'being a teacher' is not co-extensive with 'teaching'. Might it not be possible for teachers effectively to 'see that' pupils learned effectively, the actual instruction being largely given by text books, television lectures by university professors, teaching machines, and so on? But, as we also noticed, there are limits to this; in some types of learning this will not wash, and in all types the teacher must at least know what counts as successful learning, and be sufficiently familiar with the subject (as well as with the pupils) to deploy these aids to learning effectively.

This first reason for teachers needing to be educated, then, would not be best given by saying that a teacher needs to *know a lot of* (say) mathematics, science or history. He must 'know his subject' in a way that is most useful for the learning of his pupils; and whilst of course this will usually include possessing a good deal of relevant *information*, we should more naturally stress the idea of having a clear understanding of what it is to make progress in the subject — the type of reasoning involved, its logical structure, the marks of 'a good historian' (scientist, mathematician, etc.), and so forth. This, of course, cannot (logically) be gained only by *training* nor merely by the teacher having received competent *instruction*. To the extent that the teacher 'knows his subject' in this sense — as opposed to just being able to dole out facts or figures — we would describe him as *educated*. This reason, then, will be valid if, or to the extent that, we think it desirable that his pupils should also be educated in this sense; and even if we did not it is hard to see how a teacher could succeed even in less ambitious enterprises. We could easily imagine a teacher trying, not to educate his pupils, but simply to give them some useful facts and skills, but it is more difficult to imagine his selecting these judiciously and presenting them effectively unless he was himself 'on the inside of' his subject.

This is, however, hardly conclusive, and a second reason is much weightier. Whatever educational content or type of learning he 'sees that' his pupils master, he has also to transmit some kind of seriousness, care or enthusiasm for it. As I have expressed it, this sounds like advocating some special bonus in education, which it would be nice if the teacher transmitted to the pupils as well as transmitting the actual knowledge. But there is a sense in which this can be seen as a conceptual necessity. In order to learn or understand — certainly above the level of the simplest skills, and perhaps in all cases — the pupil must to some extent display care or seriousness. One could not, for instance, properly be described as 'doing science' or 'learning history' if one simply did not care at all about the results of experiments or what contemporary historical documents said. Of course, if the pupils are full of excitement and enthusiasm about science and history in general, that is better still, but the processes of learning, judging, discriminating, and becoming aware in these (and all other) subjects themselves involve some degree of seriousness or care.[15]

I incline to think that this is perhaps the most important element in anything seriously to be described as 'education'; but however this may be, it clearly has some necessary importance. Without this element of care, learning cannot go on. Necessarily also the teacher — whether or not he feels, at particular times, joyous or enthusiastic about his subject — must, if he seriously oversees the pupils' learning at all, both display and dispense the kind of care which the subject demands. That just *is* teaching, or overseeing the learning of, a subject. This too is something which could not be wholly induced in teachers merely by training. Even if we imagine teachers ruthlessly drilled into grimly 'going through the motions' of teaching science and other subjects, some element of commitment seems to be required.

Thirdly, a still weightier reason, connected with the fact that the teacher has to deal with *people* learning. This calls for some degree of personal understanding on his part; and this kind of understanding is not entirely amenable to training — which is, again, not to deny that certain types of training may be useful for helping to develop such understanding and for dealing with people in general. We might perhaps, though with some difficulty, imagine a teaching situation in which a teacher would not be handicapped by a complete lack of understanding about his pupils: for instance, teaching people to type, or doing what a drill-sergeant does on the parade ground. Even here, however, the need for such understanding *could* always arise, and it is fairly clear that, for the kind of overseeing and the kinds of learning that a teacher will be concerned with, it will be highly relevant.

To summarize these three reasons: the teacher needs to be educated (not just trained) because (1) he has to 'know his subject'; (2) he has to exemplify and transmit some degree of 'seriousness' or 'care' as part of learning; (3) he has to understand people. Only the first (and the weakest) of these reasons gives us any *a priori* grounds for specifying *what* the education of the teacher should consist of: that is, in respect of this reason, education in his teaching-subject. The other two reasons give us no such specification; in particular they give us no reason to suppose that the teacher should know a lot of 'educational theory', or that his training should be primarily 'practical', or indeed for any *a priori* views of this kind. We need to look at the notions of 'theory' and 'practice' for the intending teacher more closely.

Before concluding this chapter, however, I think it worth noting one important methodological point. To some readers — I hope, to many — much of what I have said will seem in essence wholly obvious. So indeed it is; and a lot of it would not need saying, if some educators did not seem to have abandoned a common sense grasp of these matters. A good many books written either before the current fashion for making teacher education 'scientific' and 'professional', or else in a state of blessed immunity from this fashion — Highet's *The Art of Teaching*,[16] for example, — display such common sense, and make many of the relevant points clear. Certainly they are much better as a basis for reflection than most contemporary works.

But we have to go a bit further than common sense, even if the journey may seem more wearisome than the simple appreciation of intuitive insight. First, we (or some of us) *are* in the grip of this fashion and need to recover our senses by unbewitching or — so to speak — demythologizing ourselves: no short or easy task. Secondly, for the sake of security, we need to see in detail *why* the conclusions we reach by 'common sense' or 'intuition' are correct; otherwise we cannot defend ourselves against new fashions which may distort our judgement. Thirdly, even the most apparently 'insightful' authors may have prejudices of their own. All this makes a certain kind of task necessary; *not*, as I hope to have sufficiently shown already, the task of trying to turn our common sense knowledge into 'science'; rather that of explicating this knowledge and putting it into a certain kind of framework which will show it to be *necessary*, not just 'obvious', knowledge. This is the first essential towards serious progress in the subject; afterwards, it can be 'thickened out' (as it were) not only by whatever findings of behaviouristic science are relevant, but also by whatever novelists or psychiatrists or even *raconteurs* can say to make the points more vivid. But we have to get a solid basis first.

Notes

1. *Howard's End* (in relation to the Wilcoxes).
2. Taylor (1969), pp. ix — x.
3. Taylor (1969), but only for convenience. The same points will be found to apply to other well-known works, e.g. Lomax (1973), Tibble (1971). Yates (1972) is some improvement.
4. *ibid.* p. 226.
5. e.g. McMullen, *ibid.*, p. 36 ff.
6. e.g. Bantock, *ibid.*, p. 122 ff.
7. See Chapter 2, p. 49 ff.
8. See p. 53 ff.
9. PER, p. 30 ff.
10. Hirst and Peters (1970), p. 66 ff.
11. E.g. Hamlyn in Mischel (1974), Peters (*ibid.*).
12. In Tibble (1966), p. 82.
13. *ibid.*

14. Peters (1968) p. 3.
15. I owe much here to Peters (1973 and elsewhere: see references), though there are some conceptual complexities which need unravelling.
16. Highet (1956).

Chapter Five

'*Theory*'

The current literature makes it hard for one to take seriously the idea that teachers should learn a great deal of 'educational theory' (even though this idea is widely institutionalized in current practice), in two main ways. First, there is no clear idea in the literature of any respectable, solidly-based, and demonstrably informative 'theory' at all: some moderately plausible pictures are given of this, but only at the highest level of generalization;[1] nowhere is it shown, either that any reputable theory exists, or that such theory is clearly of value to practising teachers. The former proposition we have already seen sufficient reason to doubt, in earlier chapters of this book; the latter can only be intelligently discussed *pari passu* with, or after, the task of categorizing specific types of teacher-preparation.

Even if there were such theory, it is pretty clear that most of the authors and academics who write about it or teach it to student-teachers have little idea of the methodological doubts and problems involved. Thus under a section heading 'Educational psychology', one author says that intending teachers need

> ... the rigorous, empirical perspective of the social scientist. As Taylor insists, 'psychology is a science and as such is governed by a morality or code of rules which calls for the empirical verification of its proportions'[2] [this must surely be a misprint for 'propositions']

Obviously, from this passage and the rest of his article, the author has the sort of *simpliste* conception of 'psychology' which died a philosophical death some twenty or thirty years ago; the status of 'psychology' (whatever we are to mean by it) 'as a science' (whatever *that* means) is notoriously in dispute.[3] We might think 'But why should professors and lecturers in education be well up in such philosophical disputes?' Perhaps they need not, but then they must not just assume that 'educational psychology' is useful to intending teachers in these highly questionable ways. It would be better for them to remain simply in doubt. One is inclined to guess that, just because 'educational psychology' is institutionally on the map as a 'foundation discipline', authors are prepared to accept uncritically certain standard (if obsolescent) images which make the subject look good — 'scientific rigour', 'experimental evidence', and so on.

Secondly, and I think partly because of these difficulties, even the most intelligent people who write about the value of such theory to teachers seem sometimes optimistic to the point of insanity. Hirst, for instance, says[4]

> If it is the job of educational theorists to formulate the principles, it is certainly vital for educational practice that teachers and others who both take and implement individual decisions *fully understand the principles and their bases.*

Hirst's 'educational principles', as we saw earlier,[5] are supposed to flow from the interaction of various disciplines — philosophy, psychology, sociology (and we have seen reason to suppose that this list might be extended). The suggestion that intending teachers should 'fully understand' these principles *and* 'their bases' is not merely utopian in practical terms, but logically ridiculous: *nobody* 'fully understands' the 'bases' of some of these disciplines. The criteria for competence in areas marked by 'psychology', 'sociology', etc. are themselves in doubt, and even more questionable is the relationship between these areas and 'educational principles'.

Of course Hirst knows this perfectly well, as is plain from his remarks quoted earlier ('. . . quite impossible practically, for no one could have mastered all the relevant specialist knowledge. . . ').[6] But frequently defenders of 'educational theory' for teachers find themselves writing in this utopian sort of way. Sometimes a more common sense line is adopted, but then it is often unclear exactly what is being argued for, and exactly what the arguments are. Thus Peters, writing about the philosophy of education, says

> To question its 'use' is really to question the 'use' of educational theory as a whole of which philosophy forms an essential part. Under the conditions in which the modern teacher has to operate this is not a real issue . . . Education no longer has agreed aims; procedures are constantly under discussion and vary according to different people's conceptions of the subjects which they are teaching; fundamental questions concerned with principles underlying school organization, class management and the curriculum

are constantly being raised; and in the area of moral education the task is made more perplexing by the variations of standards which characterize a highly differentiated society.[7]

We have here to distinguish a number of different theses. (1) It is not in dispute that teachers ought to think seriously, and be well informed, about the problems they face; and if 'educational theory' is a title for anything that will help them to do this, it will not be in dispute that teachers should engage in 'educational theory'. (2a) It is highly disputable that the *desirability* of this is a function of 'the conditions in which the modern teacher has to operate' — as if serious thought were only required when there was disagreement. (2b) It is equally disputable that the *inevitability* of it is a function of these conditions: it is perfectly possible to follow one's own nose, without serious thought or rational reflection, even in a 'highly differentiated society'. (I am not sure whether Peters' 'this is not a real issue' is supposed to suggest (2a) or (2b) here.) (3) It is very much in dispute whether what we *now have* as 'educational theory' meets the requirements of (1).

Arguments against the value of educational theory, as we now have it, for the preparation of teachers are not far to seek (though, interestingly, much more commonly advanced in conversation than in print). There is, first, the point that since a great deal of such 'theory' is confused or nonsensical, it is not likely to do much more than mislead the practising teacher or make him feel guilty for not living up to it. What we in fact have, under this heading, is not a set of practical principles which have been validated; this is a target which we do not yet know even how to aim at. We have a loose network of fashion, fantasy, political or social 'movements', and general 'ideas' about education, mixed in with various 'research findings' which may or may not be valid in themselves, but which are certainly insufficient to support the kind of practical principles we need.

Secondly, a good deal of such theory — even if it were sounder than in fact it is — has only a remote connection with the job of 'being a teacher'. Even in the UK, where educational power is less centralized than in most societies, 'being a teacher' has to be distinguished — in practice as well as conceptually — from being a head teacher, a curriculum adviser, a local administrator, a government official, an educational psychologist, and so forth. Many decisions, perhaps particularly those involving the political or social aspects of education (logically peripheral aspects, but much stressed by current educational theory), are simply not in the hands of teachers. Again, it is one thing to be a teacher, another to be a researcher; whatever the *use* of, say, IQ tests to teachers, the *theory behind* such tests is not the teacher's business.

Thirdly, even if the theory were both sound in itself and, in principle, usable by teachers, there would still remain immense difficulties in the area commonly described as 'relating theory to practice'. The main trouble here is that we are not clear what sort of content to give to this phrase, even in cases less complex than education. For instance, suppose I am a gardener, tending my plants and vegetables by traditional methods. Society becomes aware that various academic disciplines and practical techniques may be relevant and useful for gardening: on the one hand, chemistry, meterology, biology, etc., and on the other certain practical methods of pruning roses or enlarging marrows. To what extent, in what ways, and in what senses do I, as a gardener, need to 'know about' these? Plainly this is not — even in this comparatively simple case — an easy question. We might think that (a) I could usefully be given the *findings* of the academic disciplines, just as I might be handed bags of fertiliser, without having to understand them — and certainly without having to understand the principles and research behind them; (b) I would have to be trained to use the new practical *methods*, since it is I, and no one else, who am actually attending to the roses and the marrows; and this is fair enough as a sighting shot. But there will, even here, be many difficult intermediary cases where the 'findings' cannot be handed me on a plate; where I have to have *some* general understanding of (say) biological theory, but am still not required to understand it *as* a biologist — as it were, to take biology at A Level. I draw no conclusions here: I intend only to point out the difficulties.

If anything is clear, it is that the relationship of theory to practice in education will differ enormously from one case to another. Here I am chiefly concerned to case doubt on the vague but popular idea that, since educational matters are generally disputed, it follows that teachers must 'know a lot of educational theory'. But is not clear what this would mean or whether it is true, even in the most disputable or 'controversial' areas. To take one such area as an example: *prima facie* it is the philosopher's business to outline the aims or meaning of 'moral education' and 'religious education', and to make sure that these aims are based on as solid (philosophical) arguments as possible. It is the psychologist's business to conduct research — perhaps by extremely recherché methods — into what general factors promote these aims. It is the teacher's business to generate these factors and realize the aims. For this the teacher needs to understand what the aims and factors *are*, but he does not always need to understand the work that has produced them. At best it may help if he does, in order to accept them more wholeheartedly and with a clearer head, but he does not always *need* to. It may be more important that he should be properly trained, or educated, in a way which will enable him *as a teacher* to do the vital practical job of actually educating children in these spheres. He must master whatever practical methods have been proved, or at least *prima facie* seem, effective, and he must be able, by the use of his experience and practically-oriented imagination, to adapt them to the children he teaches, and to invent new ones where possible.

There is here, to put it at its lowest, a big difference of emphasis; as big, in its way, as that between (say) a policeman and a criminologist, or a gardener and an agricultural expert. This difference of emphasis remains where we have cases — unlike the cases of moral and religious education — in which there *is* an agreed set of aims and methods. For instance, suppose research had shown beyond doubt that the best way of getting children to learn to read was to use such-and-such an alphabet, such-and-such textbooks and methods, etc., then obviously, it will not be necessary for the teacher to understand why this is so — all he needs to be able to do is to deploy the equipment and methods effectively, much more like (though not exactly like) the gardener using the fertilisers with which chemical research has provided him. In these cases the difference is *clearer* but not *greater*. For in the other cases, where there is no such agreement and no corpus of knowledge exists, it will probably be as much of a waste of time for teachers to turn themselves into professional philosophers and psychologists as for gardeners to turn themselves into professional chemists; in the absence of known facts, both would do better to follow their instincts and hunches, and leave the research to others.

Some of the most important points lie somewhere in this area. The general intention behind laying on 'educational theory' for intending teachers might be roughly divided into (a) the desire to acquaint them with the 'hard' established facts and 'research findings' which (the story goes) we know and which teachers ought to know; and (b) the desire to improve, in some less cut-and-dried way, the teachers' awareness, insight, understanding of people, seriousness and so forth. Although almost every writer on the topic states or implies that what we do under (a) assists, or is part of, what we try to do under (b), it is at least arguable that in fact the former vitiates the latter, i.e. precisely because we pretend to ourselves, and to teachers, that we possess well-established 'theory', and because we spend a lot of time deluging them with it, we thereby succeed not in improving but in obfuscating such natural understanding and seriousness as they may have.

It is notorious that this is a possible situation; a well-known example is the deleterious effect, on the mothers of infants, of constantly-changing psychological 'theories' about, for instance, when the child should be fed, whether it should be picked up when it cries, and so forth. This is, indeed, almost a paradigm case, for it is equally clear both that *something*, of course, can be done to help mothers understand and cope with children (or teachers with pupils), and that the majority of 'theory' in this area has in fact hindered rather than helped. In just the same way, it is clear that not a few teachers are (like the rest of us) badly in need of some sort of improvement in their understanding and perceptions, but it is certainly *not* clear that educational theory has provided this. And if it has not, the chances are that what it does instead is either to provide them with fantasies or just to muddle them up.

I do not, of course, want to lay this at the door of any academic subject *per se*, but some examples may show how it comes about that any such subject may have this effect. For instance, it is at least arguable that most intending teachers — if not already corrupted by various social fantasies — are tolerably clear (in what one might call an unconscious sort of way) that human institutions require rules, and rules require punishments; that notions marked by 'discipline', 'authority', 'punishment' and so on are (so to speak) inexpellable. Now in practice the 'philosophy of education' has engaged in long discussions, supposedly of practical value to teachers, under the heading of 'The Justification of Punishment'. The actual effect of these discussions, I should guess, is chiefly to cast doubt on these inexpellable notions; doubt which is then heavily reinforced by anti-authoritarian and liberationist fantasies common in our present society. This is not the fault of 'philosophy' itself, and shows only that philosophers too are liable to mistake and fantasy. But it illustrates its dangers and reinforces the importance of seriousness, rather than (what we do not have) of a coherent body of knowledge, as a crucial aspect of the preparation of teachers.

Or consider, again, the vast quantity of sociological research which clusters round the (obscure) notion of 'social class'. I should need convincing that the affect of this, on the average teacher, was to improve his day-to-day understanding of pupils from different social strata in any teaching-situation — that is, actually in the classroom. (Indeed, it is not clear that the pupils' social class *as such* is directly relevant to education at all.) More likely is the promotion or strengthening of some fantasy, perhaps about the value of 'working-class culture' or the horrors of '*élitism*', which simply saps his common sense. Again, it can of course be said that, insofar as this happens, it is due to bad sociology in the first place, perhaps compounded by bad teaching (or stupid student-teachers). Nevertheless, this may be what actually happens.

Or again, it is far from clear that the research and 'theory' relevant to pupils learning to read and master basic mathematics has, in fact, produced more understanding and effective teachers who have hence been able to turn out pupils more literate and 'numerate' than their predecessors. Indeed the reverse may have happened: certain psycho-logical ideas and researches — in themselves vague and unproven — may simply have been used in the service of some general 'approach' or 'ideal' about how to deal with primary school children. Once more, to cast doubt on the use or validity of such 'theory' *for teachers* is not to cast doubt on (for example) Piaget — though that too has to be done.[8] But arguably, if we had reasonably serious teachers who relied on their own knowledge and common sense, and were expected to do the best they could by way of teaching pupils to read and add up, things might well be better; at least, it seems they would not be worse.

Closely connected with this is the point that, even if the 'theory' were sound, and even if it were able to be properly absorbed by intending teachers, it might still unnerve rather than help them; for they might not (all) be the sort of people to benefit from it. On any account, a great deal of teaching or 'being a teacher' is a function of the particular teacher's general style or personality; 'theory' which goes against this style may well be disruptive rather than helpful. To take a simple example: suppose we have some evidence from theory or research that an ideal teacher or expositor would, in a particular context, speak at an optimal rate of so many words per minute, use a few but not too many gestures, write in a certain way on the blackboard, and so on. Now the fact is that, to a considerable extent, how fast or slow people talk, or what gestures they use, is part of their temperament or personality. Of course they can, in some degree and with the help of various methods of training or education, change their style or even their personality in these respects, but certainly not entirely, and perhaps even not much — not, at least, without losing the kind of naturalness and enthusiasm which they originally had.

Or again, there are of course things to be said about the problems of keeping order in the classroom or 'classroom control', and about the merits of certain arrangements ('open-plan', 'team teaching', 'the integrated day', and so on). But whatever the theoretical merits of this or that system, the teacher's success will depend very much on how far a particular system *suits* him — that is, suits his temperament, his approach, his style: even, if you like, his prejudices and neurotic compulsions. Some people (I am one) find it difficult or impossible to teach or lecture if people are talking to each other or otherwise not attending; others, more tolerant, can carry on in a hubbub. Some find 'team teaching' a muddle, perhaps even a threat to their autonomy; others find it congenial and companionable.

Notice here that this point reinforces the importance of certain types of *personal* education or training for teachers. If my personal style leads me into what are demonstrably mistakes — talking too fast, or getting too upset if one or two children talk to each other when I am teaching — then what I need is not some 'theory' to show me that these are mistakes, but some kind of cure or treatment that will change my style. Similarly, if I lack elements of the kind of common-sense understanding of people, awareness of my pupils' problems, and so on which I need as a teacher, the chances are that this is due to some defect in me — in *me*, not in my ignorance of the latest research findings.

It is possible to say, and indeed is commonly said, that one function of educational theory is that it 'makes teachers think', 'prevents them from just teaching in the way they themselves were taught at school', 'opens their eyes to the complexities of child development', and so on. This is not wholly absurd, but there is an element of the grotesque about it, deriving from the notion that the only or the best way to 'open their eyes' in this way is to give them large doses of (for instance) Piaget, Bernstein and others. I have even heard lengthy courses on Piagetian 'stages of development' for teachers defended by somebody who believes, as I do, that most of what can truly be said here is a matter of logic and not empirical psychology at all; his defence was that the logical or conceptual points would only sink in if the student-teachers were compelled to wade through all the empirical data. To use Hirst's example,[9] this is a bit like saying that they would only grasp that bachelors are unmarried after having sent out enough questionnaires. In the same sort of way, it might be (is) said that intending teachers must master the interesting but not very lucidly expressed work of Bernstein, because otherwise they will not appreciate that some pupils in their care, probably of working-class origin and from 'linguistically deprived' homes, only use a 'restricted language code'. If a teacher, after knowing and dealing with his pupils for a few weeks, did not learn most of what he needed to know for himself about their use of language, I think we should be inclined to say not that he had not read enough Bernstein, but that he must have been living in a dream world.

Naturally it is not denied that the theorist and researcher can add to and sophisticate the teacher's knowledge in all sorts of ways. Nevertheless, if 'theory' is to be useful to teachers, it must rise above the level of common sense. Meteorology has no satisfactory *raison d'être* for a man if it cannot predict the weather better than the man's own rheumatism, aching corns, or common-sense knowledge. We have to face the initial question 'What can "theory" tell the teacher of average competence, insight, understanding, etc. which (1) is demonstrably correct, (2) is practically useful, and (3) he does not know already or could not find out for himself by ordinary experience and reflection?' Not much would, I suspect, survive even this question; but, remembering that the preparation of teachers will (because of time shortage) depend largely on establishing priorities, it would be fair to ask an even tougher one, *viz.* 'What "theory" satisfies (1), (2) and (3) above, *and* (4) gives teachers understanding and knowledge which could not more efficiently and quickly be given by developing the teacher's *own* powers of perception?' And even if some elements of 'theory' survived this, we should still have to ask whether these elements were important enough to spend the time on them which we do spend, when contrasted with other ways in which we could improve and prepare teachers.

Many readers may have a good deal of sympathy with these doubts about the importance of existing educational theory to teachers. Unfortunately such doubts are commonly used to argue in a direction precisely contrary to the one which seems to me correct. Roughly, the thought is: 'Yes, "theory" is not much use to teachers; indeed, as soon as they get into the classroom they forget most of it, and quite right too. So let's drop it and concentrate on practice. Let's give them more experience of teaching-situations, practical problems in schools, immediately useful "methods" and "materials" for their subject, and so on; we can leave the "theory" to researchers or "educationalists" — if indeed it's any use at all'. This thought is often combined with the (politically fashionable) idea that we should give intending teachers more general education, in order to improve their professional status (or perhaps just because more higher education is thought to be a Good Thing), after which they can end up with a year or two's down-to-earth practical training.

It needs to be made absolutely clear that these ideas are wholly disastrous. They are analogous to saying something like the following, which might well have been suggested in a pre-medical or pre-scientific era: 'Yes, we don't really have much worthwhile "theory" about anatomy and physiology or about bridge-building: so let's not waste the time of intending doctors or engineers with that — let's make their training purely "practical". They can be taught the "skills" of how to apply leeches or build towers of Babel'. The disaster lies in the severance of the practical skills from *any* serious or sustained consideration of a more general or theoretical kind: in particular, from questions about what the teacher is *trying to do* at various times and in various situations. The absurdity of such severance emerges in another parallel: one might argue 'Look, all the "theory" of theology and religion and so on is extremely misty and questionable, and keeps changing; so let's just train ministers of the church in practical matters, like how to organize choir practices or read the lessons clearly'.

We have, as I see it, to hang on tightly to two ideas at once: first, that 'educational theory' as we in fact have it is extremely questionable and perhaps largely a waste of time; second, that we cannot begin to succeed in the task of preparing teachers in any serious sense unless we get them to take certain central aspects of learning and education seriously. This follows from what we have already noticed about the three general respects in which teachers need to be prepared by education: (1) to 'know their subject'; (2) to transmit care and seriousness about learning; (3) to understand people. All these are, very obviously, not entirely covered by anything we could call 'practical training'. They may also be, in institutional practice, pretty far removed from what actually goes on under the title 'educational theory'. But they are clearly very close to the general business of serious and critical reflection about education – that is, about subjects, learning and people.

Let me try to put this a little more practically, by means of examples we have used earlier. Almost any teacher will necessarily be involved in areas roughly marked by, say, 'discipline', 'moral education' and 'the curriculum'; this could be made to follow conceptually from (1), (2) and (3) above. Now it would be equally fatal, either (a) to give them the impression that there is much sound and well-based *empirical* knowledge or 'theory' in any of these areas, or (b) to say to them 'Never mind about all this theoretical stuff, all you need to know is how to cane pupils and control mobs, how to make the pupils' behaviour respectable so that parents won't complain, how to use materials and visual aids in your teaching-subject, and so on'. (a) is simply false, and (b) would prevent or discourage them from doing much serious education at all in these areas, since to do this they would have to start by trying to get a clear idea of what 'discipline', 'moral education', 'curriculum', etc. *meant*.

The 'message' we have to 'get across' (an odious phrase, but actually much depends on the general expectations and attitudes we ourselves display about 'theory' to intending teachers) is more like this: 'Look, this business of "educational theory" is in its infancy; hardly anything is known. On the other hand, it's pretty clear that you can't operate intelligently or successfully as a teacher unless you make some sort of serious and critical attempt on various topics, at least in areas which as a teacher you're bound to be involved in. We can try to help you get clear about these, anyway, and direct you to some books which might – only might – also be helpful. You should be able, as a minimum, to get some grasp of just what the problems are, and what serious work in "educational theory" would look like; and this should defend you against the fantasies and prejudices which now beset the study of education'.

Of course this only covers *one* aspect of the preparation of teachers: what might roughly be called the 'intellectual' aspect, which we have discussed because it arose out of a consideration of the relevance of 'educational theory'. There are plenty of other aspects — for instance, the matter of personal attitude and insight (whatever ground this phrase may cover); and some of these may be more relevant to the kinds of seriousness and knowledge encapsulated in (1), (2) and (3) above. But the right kind of 'intellectual' *posture* — I prefer not to say, the right kind of admixture of theoretical *knowledge* — is obviously of immense importance; and it is this which seems to emerge as a priority from our discussion so far. Some of its implications for teaching-methods in institutions that prepare teachers are already obvious: for instance, the weakness of mass lectures, of lengthy reading in the empirical field, and the writing of massive dissertations or theses based on the latter (as if we had a lot of well-established and relevant factual knowledge), and the comparative value of conceptual clarification, discussion in sustained seminars, and — to put it briefly — a much more Socratic approach to almost every topic.

I am tempted to say that at present we do not really take educational theory (in the preparation of teachers) seriously at all. For example, in one institution (A), a philosopher lectures to the students on Tuesday; on Wednesday a psychologist (B) tells them about 'learning theory' or 'development'; on Thursday they are introduced, by C, perhaps a sociologist, to 'curriculum theory'. A thinks that a lot of what B and C say is either tautological or mistaken; B and C think that A is 'just playing with words' or 'too abstract'. B perhaps thinks that C's 'curricular theory' is not a respectable subject at all, and C that B's remarks on animal learning are 'irrelevant'. The students have not only to listen to A, B and C, but also to answer an examination paper set and marked by them jointly. They, like the lecturers, avoid overt schizophrenia only by compartmentalizing these 'disciplines' and trotting out on demand what the institution requires by way of essays or examination answers; by *not* doing what is obviously necessary, i.e. getting together and sorting out the basic methodology of the whole business, arguing, criticizing and so forth in some adequate context of communication; in a word, by not taking it seriously.

Other reactions are of course possible. Some students, anxious to pass the course and perhaps naturally deferential, seem somehow to believe that the lines taken by A, B and C can happily coexist: these are people who can cheerfully read, say, Peters[10] and Winch[11] and yet still believe in behaviouristic psychology and sociology, at least for the purposes of the examination. Others may cotton on to a discipline which fits naturally with their interests or fantasies (usually some kind of sociology), and regard the others as a waste of time. Others again may dimly perceive that the whole business rests on insecure foundations, and make unhappy attempts to think about it: attempts almost certainly abortive because not likely to be supported by the staff of the institution.

I have omitted here reference to certain more obvious difficulties; partly because they are more obvious, and partly because they tend to promote the wrong sort of suggestion. Thus it is generally acknowledged that, in practice, many student-teachers are of a lower intellectual quality than one might wish, that the same applies to many tutors and lecturers (and, come to that, professors), and that time is very short. 'How can we expect them to master three or four "foundation disciplines" in such a little time?', and so on; hence we are led to some such suggestion as that they should specialize in only one 'foundation discipline' — that at least looks 'intellectually respectable'. But of course it is not. First, we do not (as we have seen) know which 'disciplines' *are* relevant even to educational theory; or rather, insofar as we have any clear ideas about this, the most relevant kind of intellectual activity — what I earlier called 'making sense' — bears some relation in theory to 'philosophy' and 'psychology' but not much in practice to what goes on in 'philosophy of education' and 'psychology of education'. Secondly, what is the point of allowing or encouraging student-teachers to do some 'intellectually respectable' piece of work, or to 'specialize', in an area which may be totally irrelevant to 'being a teacher'? If there is a point, it would presumably lie in the general desirability of people (including teachers, but not *qua* teachers) engaging in this sort of intellectual activity, but then, they might as well (or better) choose whatever area suits them on general grounds, rather than an area of 'educational theory'. Thirdly and most importantly, the suggestion is a mere evasion: the kind of 'seriousness' and 'intellectual respectability' we want student-teachers to adopt has to be applied where it is needed — that is, to the problems of methodology and 'making sense' which in fact are central to educational theory. Of course we can duck out of this by saying to them 'Look, "educational theory" is a muddle, and anyway there is far too much of it for you to master properly; so go off and tackle *one* specialist topic "in depth", whilst making some general acquaintance with the rest of the "foundation disciplines" '; but this is a cheat, because it gains the appearance of intellectual respectability at the price of misrepresenting the actual state of the subject.

These points have all the more force because we have to resist a constant temptation, which may be roughly described as the temptation to deny or disown the problem. We are familiar with certain ideas which lead, temptingly, to certain things that can be *done*: thus, as we saw earlier, we have the idea of 'practical experience in the classroom', which makes us say 'Educational theory is in a bad way, so let's make them spend more time in the classroom' or, as we have just seen, we have the idea of 'scholarship', 'intellectual respectability' or 'study in depth', which makes us say 'Never mind about educational theory, let's get them doing *something* which is "respectable" anyway'. What is unfamiliar to us, and for various (possibly unconscious) reasons distasteful, is the idea of helping student-teachers to take educational theory seriously in the right sort of way.

'The right sort of way' has to be cashed out not in the terms now familiar to us — trying to get a proper percentage of 'theory' and 'practice', or putting more weight on this 'foundation discipline' rather than that — but in terms of a particular context of inquiry and learning which fits the subject. Precisely the same points that were made in earlier chapters, about the study of education itself, will apply to that part of the preparation of teachers which concerns such study. We shall need certain contexts suitable for inquiring into the basic methodology and 'making sense' of educational topics, in the way described on p. 58 ff.; and the general question to be asked is 'How do we achieve a context of this kind, in which this sort of work is done?' This has to be contrasted with questions of a quite different kind; not, indeed, totally unimportant in themselves, but certainly secondary, such as 'How much time should we spend on this or that topic?', 'How much psychology do they need to know?' and so on. What we are after is a particular way of working — one might say, a practical instantiation of what it is to take an educational topic seriously; if the students can be given a taste for this, it does not so much matter what particular topics are covered. Indeed, we are not even clear — and shall not be, until we have advanced the subject a good deal further — just what topics *ought* to be covered; this is itself one of the things that will have to emerge from an improved methodology.

Nevertheless, it is perhaps clear what *sort* of advantages may be derived for the teacher from 'theory'; though 'theory' hardly seems the right word for the type of initiation or education which should bring such advantages. If, jumping various guns, we assume that we have a situation in which student-teachers are encouraged to take certain topics seriously, then we should expect to be able to help them to do this by *some* kind of procedures or styles of thought sophisticated above the level of common sense. Traditionally and currently, as we have seen, these styles have been construed on the model of the natural sciences (split up under headings like 'psychology' and 'sociology'), together with a ragbag of other styles and subjects, chiefly 'philosophy' and 'history'. But this can obviously be improved upon, provided we stick closely to the question 'What sophisticated *ways of looking at people learning* can we initiate intending teachers into?' or 'In what ways can we sharpen their perceptions and understanding for the dispensation of learning (education)?'

Now of course there are many such ways, but these questions give us a different criterion from questions like 'How much philosophy (psychology, etc.) of education do teachers need to know?' Thus it is one thing to be 'well up in' or well-informed about 'the philosophy of education' (whatever that may be); one would naturally expect such a person to have read, at least, Plato, Locke, Dewey, Peters and so on, and to be familiar with standard philosophical problems in the area. It is another thing to be able, willing and competent in grasping the importance of conceptual or logical points to educational theory and educational practice; to be, as it were, conceptually alert to problems and practices concerned with (say) rules and punishment, structures of teaching-subjects, 'stages of development', 'integration', and so forth. Of course these two may overlap: it is to be hoped (though one is often disappointed) that 'philosophers of education' have something sensible and useful to say, above the level of common sense though well outside the area of fantasy, about the sort of problems that teachers meet and can recognize. But both the objectives and the methods of instruction here are significantly different.

'Philosophy', if one must call it that, can be deployed for this task with comparative ease; indeed the central importance of 'making sense' has been stressed throughout this book, and if anyone were to say that teachers could be prepared without a good deal of attention to this, it would be hard to understand him. But it is also fairly clear that in areas marked by 'psychology', 'clinical psychology', 'anthropology' and even 'sociology', there will be the possibility of developing in the teacher certain 'ways of looking' which can be of the greatest value. If — for instance — the skilled psychotherapist or the skilled anthropologist have in fact anything to offer our understanding (if they are not charlatans), this will be because they can deploy certain ways of looking or certain types of descriptions which correspond more closely than common sense to people's thought and behaviour. They will have certain concepts ('ambivalence', 'taboo', or whatever) which go along with this, certain stances and procedures for gaining information and insight, and perhaps even a corpus of generalized knowledge which might plausibly be called 'theories' — though this is much more doubtful.

It is important to be clear that the merit of this approach stands on its own feet, and that it does not depend either (a) on the actual existence of any corpus of 'established theory' within the various 'disciplines', or (b) on the existence, or even the possibility, of 'educational theory' producing general 'practical principles' which all teachers should know. One might have serious doubts about both (a) and (b), doubts which only the progress of 'educational theory' and various relevant disciplines could quell. But it would remain true that teachers should master certain ways of looking at people learning, even if these ways rarely or never resulted in across-the-board generalizations. Indeed the situation may well be that we shall never reach such generalizations (still less, causal hypotheses or laws) until we are better at these ways of looking.

Notes

1. As in the articles by Hirst and Peters in Tibble (1966).
2. Chambers in Tibble (1971), p. 75.
3. And has been for a long time. See for instance Peters (1958), Winch (1958), Fodor (1968), Hamlyn (1967), etc.
4. Hirst, *loc. cit.*, p. 56 (my italics).
5. p. 47 ff.
6. p. 48 ff.
7. In Tibble (1966), pp. 80–81.
8. PER pp. 18–19: Hamlyn (1967).
9. Hirst (1967), p. 48.
10. Peters (1958).
11. Winch (1958).

Chapter Six

'Practice'

There are various reasons (some of which we noted in Chapter 3) why people interested in education are not likely to be scholarly theoreticians; one might even say that the whole apparatus and institutionalization of 'educational theory' has, in a sense, been wished on them over the last few decades. As we saw in the last chapter, some contemporary disenchantment with or 'backlash' against 'theory' naturally drives us to put more stress on 'practice'. But on inspection it turns out that there are as many difficulties with this idea as there are with 'theory'. Some of these, at least, have to be worked through before we can see more clearly.

These difficulties (dangers, doubts) are heterogeneous, and it is important *not* to try to make some coherent or connected thesis out of them at this stage. Nevertheless, it is possible and perhaps helpful to see them as stemming from one main source. Consider (a) learning to swim, or to handle horses; (b) learning to build bridges or conduct surgical operations. With (a), it might be plausibly said that a very large part of the learning consists of the acquisition of what can fairly be called 'skills', in an unconscious sort of way: that is, not so much by following rules but — as it is thoroughly natural to say here — by practice. 'Theory' here plays a very small part. With (b), the theories and principles of engineering and medicine play a much larger part: the 'practice' or 'skill' element is still important, but is guided by these principles. Now consider (c) learning to be a parson, or a psychiatrist, or a social welfare worker — or a teacher. What could we sensibly *mean* by saying that one could learn these jobs 'by practice'?

Obviously there is one thing we could mean: namely, that there are *some* elements or aspects of the jobs to which notions like 'practice' or 'skill' apply in the sense in which they apply to learning how to swim, or how to conduct an operation. But if pressed to say *what* elements, we find it much more difficult to give a satisfactory answer. Some parsons have, indeed, to wield sacred vessels with skill, some teachers have to write efficiently on blackboards, and so on, but this hardly seems enough. The truth is, I think, that we are not at all sure either (i) how much of the teacher's job involves 'skills' which can only be learned by 'practice', or (ii) just which parts or aspects of it involve these. Now this is at least partly because we do not have a very clear idea of what is involved in 'being a teacher'; and this in turn is because the criteria of success seem less clear, or more disputable, than the criteria of success for swimming, or bridge-building, or medicine.

I say 'seem' less clear, because it is in fact possible (indeed essential) to get a fairly coherent picture of the main aspects: as we tried to do in Chapter 4, under the three general headings of (1) knowing one's subject(s); (2) being serious about, or caring for, the transmission of knowledge; and (3) understanding people. If we do not keep some such picture in mind, we are apt to relapse into talking of 'the teacher's roles' and 'teaching skills', and move into an idea of 'practice' which fits these phrases (as one might talk of 'motor skills', 'dexterous incisions', and so on) but does not necessarily fit the wider and better description 'being a teacher'. We have to remember that being a good teacher may not be a matter of 'practice' in *this* sense at all, or at best minimally.

For similar reasons, the 'apprentice' model of teacher-preparation is largely inappropriate. Certain arts and crafts, usually involving 'skills' (carpentry, stone-working, etc.), may perhaps be effectively learned by attachment to a master-craftsman, whom the apprentice copies. But are the 'things' which the intending teacher chiefly requires in principle able to be copied? *Prima facie* one could only answer 'yes' to this in a very weak sense of 'copy': we could say, for instance, 'Copy so-and-so's knowledge of his subject, his seriousness about learning, and his personal understanding', but that would not mean much more than 'Acquire the knowledge, etc. that so-and-so (incidentally) has'. This is clearly different from copying, say, the way in which a master-potter shapes a pot on the wheel, or even the way in which a good receptionist smiles politely at visitors, says 'Good morning, sir, how can I help you?' and so forth. This is not to say (i) that *some* things (skills, behaviour patterns) may not be usefully copied in this way by intending teachers, nor (ii) that it may not be useful to put intending teachers under the general supervision of successful practising teachers, for certain purposes. It is simply to deny the applicability of the 'apprentice' as of the earlier 'practice' model, at least for many aspects of 'being a teacher'.

We may still have the natural feeling that 'experience' at least must come into it somehow, if not that sense of 'practice' which fits the acquisition of 'skills'. We perhaps feel like saying 'All right, teacher-preparation isn't a matter of acquiring skills by imitation or practice, like learning to swim, but surely it's not just a matter of learning things from books. You have to learn by experience — by actually doing it'.

There is a healthy substratum to this thought, but we need to press the notion of 'experience' much harder. For we are faced ultimately with the same difficulty as before: namely, the difficulty of marrying up 'experience' with *success*. Where the criteria of success are clear, and the operation itself comparatively well-defined, this is comparatively easy: it would be hard to believe that a person with lots of experience ('practice', if you like, in a wider sense) of, say, making pottery or surgical operations would not be superior to someone with no experience. But it is perfectly easy to believe that teachers in schools with thirty years 'experience' behind them may well be worse teachers, or even worse at teaching, than inexperienced teachers.

The point here is not that there are *other* factors besides experience, which may make us prefer the less experienced teacher (enthusiasm, imagination, etc.), though of course this is also true. The point is that the 'experience' may be *bad*: that is, instead of making the person more aware, competent and so on, it may make him less so. Unless we are talking of a fairly tightly defined *techne* or craft, it seems to be generally true that the merits of 'experience' are largely a function of the person 'experiencing': age may bring wisdom, but may also bring folly. In some respects 'being a teacher', or any educational job involving people and understanding, is like a *techne*, but in some respects it is not. Parallels with being a parson, psychotherapist, parent or social welfare worker are relevant here.

The dangers of bad experience arise when we try to over-specify its content. We have to beware of the experience endorsing particular styles, methods or aims of teaching (or other practices relevant to 'being a teacher') which we have, in fact, no good reason to approve. Imagine some of the effects of a would-be teacher being inducted or initiated into (still worse, copying) the disciplinary style of a Roman schoolmaster, or the methods of a 19th-century boarding school usher, or the aims of a Nazi teacher. These may seem extreme cases, and we like to suppose that contemporary styles, methods and aims are an improvement on what has gone before. But, as I have tried to show in Part I of this book, we have little or no *reason* to think so, and consequently, few satisfactory criteria, or none, for identifying the *sort* of experience (induction, copying, etc.) we want to give to intending teachers. This is not, of course, true right across the board: for there are *some* things we can be certain about. For instance, insofar as the experience is construed as a chance of copying, we know that we would prefer to attach intending teachers to practising teachers who (a) can keep order, (b) expound their subject competently, and (c) seem to know something about children, rather than to practising teachers who do not display these characteristics. But this does not take us far. We cannot happily pick master-teachers who use this or that method of teaching history, or hold this or that general view about education, or deal with children in this or that psychological way: simply because we have no good reasons for adjudicating between them, and are as likely simply to sell some current educational prejudice or fashion to intending teachers, under the guise of 'apprenticeship' to 'professional tutors' (or whatever), as actually give them the *right kind* of experience.

Similar points apply to other aspects of 'experience'. Consider, for instance, one very general aspect which, I suspect, holds much more weight than the notion of apprenticeship or copying: namely, the idea of familiarity or acclimatization. *Prima facie* there is a clear case for 'experience' as part of teacher-preparation, simply on the grounds that it is obviously useful to 'be familiar with' the situations one is going to meet: to 'know what it's like', to 'be used to it', etc. This has various possible types of advantage: it may, for instance, lessen the shock-effect of having to face a class for the first time; it may increase one's confidence to have succeeded in 'practice' situations beforehand; it may give one data, not otherwise obtainable, on which to reflect — and so on. But here again, the possibility of increased confidence and awareness is offset by the equal possibility of smugness and reinforced misperception. One may be acclimatized to bad climates as well as to good ones.

We have also to add in the point, mentioned earlier,[1] that styles and methods of 'being a teacher' are inevitably a function of the teacher as a person; and this takes a good deal away from the picture of a specified *content* of 'experience' or 'practice' which we send intending teachers out to collect or acquire. It suggests rather a picture of intending teachers needing to *find out what their own styles are*. Of course this requires experience, but puts it in a rather different light. It is more a matter of finding out one's limitations, one's strengths and weaknesses, what one can and cannot stand — 'what suits one', in a word. This is more like discovering what sort of person one is than like learning a number of specified 'teaching-skills'.

Considerations of this kind (and there are many other such considerations) cast serious doubt on many current ideas and practices arising from a desire to 'integrate theory and practice more closely'. That moves made in this direction are likely to be premature and ill-considered is obvious, simply because we do not know (a) what sort of 'theory' is useful, (b) what sort of 'practice' is useful, or (c) what it would be, even in principle, to 'integrate them more closely'. It seems to me fairly clear that this is just one more instance of a common topical fantasy, stemming from a disenchantment with contemporary procedures and a passion for 'integration' and 'relevance'. The idea is that if only we are more active, and create structures that *look* like 'integrating' and 'relating' — making the 'theory' more 'school-based',

having more 'discussions about classroom problems', and so on — then
in some magic way student-teachers will be more effectively prepared.

More specifically, it cannot yet be clear to us — I mean, in this kind
of practical or structural way — just where or how particular
characteristics supposedly gained by 'practice' can best be acquired. For
example, suppose there are various 'social skills' of the kind described
by Argyle[2] and others, which the intending teacher needs to master: the
ability to 'dominate', to keep order, to 'project' himself, and so on.
Even when we have established a clear category or set of categories for
these (no easy task), it is still uncertain whether they can best be
learned by on-the-job practice, or by training under highly-structured
conditions (perhaps best obtainable in a laboratory, and certainly not
readily available in schools). Everything turns on being clear about just
what it is we want the intending teacher to acquire; we may then, with
careful reflection, begin to consider how, in practice, we are to set up
structures and contexts for the task.

Again, if we categorize the notion which I have loosely expressed as
'finding out what one's teaching-style is' or 'what suits one', it is still
not at all clear whether this is best done by 'practice' or 'experience', or
rather by some transmission of awareness and self-knowledge from
other adults who know one well (as, for instance, is supposed to happen
in psychotherapy or 'group dynamics'). Perhaps we need both, but here
too all depends on what we are trying to achieve, and only proper
reflection on this will start us in the right practical directions. Nothing
is gained, and a great deal lost, by adopting *a priori* attitudes to the
effect that 'it must be done in schools' — or indeed to any other
effect.

We have also to remember some criteria analogous to those limiting
what 'theory' can usefully be learned, incorporated in the general
question 'What does the "practice" or "experience" part of teacher-
preparation give to teachers *that they could not acquire for themselves
anyway just by teaching?*' Obviously it might give them *some* things
but, once more, it is not entirely clear just what they are. Thus one
might suppose that many of the advantages which we might put under
the general heading of 'familiarity', 'acclimatization' or 'knowing what
it's like' could, *per se*, be just as well gained in an actual job. Others,
perhaps including 'knowing what suits one', would be easiest to acquire
partly by a variety of teaching-experience which would be difficult or
impossible to get in normal working life. Or consider the 'copying'
aspect; it is not absurd to suppose that this might be done in an
ordinary job — particularly in some form of team-teaching — just as
well as by some form of apprenticeship.

The difficulties here again arise from the dissimilarities between
'being a teacher' and, say, learning to drive or sail a boat. In these latter

cases it is fair to say that a person could not — or not without grave difficulty and danger — learn *just* by 'experience', any more than he could learn just by 'theory'. The whole business of instruction, supervision, and acquiring bits of information and 'know-how' under the care of an expert makes sense here, because (a) the ends or objectives (what counts as success) are clear, and could not be achieved without developing some expertise, and (b) the kind of expertise required is mostly of an *ad hoc*, 'know-how' nature. If these conditions did not hold, we should not proceed in this way. Thus there are cases, like learning to swim, where it is likely that this sort of instruction cuts little ice; what counts, perhaps, is the person's confidence and desire to swim, and (given that) plenty of opportunity to practise by himself. (Indeed perhaps he learns better by himself: compare the alleged merits of teaching-machines as against teachers).

Of course it is *nice* to have some 'practice' or 'experience' before taking a job, but this in itself hardly provides us with a strong enough case for making such practice a central feature of teacher-preparation. In the boat-sailing and driving cases it is not just 'nice': it is essential. (Though even here it may be that the improvement of confidence and attitude is just as important as the acquisition of know-how.) But we cannot and should not pretend that a person cannot go out and 'be a teacher' without such practice, just as he can without 'theory'. People have been doing this for centuries; and even if various societies and governments are now beginning to insist on 'professional qualifications' (as if we were clear about what the content of 'professional' should be), we must not be conned into supposing that we have any intellectual justification for it. If someone were to say, on the analogy of the boat-sailing and driving cases, that a teacher without such experience could not be let loose on the job 'without grave difficulty and danger', he would have been conned; and it is worth noting here that any plausible 'difficulty and danger' that naturally springs to mind would not be concerned with his 'know-how' or 'teaching-skills', but with his *attitude*. We might reasonably worry about whether he was serious, or sadistic, or perhaps utterly boring. But that is a different story.

Before trying to make some positive progress, we may find it useful to cast some of the above doubts in one particular form. Suppose we raise the general question 'Who is to supervise or transmit the various things which intending teachers are supposed to gain by "practice", and who is to assess them?' There is an immediate temptation to answer this question by saying 'Of course, those who already possess these qualities: namely, expert practising teachers or "professional tutors". They must be the people best equipped both to transmit and to judge'. But then we think again. Are actors and football players most effectively trained and judged by other actors and football players? Are there not such people as theatre producers and directors, football coaches, and critics? Further, if a lot depends on the man's personal attitude and perceptions, rather than the acquisition of a set of fairly impersonal skills, are we not obliged to bring in somebody who — quite simply — *knows* the man intimately and *cares* for him? Such considerations reflect our general uncertainty on this subject; and it is much more important to be uncertain, and try to get clear, than to go overboard for some 'theory' of 'teacher-training' which will only highlight our own stupidity.

In order to gain some solid ground, we might begin by noting 'things' which are needed by 'being a teacher' and which could not, even in principle, be acquired except by something fairly to be described as 'practice (experience) in schools'. These appear to fall into three main categories:

1. *Know-how.* There are certainly some things, fairly to be called 'skills', and perhaps able to be picked up partly by copying those who already have them, which could not be *wholly* gained except on the spot. If we think of things like dominating a class, 'projecting' oneself, or even writing on a blackboard, it may seem as if these could be gained by specialized training: for instance, Argyle-type 'social skills' training might help one to be 'dominant'; or work in role-play or psychodrama (or even simple elocution) might improve one's 'self-projection'; or one could more easily be taught to write on a blackboard at home. We certainly have to examine each case of 'know-how' with this point in mind; but there is a solid reason why it is not sufficient, which might be put by saying that coping with the on-the-spot variables is an essential *part of* the know-how. For instance, what a teacher needs is not just — not even chiefly — to write on the blackboard, but to be able to write coherently on the blackboard *even when* the kids at the back of the class need watching, or there is only a little chalk of the right colour, or somebody has hidden the board duster. Similarly, it is not just 'dominating' or 'projecting' that he has to learn, but rather to do these things — or some appropriate version of them — under all sorts of unpredictable conditions. In a word, the variables are too many for any specialized training to include.

It would, of course, be possible to make the specialized training more like a school situation: for instance, by using a specially groomed class of children in the laboratory, watching and instructing the teacher through a one-way screen, and so on. [3] These variations also need examination, but they reinforce the point just made. The teacher needs the flexibility of response required by immense variety of what happens in classrooms and schools: he needs to be able to think on his feet, talk and act 'off the cuff', and in general acquire those empirical, *ad hoc* and skill-like abilities that constitute know-how in this area. Since propositional knowledge by itself is not at stake here, and since specialized training is inadequate, there seems to be a solid case for on-the-spot practice, perhaps monitored and assessed by suitable instructors.

2. *Propositional understanding and awareness.* This category shades into 1. above, and also into 3. below, for reasons worth noting. If we talk generally of 'getting the feel' of, say, what it is to manage a class (or live with one's spouse, or almost any situation of human interaction), it is in practice very difficult to distinguish between (1) ability or 'know-how', not or not obviously the result of propositional knowledge, but rather 'intuitive': that is, not a matter of the conscious following of rules and principles, but an instinctively dexterous or competent reaction to the situation; (2) conscious knowledge that such-and-such is the case; and (3) the self-confidence or other attitudinal characteristics that may or may not go with (1) and (2). Yet is is clear that these are distinguishable in principle, and sometimes in practice. In managing a class, a teacher may (1) have the knack of just telling a kid to shut up instead of (wrongly) arguing with him at length, but not (2) entertain any conscious principle such as 'Long arguments in class don't pay off'. Similarly one can (2) 'get the feel' of a class or a school without *doing* anything of type (1), whether clumsily or dexterously, and without the need for anything attitudinal (except, perhaps, a serious interest in learning what the school is like).

We have already mentioned the kinds of propositional knowledge and awareness that seem relevant here. The intending teacher needs to know (a) what it is like to teach his subject, and do other things involved in 'being a teacher', to particular types of children; (b) 'what suits him', what his teaching-style is, what sort of children he is best with; (c) what in fact different schools and classes are like (whether or not he himself has to operate in them). These are things which could not wholly be learned except on the spot in two ways. First, when one *does* something — e.g. actually has to keep IVB in order and make them learn some history — a whole host of new propositions floods one's consciousness, again so various that no specialized theory or training could accommodate them; propositions, often, about oneself and one's own feelings in relation to one's responsibility. Secondly, even without the responsibility, the mere observation of schools and classes generates propositional awareness not fully specifiable elsewhere; just as one could not fully know about a primitive tribe unless one actually spent some time with them, and any anthropologist who thought he could would hardly know what anthropology was about.

There are, in fact, much deeper and (from a more strictly logical point of view) more compelling reasons why 'personal understanding' can only flourish by on-the-spot learning:[4] reasons which cast into some disrepute most of what passes as 'educational psychology', and have — from this point of view, quite justly — caused a revulsion in favour of something more 'practical'. This does not mean we are all that clear about *how*, in fact, such understanding is advanced; all we have shown is that it is *partly* 'practice'.

3. *Confidence, caring and other dispositions*. The reasons why these cannot be wholly induced by other than 'practice' or 'experience' methods are similar to those in 2. above. Thus it is not, or not only, that we want the intending teacher to 'have confidence' or 'care for his subject' or 'like children'; we want him to have confidence *in running a class*, care for imparting historical knowledge *to the Lower Fourth*, or a liking *for teenagers*. Much of the point of 'practice' here, as we have noticed, is that this is essential for the teacher to find out just *what*, in fact, his dispositions (confidence, caring, etc.) *do* relate to. Does he really like children, or only certain types of children? In what contexts does he like them? Is he confident about his expository powers, and/or his disciplinary ones? Such questions are fully answerable only if we add on-the-spot experience.

There is also the point that one may learn to have confidence, care, and other feelings and dispositions simply by successful experience. Questions in the teacher's mind will include, for instance, 'Can I, in fact, keep this class in hand for a whole hour? For a whole term?', 'Will my interest in history survive thirteen weeks of teaching IIIB?' 'Can I learn to love these ghastly teenagers who *prima facie* look like people to be avoided at all costs?' Success, or even survival, enables one to answer such questions in the affirmative; nothing explodes, one's identity remains more or less intact, and quite a lot of it is even enjoyable. Here the 'practice' element is, in fact, much more analogous to what may happen in other cases (driving, swimming, sailing) which are in other respects quite different.

Now what needs to be done — something which would take time and teamwork, and which I am not attempting fully in this book[5] — is to list the particular types of (1) know-how, (2) propositional knowledge and awareness, and (3) dispositions which seem most central to 'being a teacher'; and then we could go on to consider the importance of 'practice' in relation to this detailed list, treating each item separately. Without the benefit of this enormous operation, however, can anything general be said at all?

I think it can, if we bear in mind what was established as central to 'being a teacher' — subject-knowledge, seriousness, and personal

understanding. The merits of 'practice', as expounded in (1), (2) and
(3) above, are not negligible, but they are surely best seen as a kind of
topping-off, or detailed reinforcement, to these central characteristics.
If the intending teacher acquires these characteristics, 'practice' adds to
them significantly; if he does not, it is not clear that 'practice' can do
very much for him. This is primarily because the characteristics are
required (empirically, and I think also for conceptual reasons) *in order
to* benefit from 'practice'.

Just as there would be no point in the whole operation if the
intending teacher did not know enough about his subject to dispense it
properly, so there would be very little point in attempting to give
(1) know-how or (2) propositional awareness to someone who lacked
the basic dispositions in (3); and though 'practice' may reinforce some
such dispositions, and make them more specific, it cannot create them.
If a person is extremely timid about other people, or has no real
interest in them, nothing is gained by 'practical' tips about keeping
order or by putting him in situations where he could (if he *were*
interested) learn more about human beings. This point has less force in
cases where human interaction is non-existent or minimal: for instance,
in sailing or bridge-building or even some kinds of medicine. In these
cases, a clear sense can be given to saying that a man is *able* to sail or
build or cure, that he is 'skilled' or 'competent' at these tasks, even
though he might be extremely uninterested in them. But it is not clear
what would be *meant* by saying that a teacher was 'skilled' or
'competent', if we also said that he was not serious about dispensing
learning, and did not have much interest in other people.

We could, in fact, only mean that he had mastered some of the
techniques (skills) that teaching normally involves, but it is obvious that
we should have badly degraded the content of 'being a teacher' if we
regarded these techniques as of primary importance. The phrase should
make us think much more in such terms as 'enthusiastic', 'fond of his
pupils, but sensible and firm with them', 'stimulating', 'well-organized',
'understanding', etc. The point about such terms is that it is virtually
impossible to sever ability from 'motivation' (attitude, disposition). It is
the kind of person you are that counts.

The temptation now arises to say 'Yes, and that means you can't
really prepare teachers at all: good teachers are born and not made; you
can't change people in those fundamental ways', and so on. This
temptation has to be resisted. There is a close analogy, at several points,
with what we noticed in Part I about 'theory'. We there had to resist
(1) the idea that what now passed as 'educational theory' was
respectable, but also (2) the idea that the whole enterprise could be
written off as irredeemable; and fought our way to some clarity about
what such an enterprise, if taken seriously, should look like — paying

particular attention to the *context of work*, and to a general understanding of the sort of work required. Here we equally resist (1) the supposed merits of 'practice' as now advertised, and (2) the notion that 'practice' is pointless because everything depends on unchangeable traits of personality. Can we now (3) say anything about what a proper general approach would look like?

One thing seems entirely clear. If the teacher's personality (serious-ness, care, understanding, 'self-projection', etc.) is central, we shall have to take much more seriously the whole enterprise of educating student-teachers in this respect. There are many dangers here, essen-tially similar to those encountered when we considered 'teacher-preparation' as a whole. First, we may mislead ourselves right at the start by inadequate descriptions of the task; thus the word used above, 'personality' — particularly if rapidly incorporated in some such phrase as 'personality-training' — , may lead us to think of the task as empowering student-teachers to adopt different 'personalities', or 'project' different 'images'. Then we should have doubts about sincerity or integrity, about the excessive severance of 'personality' from 'character', even though we might acknowledge that much or some of 'being a teacher' necessarily involved some form of *acting*. Similarly, such terms as 'character-building', 'personal development', 'emotional awareness', 'social skills' and so on are either too blank to tell us much, or too heavily loaded in one particular direction. There are *many different* things to be achieved under this heading.

Secondly, and closely connected with this danger (indeed, in a sense, just another aspect of it), we may plump for one or two particular methods that fit our partisan or doctrinaire picture of what we are trying to achieve. There are those who put their money on 'group dynamics' or 'T-groups', role-playing or psychodrama, various kinds of 'counselling' or tutorial relationships, 'the general atmosphere of the college', and so forth. Whatever the merits or demerits of these and other methods, no *one* method could conceivably suffice, simply because of the variety of things to be achieved. Nor is it particularly helpful just to add in as many different methods as we can think of, in the vague hope that the job will somehow get done; we need rather to establish one or two general points about what is in principle required for any such task.

The most important of these requirements seems to be that this kind of learning or education has to be based on (i) trust, and (ii) intimate knowledge. For very fundamental reasons, it seems inconceivable that much good could be done to the student-teacher in this area except by, or in relation to, at least one person who knew him (her) fairly intimately as a person, and whom he (she) trusted. This is of course a commonplace in the literature on this topic, and indeed no more than common sense. But it has considerable practical consequences for the preparation of teachers.

Some of these consequences we shall try to work out in the next chapter, in a fairly practical way. Here it will be worth noting one or two considerations which may help us to take the task seriously. Perhaps the most important of these concerns our own attitude. If we do not go overboard, as described above, for some particular method of 'personality-training' ('group dynamics', or whatever), we may retreat into an attitude common in higher education: roughly, that of refusing to face the obvious fact that student-teachers — even post-graduates, and even 'mature' students — are badly in need of *some* structure, context and education of this sort. We see them, and have a vested interest in seeing them, as mature, independent adults: people who neither need nor want this education, any more (perhaps) than we ourselves think we need or want it. Then there is the immediate temptation to say something like 'These aren't schoolchildren, you know, we don't want to interfere with their feelings and private lives, it would be insulting and perhaps dangerous to invade them in this way; much better to exercise a general benevolence whilst keeping our distance', and so on. We might perhaps make some attempt to 'make them feel at home' (coffee- and sherry-parties, and so on), and be available for 'counselling' or 'guidance'; we might even think it part of our job to form some sort of judgement about them as people, from a decent distance. But that may be as far as we want to go.

This attitude is understandable and correct as a contrast to some lunatic scheme which might try to *force* trust and intimacy of knowledge onto students (or anybody else, for that matter); there are, again, basic reasons why this sort of forcing procedure cannot work. But apart from that, it is not a serious attitude, and probably reflects our own fears rather than anything like a set of rational beliefs: just as the opposite desire to become more intimate than the other person wants (or can stand) may reflect our own loneliness or even voyeurism. We know quite well, when we keep our heads, that trust and intimate knowledge cannot be forced, but it can be *planned for*. Contexts can be created in which it is likely to thrive, particularly if those concerned have a clear understanding that such thriving is important. It is best here not to talk of 'counselling', 'non-directive therapy', and so on, but rather to stick to terms which are both less frightening and less partisan — 'friendship', 'trust', 'sharing', 'personal understanding', 'support', perhaps even 'love'.

It would be quite possible, I think, to maintain that this sort of enterprise was of central importance to any kind of education, because of the very close connections between seriousness (and other personal characteristics) and any kind of learning. But there are two reasons why it is particularly incumbent in the preparation of teachers. One is obvious: as we have seen, a large part of 'being a teacher' necessarily and centrally involves the development and use of these characteristics, in the way that being (say) a scholar or a bank clerk does not. If we do not prepare teachers in this way, whatever the difficulties, we are not seriously preparing them at all.

The other is almost as obvious, but more subject to particular variables. It is increasingly the case that schools are having to take over some, at least, of the tasks originally supposed to have been done by the family or by 'society'; that is, tasks concerned with the pupils as people rather than as students of a particular subject. To use the jargon, the 'pastoral role' of teachers is now of central importance, and there are reasons, which I have expressed elsewhere,[6] why this should be endorsed and not resisted or written off as a temporary failure by 'society'. There may, of course, be subject-teachers who survive happily without having much interest or ability in this area; there may even be a case for distinguishing between teachers whose primary expertise is with subjects and teachers more expert with pupils as people, rather like the housemaster/subject-teacher distinction institutionalized in British public boarding schools and elsewhere. But generally speaking, it would be hard to maintain that this 'pastoral' aspect of 'being a teacher' was not of equal importance to the 'subject-teaching' aspect; and if so, of equal importance in the preparation of teachers.

As in the last chapter on 'theory', we have not here taken many steps towards any practical or institutionalized form which might follow from these points about 'practice'. It is very important not to do this too quickly; and though in the next chapter I shall advance more concrete suggestions, any weight they may have should derive from the sort of understanding we have been trying to gain. Many, perhaps all, of the points mentioned above require a much fuller and more detailed discussion, but my hope is that enough has been said to make certain generalized arrangements obviously necessary.

Notes

1. p. 121.
2. Argyle (1967).
3. This is no doubt where techniques commonly called 'micro-teaching', 'interaction analysis' and so on would usefully come in.
4. See Hamlyn in Mischel (1974).
5. See however p. 148 ff.
6. Wilson (1972), Part 4.

Chapter Seven

Taxonomic Sketch and Conclusions

An attempt to create an adequate taxonomy or set of categories for the preparation of teachers is, obviously enough, one of those tasks in 'educational theory' which we discussed in Chapter 3; tasks which ideally require close communication between members of a sophisticated team concerned to 'make sense' (as we put it) of just this kind of topic. Lack of sophistication here has, in fact, resulted in all kinds of incompetent taxonomies in 'educational theory' (Bloom is perhaps the most notorious),[1] which contain standard errors — failure to identify items clearly, cross-categorization, logical disparity between items under the same heading, logical overlap or lack of discreteness between items, and so on.

Unfortunately lists of 'objectives' for 'teacher-training' seem usually to incorporate all these errors. I will take one example:[2] not just for the fun of destructive criticism, but because it manages to encompass in a short space (40-odd pages) mistakes whose typicality needs to be thoroughly understood. First and foremost, the authors clearly have no idea at all of *what sort of job it is* to construct such a list. The preface to the document says:

> It will be observed that the report of the work is psychological in tone. No doubt this followed from . . . the sympathy which progressive teachers have with what is often called the 'human development' approach to education. Philosophers of education will shake their heads over the unabashed use of the term 'needs' . . . Some sociologists of education will find the work sadly deficient in consideration of the 'hidden agenda' in school curricula. But I think this list of objectives will stand scrutiny because it represents basically a solid, pragmatic, middle-of-the-road approach to education, likely to gain the sympathy of the average parent or teacher. (p. 5).

Behind this remarkable passage seem to float the ideas (1) that any group making such a list must have some sort of partisan line about 'education' (here, 'progressive'), and must 'stand scrutiny' in essentially political terms: that is, in terms of whether it will 'gain the sympathy' of various people; (2) that there are various possible approaches or 'tones' (here, 'psychological'), apparently connected with the institutionalized 'foundation disciplines': so that 'philosophers' or 'sociologists' may object to a 'psychological' line being taken. Of course what competent philosophers (not necessarily 'of education') will want to 'shake their heads' about is, in the first place, this procedure itself.

One is consequently not surprised that a good deal of the report seems largely unintelligible. Thus Diagram I gives a heterogeneous and largely arbitrary list of 'the individual's needs', including items such as 'air', 'to look', 'knowledge', and 'success', and ungrammatical items like 'curiosity' and 'cooperation' (the individual does not need curiosity and cooperation, as he needs air and success; what the authors mean, I suppose, is that he needs to satisfy his curiosity or to develop the ability to cooperate).[3] Diagram II describes mathematics as a 'language skill' along with English and other languages;[4] under the teacher's 'professional attitudes' the last three items read 'a strong moral sense, punctuality, appropriate standards of dress'[5] [*sic*], and under the heading 'flexibility and adaptability' one item is 'courage' — though the next heading is 'Confidence'.[6]

This sort of cross-categorization and other muddles persist in the somewhat more interesting 'list of teachers' skills and techniques'.[7] Almost every item in this 24-page list begins either with the word 'skill' or the word 'knowledge', even though the items are all headed 'The professional needs of the teacher' — as if 'skill' and 'knowledge' represented the only possible characteristics which teachers needed.[8] This does nothing to inhibit grotesque overlaps such as

> Knowledge of scientific principles and their application . . . ;
> Knowledge of the 'facts' of Science . . . ;
> Knowledge of the principles of classification . . . ;
> Skill in relating phenomena in Science and in seeing connections and influences;[9]

— as if one could somehow 'relate phenomena in Science' (whatever this means) or have 'knowledge of scientific principles and their application' without knowing the 'facts', or vice versa. The whole idea of producing *clear and discrete* items does not seem to have struck the authors at all; and they seem not to have read, or certainly not to have understood, any of the work done in this area by people like Hirst.[10]

All this may seem harsh, and I do not deny the difficulty of such a task. Of course it is easier to criticize than to construct. But these deficiencies, which are entirely typical, show the terrifying methodological naivety or lack of seriousness which I have been emphasizing throughout this book. The work I have been criticizing is claimed to be 'the fruits of two years of hard thinking by a group of experienced college lecturers and school teachers',[11] and I am sure those concerned[12] are neither stupid nor lazy. Yet it is utterly plain that they have no idea at all of some of the most elementary conceptual (logical, methodological) requirements for any kind of effective taxonomy or classification; almost as if they thought they were making a shopping list.

I must stress that these points are not (as they say) 'academic'. Just as every person has, however unconsciously, some set of principles or 'moral philosophy' which guides his actions, so any taxonomist or list maker will have (or be conned into adopting) some sort of pattern or criteria in the back of his mind which determine the items on his list. One such pattern may emerge from the unconscious idea that 'being a teacher' (or 'professional competence', or whatever) consists of separate items, or 'skills', or bits of 'knowledge', which are logically on all fours with each other and hence can be simply listed one after another — like carrots, turnips, peas, and so on. This is accompanied by the vague perception that other things ought somehow to go in, even if they seem a bit different: so that the list then reads rather like 'carrots, turnips, peas, vegetables, beans, pulse food, cheap provisions, vitamin C . . . .' and so on (where five criteria of items have replaced the original one). What inevitably happens is that the original pattern distorts and misplaces the items, unconsciously squeezing some into improper categories (or devaluing them until they fit the categories), and leaving others out altogether. The 'skill' pattern, though perhaps the most fashionable (as representing a down-to-earth, no-nonsense approach), is not the only one: we can see others at work in, for instance, list items like 'enthusiasm', 'a strong moral sense', 'confidence', and so on.

As I tried to show in Chapter 4, there is no short cut to sorting out the different *kinds* of 'things' required by 'being a teacher': and here, yet again, we bump into the notion of seriousness and the various temptations not to be serious. We have to recognize our *a priori* or doctrinaire prejudices, the bewitching models or pictures that dominate us, and (as the psychoanalysts say) 'work through' them. A person may have the picture of a set of 'skills' or 'teaching behaviors' (spelled thus, because characteristically transatlantic) or 'end products', on some sort of mechanical or industrial model; the picture of practical, common sense 'competence' or 'professional competence', on the model of horse trainers or nurses or carpenters; the picture of 'teachers are born, not made', 'the magic spark', etc., apparently on the model of Museinspired poetic and other activities. These and other models — there are plenty more — may be all the more hard to relinquish, as they are certainly more hard for the individual to detect, insofar as they are unconscious and hence less overtly challenged.

An intelligent sociologist or social psychologist ought to have a lot to tell us about predisposing causes for the popularity of this or that model. It seems fair to say, for instance, that in most pluralistic and liberal societies nowadays an accepted 'democratic' procedure replaces the hard work of effective taxonomy. Roughly, the line is that one assembles a 'working party' of various kinds of people — lecturers, teachers, perhaps an occasional professor thrown in, a psychologist or two, and so on — and tries to find 'common ground'. This avoids any unfashionable implications of 'authoritarianism' or indeed of any expertise at all; a general, and hence necessarily vague, 'agreement' is supposed to emerge. Political questions are often in the background, sometimes more prominent. Will the teachers' unions go along with what we do? What will the DES say? Is it 'acceptable' to parents?

That way, as indeed we tried to show in Chapter 3, madness lies. Much more important than any particular taxonomy (including my own sketch) is the general understanding that there is such a thing as expertise here; that what we have called 'making sense' is an art in its own right, which can be pursued well or badly, and which some people are better at than others. The *recognition* of this is more than half the battle: if the individuals concerned feel themselves incompetent, they can call for the right sort of advice.

In what follows I can do no more than attempt a basis or sketch of an adequate taxonomy, for two reasons. The first, already mentioned, is that this could only be the end-product of a long-term and properly organized research project, conducted along the lines in Chapter 3. The second is that, to *some* extent, no single taxonomy would suffice for the preparation of teachers in all societies and under all spatio-temporal conditions. 'Being a teacher' may be one thing in Somaliland and another thing in New York; one thing in 1975, another in 2001.

It is important, however, not to use this second reason as an excuse for reneging on one important principle, which I hope to have established in Chapter 4: that is, the principle of taking what is logically or conceptually required by the notion of 'being a teacher' as a basis for teacher-preparation, rather than any notion about 'what society demands', 'what the general consensus is', 'what is politically viable', and so on. Not that we must disregard claims of this kind, but we must distinguish them clearly from the claims of logic. In fact, this makes the difference between items in taxonomies suitable for different social or spatio-temporal conditions pretty small, as we shall see; it is more a matter of filling out the same logical categories with different items than of constructing different logical categories. Hence it is fair to say that *one* general taxonomy will serve the purposes of teacher-preparation, in a way which is not severely time-bound or culture-bound.

A parallel may help here. In trying to spell out or taxonomize what counts as a 'morally educated person', it would clearly be disastrous to base any categories on the particular moralities or social pressures of any social group, or to base them on a 'general consensus' between various societies or opinions. We can only draw our categories from a conceptual basis: that is, from what is logically required by the notion of a 'morally educated person' itself. If some society or 'consensus' pressurized people in various ways which did not fit these conceptual requirements — if, for instance, it indoctrinated citizens with a belief in the absolute rightness of the Führer, or persuaded them that morality was a matter of taste and not subject to reason at all — , then we should say, not that the society 'had a different idea about moral education', but rather that it was not interested in anything properly to be described as *education in morality* at all. In the same way, if a society insisted that teachers spent most of their time in brainwashing their pupils, or giving them sweets, or just trying to keep them under control, we should say that such a society was not much concerned with the notion of 'being a *teacher*', since there would be only a tenuous link (or no link at all) between that phrase and any idea of *teaching*, or dispensing *learning*; perhaps what the society really wants is child-minders, or indoctrinators, or something of that kind.

Nevertheless we should take the social pressures into account, whilst not regarding them as *authoritative*. Thus one obvious characteristic required by the morally educated person is awareness of the 'hard' facts, relevant to people's needs and interests, with which as a moral agent he has to deal: for instance, facts about what the law is, about health and safety, and so on. Clearly these will to some extent vary from society to society, climate to climate, and time to time. So we establish one category — 'knowledge of hard facts' — which will serve as a culture-free and time-free taxonomic heading, but would obviously *fill out* that category with somewhat different items. Thus certain facts that a teacher needs to know will include facts of a social or institutional kind, which may vary: in one country the law lets you do this and that to pupils, in another it does not; in one age certain sexual behaviour will get you the sack, in another it may be tolerated — and so on.

The parallel with the taxonomy of moral education, which I have discussed at length elsewhere[13], is in fact remarkably close at many points, and may serve to introduce the problems of an adequate taxonomy for teacher-preparation. 'Being morally educated', like 'being a teacher', is obviously to *some* extent a matter of performing well in various particular tasks or 'roles' — being a good father or mother, a good citizen, a good soldier in time of war, a good driver and so on. But it would clearly be disastrous to suppose that the phrase could be exhaustively, or even primarily, translated in this way. It is better to start by saying that we want the person to 'do well' or 'be serious' (competent, reasonable, etc.) *in a particular mode* — that is (for morality), in relation to the needs and interests of other people. This 'seriousness' (competence, etc.) will, of course, cash itself out in specific tasks or roles, for which the morally educated person may need special training or information, but clearly the first taxonomic task is to break down the notion of 'seriousness' into a number of specific characteristics or components — into a list of the different kinds of things a person needs if he is to be 'serious'. Thus the 'morally educated person' will need certain concepts, attitudes, abilities, factual knowledge, skills and so on; and he will deploy these *in* particular roles or situations.

With 'being a good teacher' we are, of course, operating on a narrower front than with 'being morally educated'; arguably, one can — and we must remember this, before we get carried away by some picture of a good teacher as some kind of saint or hero who just happens to be teaching — be a good teacher but a bad man. Certainly one can be a good teacher but a bad parent, friend, business man, politician, citizen or husband. We are talking about a certain kind of virtue, or group of virtues, adumbrated in Chapter 4 under such headings as knowing one's subject, transmitting seriousness, care or love of learning, and understanding people (at least, *qua* pupils). These were strictly logical requirements, folowing fairly obviously from the notion of educating or dispensing learning, itself logically central to 'being a teacher'. What we have now to do is to distinguish different types of characteristics which this group of virtues logically necessitates.

Unsurprisingly, these fit into categories much like those required for 'being morally educated', though with the restrictions mentioned above. 'Being a teacher' involves a particular genre of practical action, which (as I hope to have sufficiently shown) is logically more like, say, being a social worker (parson, parent, psychotherapist) than like being a carpenter or even a nurse. It is thus likely to require characteristics which are very various, and bring in all the categories required for practical action generally, when such action relates directly to other people's minds and personalities. Our taxonomic sketch here might look something like this:

A. Basic attitude to learning and people. I refer here to what might be termed a conscious or acknowledged commitment or seriousness about what 'being a teacher' logically entails. The person would have to think (and to some extent feel, if his thought was to be genuine or sincere) that learning, rationality, being educated, etc. were important, and that people were also important, at least *qua* learners. To think this is not just a matter of saying it, or saying it with feeling. It is a matter of understanding, and quite complex understanding at that. He would have to know, and show that he knew, what 'rationality' or 'education' or 'learning' were, and why they were important: and he would also have to possess an adequate concept of a person *qua* learner. A teacher who only had a general idea or feeling that 'education was important', or who regarded it as only a necessary tool for social advancement, could not have this attitude: nor could one whose idea of a person was dominated by improper considerations of race, colour, class, sex and so on.

It is this which best deserves the term 'professional', though as this term is often used it may be misleading. We are talking about the teacher's attitude to his job, with particular reference to his *understanding* of it and what I have called his 'conscious seriousness' about it. To talk of 'caring' or 'concern' or 'commitment' may also mislead: we are not describing some 'brute' emotional stance, but the grasping and taking seriously of certain kinds of concepts and reasons for action. Briefly, he needs to know what education is and why it is important, and to acknowledge the relevance of all this for him. This involves a very high degree of clarity, freedom from prejudice and fantasy, and a certain amount of conceptual sophistication; much of this along the lines we have travelled earlier in this book. Without this, seriousness is impossible.

B. Personal knowledge. We are talking here of that particular kind or form of knowledge which concerns the intentions, purposes, emotions, moods, beliefs, etc. of *people*: that is, of people *qua* rational creatures, not *qua* physical entities, or *qua* statistical items. The teacher needs to know 'what is going on in the heads' of people; and for this a particular kind of understanding is required, mentioned earlier[14] and now quite well documented in educational literature,[15] which is by no means co-extensive with 'psychology' or 'sociology' as these terms are normally used. It is important to add that this knowledge must operate in various dimensions: the teacher needs knowledge of himself as well as of other people, and of his and their unconscious or semi-conscious as well as conscious minds. He must clearly have the concepts of various emotions at his fingertips, and be able to identify them in practice. These requirements are also more fully explained elsewhere.[16]

C. Knowledge of 'hard' facts and concepts. This heading, somewhat unclear as it stands, is intended to cover propositional knowledge not included under A or B. There is of course an area of blur or uncertainty here, inasmuch as the notion of a 'fact' runs through most or all disciplines or 'forms of knowledge'; for instance, there are 'facts' about people's sensations, about institutions, even 'about life'. But the notion of a fact or a 'hard' fact has, perhaps, its most natural home in the world of physical objects, and is connected with such terms as 'empirical'. The category here would include, for instance, knowing whether pupils come from poor or rich homes, or how far they have to travel to school; knowing the basic facts of one's own teaching-subject; knowing what materials, visual aids and other resources are available; knowing what a child's vocabulary is likely to be; knowing something about the powers of a local education authority, or the provisions of an Act of Parliament. These are 'hard' facts, inasmuch as they are not beset by much or any conceptual complexity, and do not depend on the more subtle (or at least different) procedures and insights of 'personal knowledge' or phenomenological clarification. However, of course a grasp of the relevant concepts is also involved (indeed, is inherent in the notion of a 'fact'); particularly important here will be those concepts which figure in the person's teaching-subject.

D. Know-how. This covers non-propositional knowledge, or what one is tempted to describe as the 'skill' or 'practice' element which is a necessary part of successful performance in many activities. Words like 'skill', 'competence', and 'ability' may all be used here. It is simply the case that many activities contain this element; not only writing on the blackboard, but also what one might roughly describe as 'managing' or 'organizing' a class, thinking on one's feet, 'projecting' oneself, 'getting on with' colleagues in the common room, parents, and so on. This is not to say that propositional knowledge may not be useful for improving one's competence for such tasks, but only to say that such knowledge is not enough: the need for some 'know-how' — what one might call 'facility' — remains.

E. Bringing-to-bear or 'motivation'. It would be possible (indeed, it is often in fact the case) that a person can possess the attitudes, knowledge, and abilities in A-D above, yet not actually deploy them adequately in practice. This is not a question of his lacking skill or experience or further knowledge, but rather of how deeply-rooted they are in his mind and personality. Thus he may have a fairly adequate conscious understanding and commitment, as in A, to what is central to 'being a teacher', but even though this is, so far as it goes, sincere and genuine, it may not be backed by enough emotional weight (so to speak). He may be subject to other desires, fears or 'pulls', conscious or unconscious, which prevent this understanding and commitment from being properly brought to bear on actual situations in school or elsewhere. Of course this (as with A-D) is a matter of degree, the degree of seriousness which the person has; how much, one might say, the person really wants or is mentally geared to the actual use of A-D; how much he really *cares* about it.

These categories[17] are all categories of characteristics or qualities which can to *some* extent be acquired by *learning* — that is, by various types of education, training, drill, 'experience', psychotherapeutic transactions, or whatever. More importantly, many of the characteristics — and, in my view, most of the most significant ones — cannot be acquired *except* by learning. By 'cannot', I do not refer to empirical difficulties, such as the absence of proper training techniques. There are clearly logical or conceptual reasons why understanding (and such understanding plays a central part in almost every one of the characteristics) has to come by learning, and that of a fairly sophisticated kind. It seems reasonable, therefore, to make these categories central to any notion of the preparation of teachers. What teachers need, on almost any account, will consist largely of characteristics involving understanding and knowledge; in a sense, the categories are simply an attempt to list these properly.

However, we have at this point to note two extra considerations. First, teachers may need other things besides learning-processes in order to acquire these characteristics. Certain preconditions may have to be established before a person can even begin to acquire the relevant knowledge, or may have to persist throughout the process of acquisition; for instance, a person might be too deaf, or alarmed, or hungry to be in a good position to acquire it — so that we would have to equip him with a deaf-aid or give him a tranquilliser or food, in order to make the learning possible or effective. Secondly, teachers may need *other* things besides these characteristics, things which cannot be acquired by learning at all: for instance, health, money, food, self-confidence, and so on. Giving them these things, whether because they were important *per se* or because they were important for the acquisition of our categorized characteristics, might perhaps count fairly as part of 'preparation' for 'being a teacher'.

In most practical cases, I think, these (non-learned) things would be relevant to institutions for teacher-preparation only insofar as they had to do with the person's general mental or psychological state. It is hard to draw clear dividing lines, but it seems plausible to say that, for instance, it is not such an institution's job to ensure that the person had enough vitamins or clothes, but that it is very much its job to do what it can to give him such things as confidence, successful relationships with other people, self-esteem, common sense, and so on. Some of these, in some measure, can of course be seen as learned, but a large part of many of them cannot. They necessitate rather certain types of social or psychological arrangements which ensure that the right things happen to the person.

These other needs form two categories, roughly distinguished as above, which we must add to our taxonomy so far:

F. Personal (psychological) preconditions for learning, and
G. Other personal (psychological) needs.

Particular items in these categories would require a whole book to discuss, but their importance for any complete taxonomy is surely clear.

Much more difficult than this set of categories is the problem of determining what other categories we need — the categories *in* which the teacher must have and display A-E above. Are we to talk here of roles, or tasks, or situations, or modes of operation, or what? Are there a number of 'jobs' which the teacher does, or a specified number of 'objectives' which he has? For instance, we could try to run a set of categories classifying the sort of thing the teacher would be doing, with headings like 'explaining', 'controlling', 'motivating', 'evaluating', and so on; or we could distinguish 'situations' by some criterion of social psychology, perhaps separating 'face-to-face' situations from others; or make rough pragmatic distinctions like 'inside the classroom' and 'outside the classroom'. Various writers have produced lists based, consciously or unconsciously, on such criteria: usually with disappointing results.

There is a degree of pressure here, which ought to be noted if not wholly yielded to, in the direction of abandoning the attempt at this point. One might not unreasonably say: 'Look, on any account the teacher will have an immense variety of 'roles', 'tasks', and so forth; and any attempt to categorize them is all the more dangerous inasmuch as (a) schools and society may change, creating new tasks and abolishing others, and (b) some of the tasks perhaps *ought* not to fall under the rubric of 'being a teacher', so that we might not want to endorse these by preparing teachers for them. What we should do is to give student teachers, so far as it is within our power, as much of characteristics A-E as we can — if you like, in a fairly 'pure' form: that is, without much reference to the actual *job* or jobs they will confront. For instance, we may try in a general way to improve their interpersonal perception (B), or their seriousness about learning (A and E), without trying specifically to prepare them for the perception of (say) teenage adolescents, or the learning of primary school children. We cannot in fact predict with much precision what their specific tasks will be — some students may not in fact be teachers at all. It is best to concentrate on these general characteristics, give the students a bit of practice and experience, and let *them* decide or see how their particular 'roles' and 'tasks' work out'.

I have a great deal of sympathy with this position, and my guess is that the preparation of teachers would indeed be much improved if this sort of approach were adopted; certainly it would be better than any *incompetent* attempt to specify tasks, roles, skills, etc., and gear the preparation to that. For such an attempt would almost certainly result (I think, is actually resulting in many institutions) in omitting or devaluing what is of general importance in A-E above; in particular, the characteristics of A, B and E, which are (roughly) to do with seriousness and understanding rather than 'facts' and 'skills'. Certainly any institution would be ill-advised to attempt such specification, and still worse advised to act on it, unless and until its members had thought properly about these other characteristics, and done their best to transmit them.

We continue, therefore, with even more hesitation than usual. Nevertheless it seems that we have to continue, because clearly these characteristics are to *some* degree specific to 'being a teacher'. One might hold, not without plausibility, that more or less any job closely concerned with people and some kind of learning and rational change — being a parson, a social worker, a guidance counsellor, a youth leader, a psychotherapist — required above all certain common characteristics; so that intending parsons, teachers, etc. could in principle be 'trained' or prepared together, without job distinctions, for a large part of the time. Nevertheless, there will (to say the least) be differences of emphasis; differences immediately apparent when we consider the — perhaps less important, but still important — sets of characteristics under C and D, the relevant factual knowledge and the relevant know-how.

When we consider listing the tasks (roles, modes of operation, etc.) involved in 'being a teacher', we shall of course be generally guided by some of the broad notions discussed earlier — knowing one's subject, caring for learning, caring for people *qua* learners and so on. Concentration on the gap between these general notions and specific situations or tasks suggests one important distinction, which may help us to bridge this gap without grotesque omissions or prejudices in favour of 'theory' or 'practice'. The distinction is simple: on some occasions the teacher can and should *think about* what he is doing, and on other occasions he *does* it. Now this distinction does not everywhere hold up: there is, for instance, obviously a clear sense in which, when teaching (say) English, he is both 'thinking about' what he is doing and doing it. But this situation can be roughly distinguished from situations in which he reflects on or discusses his particular lessons, or thinks about what it is to teach English, or about the home backgrounds of his pupils, or whatever. Similarly, it is one thing actually to control or keep order in a class during first period on Monday morning (although of course this involves thinking), and another to reflect on discipline and control either in this particular instance or more generally.

This more or less corresponds to a distinction between 'face-to-face' situations and others, though even this does not work exactly — for instance, a curricular working party or a staff discussion would be both 'face-to-face' and a situation in which reflection was expected. But as a sighting shot, at least, it may prove to be of some value. In 'face-to-face' situations of most types that a teacher meets — coping with pupils on the spot, mixing in the staff room, dealing with the headmaster or with parents — a large percentage of what he does will inevitably be automatic, 'reactive', 'off-the-cuff', or whatever it should properly be called. There is rarely time (particularly in the classroom) to reflect, even if there is in some sense time to think. On the other hand, there are plenty of occasions on which there is time; not only when preparing lessons or marking homework or deciding what to say to the headmaster, but in a much more general way — when he tries to achieve more understanding of what he is doing, and to adopt some attitude towards it.

With this distinction in mind, then, it may not be too dangerous to attempt an initial sketch of what 'being a teacher' seems centrally to entail, in terms of 'roles', 'tasks' or (better) 'things to do'. Something like the following might at least be a start:

1. *As a dispenser of knowledge.* The teacher acts thus most obviously in the classroom (a face-to-face situation), but also in more reflective situations: e.g. when preparing or evaluating work, taking or assisting in decisions about the curriculum, keeping up with his subject, and so on. Under these headings would come, for instance, such requirements as showing enthusiasm, knowing one's subject, familiarity with teaching-methods and visual aids, knowledge of the pupils, sophisticated understanding of curricular objectives, 'class management', and a number of 'skills' (writing on the blackboard, clear diction, 'projection', etc.).

2. *As a controller.* This task is different both from 1, above and from anything properly to be called 'relationships' or 'pastoral care' (3. below). The teacher has (not only in class, but most obviously there) the fairly specific job of controlling pupils and being obeyed by them, a job which would only lapse under highly unusual circumstances — I suppose, either an entirely voluntary system of pupil-attendance, or a

system including only obedient saints. It requires a number of personal characteristics and skills, very difficult to specify; together with some understanding of the notions of discipline and motivation.

3. *In other relationships.* Such 'relationships' may be sub-headed roughly as follows:
   (a) Relationships with pupils *qua* people ('pastoral care');
   (b) Relationships with colleagues (superiors, subordinates) in school;
   (c) Relationships with those outside the school (parents, LEAs, etc.) including some 'professional' relationships, i.e. as a member of a professional body, a teachers' union, etc.
Characteristics here obviously include some knowledge of 'hard' facts and a good deal of 'know-how', but would be mostly in the area of personal understanding and attitude. It is important to stress again that we are not talking only of face-to-face situations. For instance, a teacher has to reflect about the general desirability of (say) house- or tutor-group systems, what sort of contexts are satisfactory for informal contact with pupils, and so on.

Before going further, I must emphasize the dangers of giving any pre-eminence to any of these categories over others. Thus one temptation is to suppose that 1 is pre-eminent, perhaps because it is much easier to fill it out with all sorts of items, or perhaps because we might think of 2 and 3 as somehow more 'optional'. Clearly, teachers may shine more in one category than others, but somebody who was a complete failure in 2 or 3 — somebody, say, who could not control his pupils at all, and caused havoc by his relationships with pupils, parents, and colleagues — would be just as useless as somebody who could not dispense knowledge. Of course in practice, 1 is going to involve some competence in 2 and 3; one cannot dispense knowledge, or at least one would find it hard in most schools, without some ability to control and at least a minimal ability to relate to people. Nevertheless, the categories are in principle discrete; we could, as it were, score or rate teachers in each independently.

I shall now try the experiment of marrying up these two sets of categories, A-G and 1-3, in relation at least to *some* items; there is no pretence here of any attempt to 'make a list', much less an exhaustive list. By this operation I hope to show some of the difficulties of a full taxonomy, and also to arrive at some general conclusions about 'what the teacher needs' and how to minister to such needs. For this purpose the important thing is to see how the two sets of categories mesh together.

Suppose we start with 1, the teacher *qua* dispenser of knowledge, and put down some such item as 'caring for one's subject'. Then it is at once apparent that this involves category A, the teacher's basic attitude, and some of the 'motivation' in category E, but it must also involve knowledge of the facts and concepts of the subject (category C), which in the case of certain subjects in the humanities would also involve personal understanding (B) – everything, in fact, except 'know-how' (D). The item 'transmitting care for the subject' would involve all these and 'know-how' as well. 'Knowing one's pupils' clearly entails not just factual knowledge (C), but personal understanding (B): and it is hard to see how these could be of any significance unless the teacher thought it *important* to know his pupils – which brings in categories A and E again. Expounding or explaining a subject well might primarily involve a clear understanding of the subject's facts and concepts (C), but also 'know-how' (D), and an understanding of the audience (pupils) (B); and again, it is difficult to see how this could be entirely divorced from being committed to, or enthusiastic about, explaining – A and E yet again. Even marking or evaluating will entail, besides factual knowledge (C), some degree of understanding about evaluation in general and some degree of conscientiousness or willingness (A and E). In fact, the only things we can list which involve only one or two categories are skills like writing legibly on the blackboard, which is mostly 'know-how' (D) – though even here motivation may be as important as skill or ability.

This emerges even more clearly in 3, where almost any 'relationship' – perhaps particularly in areas commonly marked by 'pastoral care', 'counselling', etc. – is obviously going to involve more than just a knowledge of a few 'hard' facts and a few 'social skills'. Whether a person makes a good tutor or housemaster, or even relates well to pupils on a few informal occasions, will depend more on his attitudes, commitment and understanding (A, E and B) than anything else, even though a certain 'know-how' is also important. Even in 2, 'discipline' seems to be more a function of personality (confidence, sincerity, having nerve, being clear-headed, etc.) than anything else, however useful certain 'skills' or tricks may be.

It seems pretty clear from all this that we have only two possibilities. First, we can try to list 'items' under 1, 2 and 3 in something like the way exemplified above. We can say, as it were, 'As (1) a dispenser of knowledge the teacher will have to "do" the following "things": care for his subject, transmit such care, know his pupils, expound his subject, evaluate, write legibly on the blackboard . . . ' and so on, or 'As concerned with "relationships", he will have to be a housemaster, have meals with the pupils, "counsel" them, mix informally with them . . . '. The obvious difficulties with this procedure are (i) that we shall not be able to keep the items discrete (writing on the blackboard is *part of* transmitting care for a subject, or explaining), and (ii) that we shall pre-empt a set of 'roles' or 'tasks' unfairly; in 3, for instance, it is not at all clear that there is a *finite* number of *set* 'relationships' with pupils or colleagues, and any attempt to specify the 'best' or 'right' roles or tasks here would clearly be premature and dangerous. I do not say that it will be a waste of time to specify *some* items, as indeed we briefly did when describing categories 1, 2 and 3 on p.154 above. *Some* things are 'set' in this way: for instance, we might itemize (under 3) 'dealing with parents' and 'dealing with the head teacher'. But to specify particular tasks under those sub-headings would be to over-specify; not just because much depends on local conditions, but because much depends on how the teacher stands in relation to the very basic categories involving personality, attitude and understanding (A, B and E).

The other possibility, though I shall not attempt it here, is to adopt something like a 'case-study' approach. This is not strictly a taxonomic enterprise, but may nevertheless be useful. Given our three basic categories 1-3, and the earlier categories A-G, we could try to select typical cases or situations in which teachers would, or ought to, find themselves. We could then analyse these cases, fairly easily categorized under 1, 2 or 3, and see which of the categories A-E were involved. This procedure, though it could not be regarded as even attempting an exhaustive list, might nevertheless enable us to cover most of the ground. In particular we might be able to identify the most common causes of failure – in terms of categories A-E.

To link this approach prospectively with some conclusions I want to draw: the process might remind us of what happens when a supervisor visits a student on teaching-practice. Such a supervisor could, I think, roughly score or rate a student in categories 1, 2 and 3, with some appropriate sub-headings (e.g. those mentioned on p. 155). He could also, though with more difficulty, make some shot at guessing what was wrong with the student, in terms of categories A-E. What he could not do, in my view, is to operate an exhaustive checklist of 'tasks', or any checklist much fuller than the one given above. The student might, for instance, leave some children on their own for too long, or show some lack of insight when dealing with young girls, or just sound rather bored. These are not best classified as failures in tasks, although of course we can make it look as if they were by adding 'items' *ad hoc* ('proper management of individual pupil time', 'taking proper account of sex-differences', etc.). The supervisor would be much clearer if he tried to pin down failures a bit more precisely in terms of what the *student* lacked: that is, in terms of A-E.

Two things, I am sure, emerge from what we have just said. First, it looks as if what we have all along suspected is correct: namely, that 'being a good teacher' is much more a matter of basic attitude, personality and understanding than it is a matter of particular pieces of factual knowledge or 'know-how'. In almost any important 'task' that can be fairly defined, categories A, B and E enter. We are brought back, and very properly too, to the overriding importance of general notions like seriousness, love and personal understanding. Not that 'know-how' 'skills', relevant 'hard' facts and so on are not important, but their importance would be negligible, or much diminished, unless backed by these more significant general characteristics.

Secondly, it is clear (if only from the example of the teaching-practice supervisor) that we cannot even identify the particular faults or failure-types in student-teachers *unless we know them fairly intimately*. We can, indeed, sometimes identify failures in particular cases of 'skill' or 'hard' factual knowledge, either by observation or examination, but we cannot be at all clear whether a person lacks some basic conceptual understanding, or an understanding of people, or a proper care for learning, or whatever, in a great many situations unless we know him. Thus, if a particular lesson seems to go badly – if, as we intuitively say, there is 'nothing happening', 'no rapport', 'a lack of interest', etc. – we want to know whether the teacher (a) cannot really understand his pupils, even though he wants to, (b) does not want to understand them, (c) is not really interested in his subject, (d) lacks self-confidence, (e) cannot 'project' himself even though he would like to, (f) is just tired, and so forth. How could one begin to judge here, without some intimate knowledge?

These two points surely enforce on us the necessity of taking what was said at the end of the last chapter with much more seriousness than is customary. As a sighting shot in the direction of some practical conclusions, let us first say that we need a 'working group' as the central context or instrument of teacher-preparation; that is, a group of students sufficiently small to allow of close personal knowledge, sophisticated discussion and other activities which we might need, presumably 'supervised' (or 'led', or 'taught', or whatever verb may be most appropriate for the activity) by one or more members of staff.

It is important to distinguish different reasons which lead us to this conclusion. First, as we have already noted in Chapter 6 (p. 141 ff.), and immediately above, the most significant characteristics in our categories A–E (a) cannot be *identified* except via intimate personal knowledge; (b) cannot be *made known* to students; and (c) cannot *form the subject matter* of education or personal change, except in a context of trust and understanding. Secondly, the kind of (non-learned) preconditions in categories F and G – psychological and other needs which the student has – cannot be met or identified. In plainer English, we cannot even begin to prepare them seriously as people; and I am tempted to add that anyone who denied this could not have reflected sufficiently on what 'being a teacher' *was*.

I say 'in plainer English'; but it is very important to see (I hope, already to have seen during the course of our taxonomic wanderings) in what *specific respects* or categories this need has to be met. Most institutions and staff-members will cheerfully agree about the importance of 'personality', 'self-confidence', 'personal development', etc.; but, I think, find it difficult to institutionalize proper contexts for these vaguely-expressed aims, partly at least because they *are* vaguely expressed. We have to have a much firmer grasp of the crucial categories and sub-categories in A, B and E, if we are to do more than pay lip-service to this necessity. Only then can we begin to see the kind of concepts, relationships, and learning that is required.

A third argument must be brought in here, of a different but not wholly disconnected kind. It is clear from previous chapters that the kind of 'theory' — or let us more safely say, 'intellectual work' — that intending teachers need will not for the most part consist of 'facts', 'research findings', or 'theories' which allegedly represent the gaining of solid ground in 'educational theory'. We have seen that little or no such solid ground exists. In Chapter 5 we attempted to show that this should lead us, not to the abandonment of any serious 'theoretical' or 'intellectual' study, but rather to an alteration and intensification of it. We have to get students to take educational problems with much *more* intellectual seriousness, and to initiate them (as we there put it[18]) into whatever 'sophisticated ways of looking' that we can find, not the acquisition of supposed chunks of knowledge in 'the philosophy (psychology, sociology, etc.) of education'.

Now this is certainly very difficult (though there is no honest alternative); but it stands no chance of success whatever unless a close context of communication is used. For this even the word 'seminar' is too weak, and certainly mass lectures, the writing of long essays and theses and 'projects', and most of the usual apparatus of teacher-training are demonstrably not suitable vehicles for it. Here again, we need a closely-knit group, working over as long a period of time as is possible, intensively reflecting, and trying to sort out the problems. We are reminded, surely, of the 'teams' for the study of 'educational theory' delineated in Chapter 3. Most of the 'intellectual' ('theoretical') side of teacher-preparation will have to look something like the operation of these teams, though of course because of shortage of time and perhaps ability we cannot expect results of such a high standard. What matters is that the 'results' will have a better chance of being *real*; that the students will actually have thought critically and honestly, and in a methodologically appropriate way, about the problems.

To descend still further towards the practical has its dangers, because much will clearly depend on variables such as time, staff-student ratio, the particular identification of intending teachers (with one or more subjects, or with a certain age-group of children), and so on. Nevertheless, I think we can map out a rough practical stucture which, so far as I can see, seems to follow with something like conceptual necessity from what we have established so far.

It needs first to be said — and this is one reason why we spent so much time on it earlier in this book — that we must clear the decks, as it were, of a great deal that now goes on under the headings of 'theory' and 'method'. Once we have seen through the fantasy that there exists a large and solid body of 'theory' and 'method' which is intellectually respectable, we gain (a) the possibility of seeing a more reputable content which we could give our students instead, and (b) the more obviously practical advantage of saved effort and man-hours previously wasted under these headings. I am going to assume that we have cleared the decks completely, and are starting from scratch.

The prime working unit will be a group of, say 10–20 students. If the group is to operate effectively in the ways described above, we have to observe two principles. (1) A good deal of time must be spent initially by the group and its staff 'leader' ('supervisor', 'tutor', or whatever) in establishing trust. Much might be said about how to do this; it is perhaps enough to say here that the job is best done in an informal atmosphere, not always within the institution, and not just by talking (or 'social' activities); it works better if they undertake some simple and preferably physical tasks in common. (A naive but effective example: take them to visit a school or two in the country; camp out; climb a mountain or two; go to the pub in the evenings; run a few simple games.[19] (2) The students will need a lot of contact hours. The whole subject of our discussion is extremely complicated, and it is only too easy for even the more able students to get lost, or become intellectually autistic, in the morass of 'education'. This is true even of post-graduates: we are not dealing with a clear-cut discipline, which they might reasonably be expected to pursue clear-headedly for themselves in libraries or at home. They need a great deal of support. I should regard 20 hours a week as a minimum.

They need two main types of work or experience: a serious attempt to grapple intellectually with educational problems, and a serious attempt to understand (and so far as possible control or at least allow for) their own personalities. It may be unrealistic to suppose that the same tutor can do both, just as it is (more) unrealistic to think that 'courses on communication' or mass lectures in 'the philosophy (psychology, etc.) of education' can take care of these needs, without a working group having been properly established in the first place. We need, therefore, at least one tutor who is intellectually competent — or as competent as we can get — at the first general task, and one who is competent (more *qua* therapist than *qua* theorist) at the latter.

If either of these happens also to be expert at the student's specific teaching subject (assuming he has a specific one), so much the better. But this is not the chief criterion to use. For the first task, we need somebody who is of high general (theoretical) intelligence and ability, someone who at least takes seriously the task of 'making sense' of education and can help the students to do so. He may (no doubt will) know something of 'the philosophy (psychology, etc.) of education', but the important thing is that he is committed to truth and learning, and to the encouragement of these in the students; it is sufficient if he is aware of, and can lead students to, the (extremely few) books and articles that actually make sense and are intellectually helpful. For the second, we need above all somebody who is himself acceptable as a person — 'good at personal relationships' or 'good with students' convey false images, but may make the point clear: someone who generates trust and who is concerned that the students become as good teachers as it is within their power to be — if you like, some kind of 'parent-figure'.

In this second person's hands will be the business of adding to the student's preparation whatever cannot be achieved within the group. This might include such things as: any sound knowledge of 'method' worth looking at; familiarity with materials, visual aids, and so on; basic facts of a 'professional' kind (about the legal position of teachers, unions, etc.); and, most important of all, the various types of experience or 'practice', inside and outside schools, that are necessary. It will be to him that the students will chiefly look for any kind of *ad hoc* or long-term assistance, necessary experience, or piece of learning; and, provided always that the group is properly established, most of these (not all) can be achieved by the students themselves, under his guidance.

These two types of work (experience) are of course much more closely connected than I have made them appear here. As we have seen earlier in this book, the ability and/or the will to take the very difficult problems of education, or 'educational theory', with appropriate seriousness is closely bound up with factors of character or personality. This is why it is above all important to keep our eyes firmly fixed on the main aims. To put these briefly: we are after teachers who know their own subject, are serious about it and about learning in general, and understand pupils above the level of common sense. In order to achieve these aims, students will require an immense amount of support, confidence, the ability to tolerate doubt, and clear-headedness. These are central; the rest — even making further progress in their own subjects — is peripheral.

There is a great deal to be said, though I shall not say it here, about all kinds of problems which naturally arise. Most of these can be resolved only by getting clearer about the different contexts of communication which satisfy different items in our taxonomic sketch. In some cases this is easy: 'hard' facts can be mugged up from books or hand-outs, and certain skills can perhaps be gained by training or practice of various kinds. In others it is difficult. We have, for instance, to distinguish different contexts with different purposes, contexts now often confused and lumped together under headings like 'group dynamics' or 'discussion'. There will, for instance, be temptations to turn too much of the time into 'personal confrontations', or into purely intellectual discussion; the remedy is not to find a 'middle way', but to map out different ends served by different types of interchange. Some of the time, or much of it, we shall be wanting to satisfy those items which fall under some such general headings as 'educating the emotions' (and even within this category there are plenty of very *different* methods);[20] some of the time we shall be taking emotions and personalities for granted, and discussing intellectual problems without *ad hominem* implications.

A vast amount of work needs to be done here, some of which might certainly be described as 'trial and error', though most of which needs to take the form of a sterner intellectual effort to make sense of these contexts and aims. But I should not think it fair to describe these suggestions as 'experimental' or 'controversial'. It seems entirely clear, at least, that something like this sort of basis is required. If someone were to deny this, I should want to take him back to some of the ground I hope to have covered, and try to persuade him that the basis followed necessarily from a number of notions — 'being a teacher', 'being serious', 'trust', 'personal knowledge' and so on.

Some other general points can be added, more or less at random. First, our taxonomic sketch gives us some idea about what categories of things can sensibly be examined (by written papers). We should expect intending teachers (a) to know, and have readily available to memory, certain 'hard' facts about their professional tasks; (b) to know whatever 'theoretical' facts or findings are clearly valid, important, and above the level of common sense; and (c) to be able to show that they can think and criticize seriously and intelligently, again above the level of common sense, about educational problems. How many, and what, items there are in these categories is disputable. I have argued chiefly for the importance of (c), which consists not so much of a set of items but of the learning of a general approach ('making sense'); and plainly there are *some* important items in (a), if not very many. I am willing to be convinced that there are more items in (b) than I now think there are. But this does not matter here; the point is that these categories exist; they can and should be examined.

Ratings can be given under our categories A—G, in the departments 1—3, though obviously with more hesitation. Some independent assessment would presumably be needed, in case the group's supervisor (despite his intimate knowledge) is unjust or imperceptive. It seems entirely reasonable to allow some of this, at least, to be done by a supervisor or tutor on the staff of the school where the student does some practice teaching — particularly if the student is there long enough to become reasonably well known as a person to the supervisor.

This raises the well-known and much-discussed practical question of what sort of 'practical experience' is most desirable. It is not possible to give an across-the-board answer to this; much will depend on the particular student, and it is a decision which ought ideally to be left to the group supervisor. But the chances are that, in most cases, the student would learn most from (1) a long-term practice (a whole school term), in which his experience is as much like the real thing as possible, and he takes on long-term responsibilities; (2) a series of very rapid 'immersions' or 'experiences', with the rather different aim of getting him to see as many different kinds of schools, children, and general contexts of education as is desirable.

Such practice, however, will only be of minimal value unless it is used in the way described earlier: that is, in relation to the student's personality and attitudes. Some useful skills may be learned, and some disasters averted, but we need to give the students a kind of learning which they could not have gained for themselves anyway simply by taking an ordinary job as teachers. This brings us back at once to the kind of group work we have been talking about, and highlights the need for close and intimate knowledge. Without this, and without the seriousness and understanding which it may generate, institutions of teacher-preparation really have very little to offer. Most 'theory' and 'method work', as it stands, is rubbish, and most 'practice' gives the student little that he cannot better pick up for himself in a 'real' job. I cannot say that this task is easy, but it is at least a serious attempt.

The question may be raised as to *where* all this is to be done. It will be clear, I think, that most schools as they are could not do it effectively; not so much because of shortage of time, or because those who teach in them are necessarily less intellectually 'high-powered' than those who lecture in Colleges (Departments, etc.) of Education — a doubtful proposition — but rather because schools are, very properly, geared to practical education. Our arguments have suggested that, though to *some* extent becoming a good teacher involves practical experience, the process cannot reasonably be construed on anything like an 'apprentice' model; and the extent is not great enough for schools to be a natural home for the enterprise. Nor does it seem to me likely that the addition of 'professional tutors' would do much to change the situation; whatever the merits of this idea, it retains the false implication of the 'apprentice' model.

The current fashion in favour of this model has to be resisted, for reasons we have already given; and anyone who is prepared to say flatly, as one writer does, that 'Teacher training and teacher trainers need to be based in schools, *and in schools as they are*'[21] does not seem to me to display much understanding of what is implied by the concept of a good teacher. But this is not really an argument about institutional titles: to think that intending teachers should be prepared in Colleges (Departments, etc.) of Education *as they are* would be equally absurd. If, improbably, schools were to receive an influx of the right kind of 'theorists', and the work of student-teachers were arranged along the lines I have just sketched, one would not object just because they were prepared in an institution which was *called* 'a school' — and no doubt it would be convenient to have the 'practical' side of their preparation so close at hand.

The point is rather that we need institutions — be they called what they may — which are dedicated to the kind of programme outlined: which take the concept of a good teacher seriously, and seriously try to prepare teachers in these ways. A 'campus' which included both colleges for teacher-preparation and a variety of schools would obviously have some advantages here, but it is much more important that those preparing the teachers concentrate on the right elements, and are staffed with people who can do this well. My guess is that, in practice, they would have to spend most of their time in constructing viable and potent working groups of students, which would involve intensifying their internal institutional arrangements rather than constantly trying to make students 'relate to' or 'have practical experience of' what some call 'the real world' (*sc.*, I suppose, 'schools as they are', though anything more nightmarish and unsatisfactory than some schools as they are would be hard to find).

On the whole, then, I should be inclined to put my money on trying to improve existing institutions for teacher-preparation in this sort of intensive way. Certainly we have to resist a very general contemporary fashion for mixing up ('integrating') everything with everything else. This may make some people feel less restricted or isolated, or that we have successfully 'broken down artificial barriers'; and no doubt various types of mergers are administratively and economically convenient. But it rarely corresponds to any clear-headed idea of specific tasks — whether the task of teacher-preparation or any other.

As with our discussion of the research-teams in Chapter 3, this highly generalized sketch is apt to leave us with the question 'But what will these groups actually *do*? What will their work be *about*?' One can, of course, make brief sketches of a slighly more specific kind which go some way towards answering. Suppose, for instance, that we have a group of student-teachers who are going to be teachers of science. Then their 'theory' supervisor will at once appreciate that they need to be clear about what 'teaching science' *is*, about what is to *count as* 'teaching science'. What enterprise are we talking about when we talk of 'science' — as against the enterprises marked by 'history', 'sociology', 'politics', 'technology' and so on? Would a discussion of the morality of pollution count as 'teaching science'? Are we to aim at producing pupils who 'know a lot of science' (whatever that may mean), or pupils who are competent at 'scientific method'? What concepts, facts, procedures and structures of thought does 'science' actually consist of?

The 'theory' supervisor will be aware (following the principles laid down in this book, or his own common sense) that this is the *first* thing which these students need to do. For how could one be a serious teacher of science without proper understanding of, and care for, science itself? It will then, but only then, be both possible and important for them to consider whatever may be usefully looked at under the description of 'methods' of teaching science, and to be given some 'practice' or 'experience' of such teaching. For, unless one was clear about 'teaching science' in the first place, how could one possibly know *what* 'methods' or 'practice' or 'experience' was relevant? We have first to know what it is we want these things to be *about*. The supervisor might then bring to the students' attention various other tasks, perhaps not properly described as 'educational', which they may be called on to perform — if not, strictly speaking, as teachers of science, then at least in their actual jobs: for instance, training sheet-metal workers, giving pupils some idea about how to repair their cars, and so on. There would naturally be a lot of discussion about possible overlaps in seeking to achieve these various goals, or how the goals themselves are to be weighed against each other, and also about whatever psychologists and sociologists can tell us (perhaps not much) which bears on 'teaching science'.

It is fairly plain, I think, from even this brief sketch that the bulk of the work will have to take place in a group of the kind described earlier. This does not of course imply that other contexts may not sometimes, perhaps even often, be appropriate. Thus, there are obviously quite a few points of a general kind about what it is to teach X (where X is any subject, as here the subject 'science') which a philosopher might want to make in a mass lecture: so too with other disciplines. Conversely, individual tuition may often be useful if somebody is being left behind by the group, or is so far ahead of it that he needs special attention. But the centrally important business of what I have called 'making sense' — in this case, making sense of their teaching-subject — clearly requires a great deal of intense and prolonged group- or seminar-work of this sort. We might even hazard the view that groups for 'theory' should be subject-based: both because they will have a common background and commitment, and because we have seen that the desire and ability to understand and transmit one's teaching-subject is crucial to the notion of being a teacher.

Or suppose we are dealing with the students' 'images' or 'presentations' of themselves to their pupils and colleagues. The 'personal' supervisor will quickly become aware — particularly if he gives them some practical experience right at the beginning of the course — that one student is too anxious to please, another apt to be sarcastic and perhaps a trifle bitter, another in too much of a hurry, and so on. What does the group do? Well, we shall probably not want to plunge too hastily into 'personal confrontations' or the more potent kind of 'T-groups'; but at least we can start by pointing out these facts to each other in a fairly calm and objective way — the group-members should be able to trust each other enough for that. Then, perhaps, in some cases the student will need only some practice or training in 'social skills' — he can be trained to stand up straight, speak clearly and slowly, possibly even to control his tendencies to sarcasm. Perhaps also, by fairly impersonal or even 'academic' methods, the group could usefully consider various emotions or 'images' in the abstract, with the help of literature and visual aids. All this would at least enable them to *know* what their 'images' were, to perceive their own merits and deficiencies, to be able to admit to them, and perhaps even to control or inhibit some of them.

One could also go further. Arguably certain techniques and contexts — drama or role-playing, for instance, or some types of group encounters — may help to make this self-knowledge more 'real', more fully understood and perhaps thereby more able to be controlled. If we all 'have a thing about' some psychic area marked by such terms as 'authority' or 'dependence' or whatever, which is more or less bound to handicap our judgement and behaviour as teachers, then we can explore that in common: not only with our intellects (though not abandoning these), but by allowing the emotions to flow rather more freely than most contexts permit. What are we (or is he or she, or am I) rebelling against, or frightened of, or defensive about? What are the real, perhaps unconscious, targets of these feelings? How have the feelings seeped not only into our classroom behaviour and behaviour towards colleagues or superiors, but also into our 'theoretical' opinions on morals, politics, and (doubtless) education? The tutor here has to help the students to *connect* what they learn from these (very varied) contexts of inquiry: otherwise they will merely have a set of 'experiences' without having *learned* anything.

Here too it is clear — despite the absurd brevity of such general sketches — that we confront a task which essentially involves working in fairly close-knit groups. Again, it is quite possible that mass lectures on (say) certain emotions particularly relevant to 'being a teacher', or on how various fantasies have affected, and still affect, 'educational theory', would be useful: as would 'one-to-one' tutorials (if 'tutorials' is the right word). There are advantages, as well as some disadvantages, in group work rather than a one-to-one situation: even if we could provide each student-teacher with a dedicated and qualified psychoanalyst this would not necessarily be desirable. At the same time, we have to recognize the limitation on the *kind* of things that a mass lecture can do. We have, I suppose (if only because of shortages of staff and time), to steer a sort of middle course between a thorough-going psycho-analysis on the one hand, and the handing-out of generalized information by means of lectures or books on the other.

Nevertheless, we have to admit (with eagerness rather than reluctance) that at present there is a sense in which we do *not* know what the work of these groups should 'be about', except in these general terms. The reasons for this relate to what has been said earlier in this book about our general ignorance of the whole subject of education. To put these in a way more specific to this particular context: an obvious first step, in trying to draw up anything like a 'course' or 'syllabus' for our 'theory' groups, would be to make a list of those topics which seem to have special relevance to 'being a teacher'. Thus we might list 'discipline', 'motivation', 'concepts of education', 'the relevance of internal school structures to learning', and so on, together, of course (as we have just exemplified), with a consideration of the students' teaching-subject. But the truth is that we are not yet clear, in any detail, about what worthwhile contributions to these topics actually exist. This means that we can only cling to a generalized idea about *procedure*, rather than feel safe in specifying *content*: which is why I have throughout been stressing the former rather than the latter.

In the case of almost any of these topics — say, 'motivation',[22] or 'discipline',[23] or even the 'teaching science' case outlined above — I should firmly maintain (a) that we were often not even conceptually ('philosophically') clear what we were talking *about*; (b) that even where we are clear in this way, we are not clear whether there are any valid 'facts' or 'findings' derived from the empirical disciplines which are of direct importance to teachers. All one can honestly do in this situation is to try to initiate the procedure by making some conceptual sketches, so that at least we do not remain stuck in the confusion of (a);[24] but even then almost all the work remains to be done. This does not mean that we ought not to list relevant topics in this way — of course we ought, otherwise we cannot even start. Nor does it mean that a lot of current psychology, sociology, etc. may not be in *some* degree educationally relevant to these topics and to teachers — of course it *may* be. What it means is that we cannot tell in advance how a serious consideration of these topics would work out in practice; and to pretend that we can by filling each of them full of detailed content is simply dishonest.

The same goes, even more obviously, for the 'personal' groups. All we really have here is the vague, if obviously important and correct, idea that we ought to do something about the students' attitudes, personalities, 'self-presentations', and so on. Again, all sorts of somewhat more specific ideas are current, including those mentioned above — 'T-groups', role-playing, academic study of particular emotions, and so on, but quite obviously we are still in a muddle about this. The whole business of 'educating the emotions' or 'personal relationships' is both conceptually and empirically very obscure.[25] Once more, this is not a reason for total inaction, or even for undue caution: we shall not be likely to find out much unless we try things in practice, whilst simultaneously using our brains to clear up the confusion and avoiding any semi-religious dedication to one particular 'method'. But it is a reason for supposing that we cannot *now* specify the content of 'courses' or 'discussions' or 'encounters' with any certainty about detail. Indeed we cannot even be sure that such terms ('courses', etc.) are the ones which best fit what we shall actually want to do. We are not yet clear about the many different kinds of interactions which may be useful, and about the different rules which should govern them.

I am very much aware that this descent into the practical has been brief, and will seem to many disappointing because over-generalized. However, this is deliberate. It is not just that (i) some of the working-out of this in detail generates difficult problems which require fuller discussion, nor that (ii) much depends on local conditions. It is rather that (iii) little or nothing, at this stage, would be gained if I (or anyone else) were to spell out more practical details, even if I felt wholly competent to do so. For everything turns on whether the staff of an institution *sees the point*: I mean, on whether they are convinced, for the right reasons, that this is the *sort* of thing that needs to be done. If they are convinced, and have a thorough understanding of the background which leads to such conviction, I should be perfectly sincere in saying that they, not I or anyone else, would be best placed to decide the details: naturally with whatever help or advice they can get (chiefly, one would hope, from clinical or social psychologists of good standing).

It would be somewhat disingenuous to say this, however, without referring once more to the vicious circle mentioned earlier. To say blithely that 'everything turns on whether the staff of an institution sees the point' is all very well, but the ground covered by 'seeing the point' is pretty wide. 'Certainly', it might be said, 'if — a big "if" — all or most of the staff were clear about the methodological foundations of the study of education, and about what was needed for the preparation of teachers; if they could shake free from fashion and fantasy; if (to speak more practically) they could identify even a handful of books which talked sense about education and could be used with their student groups, and agreed on consigning the rest either to the wastepaper basket or the remoter library shelves: if, in general, they were both clear about and in accord with the general principles laid down — always assuming that you have laid them down correctly — then, indeed, this would be possible. But then we should be doing it already. What you suggest implies a whole new generation of lecturers and tutors and so on, with quite different training and background. You ask for the impossible'.

Well, of course there is *something* in this, and one must beware of utopian fantasies. But any implication that there are *no* moves that can profitably be made in the required direction would stem from some fantasy of despair or denial. One could, for instance, fall back on the defence that these principles could, at least, be borne in mind (by those who understand and accept them) when selecting new staff, or when we have the chance of creating new institutions or altering old ones. But I do not think we need retreat to such a last-ditch defence. In Part I, where we were specifically concerned with the study of education, we saw[26] that a start could be made just by identifying one or two people of the right kind and forming them into something like a 'team'; that we could make some serious attempt on the subject without waiting for a 'whole new generation' of educational theorists or totally dismantling our existing institutions. Are there not some similar moves which we can make in respect of teacher-preparation?

I think the answer to this is of the form 'Yes, if . . . ', and that the 'if' here hypothesizes not so much any profound or subtle intellectual understanding on the part of the staff, but rather a certain willingness and honesty. It is not absolutely necessary — I am not clear that it is even entirely desirable — that the 'personal supervisors' of student groups, as we may call them, should have been through lengthy courses in 'group dynamics', 'counselling', and so on, nor that the 'intellectual' or 'theory supervisors' should thoroughly understand all the philosophical, psychological, sociological and other angles on (say) 'motivation', 'the curriculum', or whatever topics might be thought important for the preparation of teachers. What seems to be needed is the acceptance of a certain kind of responsibility: the responsibility of, in the first case, trying to understand, help and prepare the students as people who are going to be teachers, and in the second of helping them to approach problems about education with honesty and seriousness.

This is primarily a question of attitude: 'seeing the point' certainly involves a minimum of understanding — the understanding that these tasks are central and necessary — but it need not involve much more than that. To gain this understanding and the attitude that should go with it, the first thing is to *see through* a great deal that we now do — to perceive it as non-serious, sustained by inertia or misconception. One does not need a treble First in Educational Methodology to appreciate, for instance, the unreality of behaviouristic psychology as applied to education; the irrelevance of much sociology; the absurdity of listing 'teaching skills' in the way described earlier; the difference between reproducing the orthodox views of 'philosophers of education' and actually approaching conceptual problems for oneself with honesty and diligence. Most of the points I have made in this book are, I sincerely believe, entirely obvious: obvious, that is, not only to 'philosophers' or 'methodologists' but to anyone who is prepared to look at things with a straight eye and a clear head.

Just as (I believe[27]) teachers in schools, if given a good deal more power and responsibility over groups of children in their care, would respond more than adequately in controlling and caring for them as people and as learners, so the staff members of institutions concerned with teacher-preparation are not too stupid or too unwilling to take on this kind of responsibility. Many would, perhaps, prefer it to the constant multiplication of courses, lectures, seminars, workshops, committee meetings and so on that at present dominate their lives: just as many teachers might prefer a wider responsibility for their pupils than the responsibility of keeping them somehow engaged by a succession of periods from nine to four from Mondays to Fridays. To take responsibility as a 'personal' or 'theory' supervisor along these lines would itself encourage the staff to develop their own personal and theoretical understanding — and, more important, to develop it for themselves and their student groups, rather than accepting it as handed down from on high by supposed 'authorities' in educational theory or the preparation of teachers.

Anyone who adopted this attitude would not, I am sure, find himself at all short of ideas for teacher-preparation that would have an immediate and practical value. To take just one example of this, it seems quite clear that student teachers could derive much benefit from reading works of fiction which are both good in themselves and cast some special light on children and education. There are a fair number of possible candidates here, and obviously we should want to argue about them — or perhaps profit from the advice of a literary critic or other expert. My point is that anyone who was really serious about wanting to develop his own or another's insight into the minds of children could hardly fail to explore this area more thoroughly than we now do. If someone said that he was desperately anxious to 'get the feel' of, say, what went on in the minds of boys of preparatory school age, but that he had no interest in Golding's *Lord of The Flies*,[28] we should have doubts about his sincerity. Exactly what books, for what student-teachers, would emerge triumphantly as 'set texts' is not at issue here: the crux is that both tutors and students must take the approach seriously if they are to count as serious about their jobs.

Another possible reaction moves in an opposite direction. 'But you are preaching to the converted: we *have* seen the point of all this, and just this is precisely what we are trying to do in our College (Department, Institute, etc.). We spend a lot of time with our students in group work and seminars, we have 'personal tutors', we are very much concerned about the general 'atmosphere' of the College, and so on. At least we are moving in this sort of direction, and our difficulties are shortage of staff, time and money (apart from being constantly messed around by politicians and administrators) not lack of clarity'. Of course I accept this reaction also, in some degree, and I do not at all want to suggest that these ideas are strikingly original, or have not been in the minds of many of my colleagues in the business. But I should still claim that things are often impeded by a certain lack of clarity or perhaps of determination.

Most institutions have been driven (usually by no fault of their own) to acquire the appearance of intellectual or academic respectability, and inevitably, over the last few decades, this has meant attaching themselves deferentially to the supposed 'authorities'. If (as I have argued throughout) these 'authorities' and their institutionalization in educational theory and teacher-preparation are in fact largely bogus, this cannot but have had an unfortunate effect. Very often the staff themselves are much better placed to prepare teachers on their own initiative than by such deference. Some staffs, perhaps, lack the clarity and nerve to 'go it alone' (and are, of course, under pressure from various central bodies which are trying to control 'academic standards' by methods more appropriate to the control of factory-production or industrial waste). Others again may have the nerve – indeed, are often quite virulent about 'the authorities' – but tend too often to opt out of the serious *intellectual* problems altogether; sometimes preferring some 'counter-culture', or quasi-political or 'social' set of 'values', to the hard work of 'making sense'. Again, I am not saying that many such institutions do not do a remarkably good job under extremely difficult conditions, nor that there are not plenty of good ideas floating around. But most would, I think, agree that there is a long way to go.

All this brings us back, for the last time, to the notion of seriousness and the willingness to 'make sense' of these and similar problems; and I want to end by stressing one central point. Naturally I am persuaded that the particular suggestions here advanced, however tentative and over-generalized, are correct. But if I have failed in presenting them as compelling, I hope at least that the reader will have gained some insight into what I regard as much more important than any specific conclusions — namely, a certain method of working which I take to be the only appropriate one. In trying to 'make sense', we have to start with certain points which can be regarded as 'necessary', in a broadly conceptual way; and then move, slowly and carefully, towards filling these out empirically, until we have got something which is both 'practical' and *makes* sense. The only alternative to such a procedure, I think, is the continuous advancement of new 'theories' of teacher-preparation, which are vitiated from the start because they are conceptually blind or naive. As I have been trying to show throughout this book, we have suffered long enough from such methods in education generally: problems about the preparation of teachers offer only one example out of many. It is about time we started being serious.

Notes

1. Bloom (1956); cf. PER, p. 104 ff.
2. See under Hollins (1973): but the work is the product of many hands.
3. *ibid.*, p. 11. The 'needs' approach is a non-starter, for fairly obvious reasons: see, e.g., Hirst and Peters (1970), p. 32ff.
4. Hollins (1973), p. 13.
5. p. 17.
6. *loc. cit.*
7. p. 21.
8. p. 23 ff.
9. pp. 32–33.
10. See Hirst and Peters (1970), p. 60 ff. (with references): Hirst (1974).
11. Hollins (1973), p. 5.
12. *ibid.*, p. 7, for a list of participants.
13. Wilson (1973).
14. p. 56 ff.
15. See Mischel (1971) and (1974), Wilson (1971), Harré and Secord (1972), etc.
16. See Wilson (1973), p. 51 ff.; also Wilson (1971), p. 99 ff.
17. Some clear terminology or notation is required to mark these

five logically distinguishable 'things' (characteristics, sets of characteristics, 'components', 'constituents', or whatever). One might follow a notation used for moral education, and use PHIL for the basic attitude (A), EMP for personal knowledge (B), GIG(1) for knowledge of 'hard' facts (C), GIG(2) for 'know-how' (D), and KRAT for bringing-to-bear or 'motivation' (E). I do not of course think this notation is *per se* important; but any preferred notation must be clear, in a way that (I think) general terms like 'concern', 'sense of responsibility', 'professional attitude', 'competence' and so forth are not clear.

   18. p. 127.
   19. See Wilson (1972), Part 4.
   20. Wilson (1971), p. 241 ff.
   21. Harry Rée in the *Times Higher Education Supplement* for 2.5.75, p. 17 (my italics).
   22. See PER, *ad loc.*
   23. p. 42.
   24. PER *passim*.
   25. Wilson (1971).
   26. p. 84 ff.
   27. Wilson (1972), Part 4.
   28. I give one of the most popular candidates. Others might include Tolstoy's *Childhood, Boyhood and Youth*; Bronte's *The Professor*; Walpole's *Jeremy* books; L.P. Hartley's *Eustace and Hilda* trilogy; Julian Fane's *Morning*; Angus **Wilson's** *Late Call.*

A NOTE ON 'MAKING SENSE' AND 'DEFINING TERMS'

Almost all of this book rests on the notion that, in the vast proportion of work undertaken in educational theory or teacher-preparation, we have to start by what I have described as 'making sense' of the topic: in effect, by pursuing the question 'What is to *count as* X?' (where X may be 'intelligent', 'good at English', 'morally educated', 'literate', or any other phrase that might form the title for discussion or research). Elsewhere I have tried[1] — very briefly — to explain this procedure, and opposed it to other procedures such as making 'operational definitions' or 'reaching a general consensus'.

I must frankly say that unless and until the nature and importance of this are properly understood by those concerned with education there is not, in my judgement, much hope of any solid progress in the subject; so I must do my best to explain it more fully, particularly since reactions to the idea (in seminars, conferences and so on where it has come up for discussion), persuade me that some people find it extremely hard to grasp. Some, not all: to many it seems, as it were, the most obvious thing in the world that we should undertake such a procedure. They will say things like 'But of course we've got to be clear what we're talking about before we go any further', or 'Obviously we have to get the concepts sorted out first'; whilst others will say 'But how can one answer be better than another?', 'Don't all definitions simply represent prevailing social values?', and other remarks which suggest that the nature of the procedure is not sufficiently clear to them. It may be that 'philosophers' find it obvious, and some of those who represent empirical disciplines regard it as either impossible or dangerous; but in the remarks which follow, I prefer not to associate the procedure with any particular 'discipline'. As I see it, the task is one which is demanded, of any person, by common sense and seriousness. I hope that the following points will at least clear up one or two misconceptions.

1. First, there may be *some* cases in which this procedure need only be brief, or perhaps in which it can be skipped altogether. Phrases like 'passing O Level', 'being able to spell "cat" ', or 'scoring over 100 on such-and-such an IQ test' do not require it, because we all know well enough how we would verify the content of such phrases. 'Being able to spell "cat" ' might require some discussion: we would want to know, for instance, whether a subject counts as 'able to spell "cat" ' if he only spells it right sometimes, whether we would accept his oral enunciation of the letters C—A—T or insist that he can actually write 'cat' accurately, and so on. But if we compare phrases like 'knowing a lot of Latin', 'being literate', and 'being intelligent', it is obvious that we are a

good deal less clear. How much is 'a lot'? Does 'Latin' include knowledge of Roman baths, or just Latin grammar? What are we going to count as 'literate'? When we call someone 'intelligent', do we include or exclude the idea of being quick, or the idea of having a good memory? These and many more questions have to be answered before we know what we are talking about.

There is no formula which will enable us to know *how much* time or effort we need to spend in this way (even though, as in the examples above, some cases seem even *prima facie* more likely to cause trouble than others). All we can do is to operate the procedure, and stop it only when we have adequate answers (for 'adequate', see 2 below). There is a fantasy here, I think, that *all* cases of operating the procedure must be so 'philosophically' complicated that we shall never reach this point, but spend all our valuable research time 'arguing about words'. This is certainly not so. Given a minimal understanding of what the procedure is, some degree of enthusiasm and intelligence, and a satisfactory context of debate, there are a great many cases that can be cleared up quickly enough.

2. That the procedure can be *effective* — that it can result in more or less 'adequate' conclusions — is, in a way, something which we already know very well. It is testified by our ability to recognize cases where the work is *not* adequate. We recognize these by noticing, as it were intuitively, that a person seems to be ignorant or heedless of what is entailed by a particular word or concept. Thus to assess 'happy marriage' by how often the partners call each other 'darling' is ridiculous, because the assessment is not *part of what is meant by* 'happy marriage' — one can say 'Darling!' with love to one's spouse (which might be part of the concept, and is at least a candidate for good evidence), or one can say 'Darling!!!' with fury or gritting one's teeth; the number of times the word is used does not constitute evidence in this case. To verify or collect evidence for X involves having a proper grasp of what 'X' means — for otherwise how could one know that it was evidence *for X*?

Hence, whatever we may think about the possibilities of reaching some final, definitive and totally perfect 'conclusion' or 'definition' of any phrase, we do at least recognize that the job can be done more or less well or badly. We recognize *mistakes*. If someone said that 'being happily married' *meant* 'calling each other "darling" ', or that 'being educated in morality' *meant* 'obeying the Führer', or that 'being intelligent' *meant* 'getting right answers to such-and-such tests', we should say that he was in error. This, at least, is not what these phrases mean. There is, then, some possibility of doing better, of giving at least a *more* 'adequate' account.

3. By what right, then, do we call these 'mistakes' or stigmatize them as 'inadequate'? The natural answer is to say 'Because this simply isn't what we mean by "happy", "intelligent", etc. Look at the dictionary, or note how average English speakers use the word, and you'll see that it's different'. This is a correct answer, but it does not imply that there is something divinely authoritative about 'ordinary language' or the 'we' who use it. What it implies is simply that people have an interest in particular phenomena, often in the same phenomena: they can communicate with each other, and describe these (roughly) under titles like 'happy', 'intelligent' and so on. In order to pin the phenomena down (so that we can discuss them or do research on them better), we have to get clearer about them; and we do this by saying, in effect, 'Well, we've said we're interested in "happy marriage" or "intelligence", and we must know roughly. what we mean (since we all use the same word): so let's now make it less rough and more precise by considering *exactly* what phenomena we're going to allow under this heading'. Just because we do use the same words, in the vast proportion of cases we should in fact agree what phenomena to allow — once we undertake the procedure and start considering cases. We have, as it were, a kind of unconscious awareness of what ground the word covers, which needs to be made conscious and explicit.

Suppose now somebody says 'But that's just *your* use of "happy", "intelligent", etc. Why should I go along with it? Maybe it's also the use of your society or social group, but why should I go along with that either? I shall mean something different by these terms, if I want to'. The first point here, perhaps, is that such a person may be mistaken about *his own* use of the term — which is very likely to be similar to that of others who have learned the same language. But the right way to answer him is something like: 'Yes, of course, you can make words cover whatever ground you like (though, if you're departing from what we normally mean by them, it would be nice if you told us what *you're* now going to mean). You can use the letters "h,a,p,p,y" to stand for anything you want. But the important question is what *phenomena* we're talking about. We're talking about those normally covered by the word "happy", as that word is used by English speakers. If you want to talk (do research) about some other phenomena, perhaps covered by your (peculiar) use of "happy", well, of course that is also perfectly all right, but it would be to some extent a different topic'.

Discussion of anything is only possible by sharing, in some degree, a common language. The person who wants to use words outside what is thus shared makes a 'mistake' only in the sense that, *if* he seems to be giving an account of ground normally covered by (say) 'happy', the account is wrong. If, on the other hand, he proposes to change the meaning of the word, we shall have to re-negotiate the language to that extent. We could, I suppose, use 'happy' to mean what we now mean by 'miserable', and 'miserable' to mean what we now mean by 'happy'. As long as we all agreed to do this, and were clear about it, no harm would be done. But there are reasons why we have to be extremely careful here, and why it is usually better — certainly to start with — if we stick to normal usage so far as possible.

4. These reasons are not, again, to the effect that this usage is sacrosanct or perfect. The point is rather that we do in fact have quite a sophisticated 'ordinary language' which (like all natural languages) has the immense advantages of being able to describe the world of phenomena and make distinctions in it, in a way which is understood by those who speak the language. In fact this is a considerable achievement. Much of the clarity we need is *already enshrined in* our language, if only we will take its terms and distinctions seriously: it represents important interests and concerns which it has been evolved to describe and identify. We can of course refine it and add to it, when we are clear enough, by subtler distinctions or 'technical terms', but it already contains resources which we have to use.[2]

Thus it is not the words *in themselves* of 'ordinary language' which are important, but the fact that they mark a set of concepts and distinctions which map out the phenomena in which we are interested. For, unsurprisingly, the identification of human interests and concerns goes hand in hand with the process of marking these by language. There may be times when we want to say 'I can see something here for which there is no word, and which I want to investigate' (though the process of making sure that there is no word takes time): then, perhaps, we borrow a word from French, or some other natural language, which covers this new ground, or perhaps we actually invent a word (possibly a 'technical term'). But these are rare occurrences, and when we really do need to do this, we can nearly always see quite clearly why we need to do so. Maybe we have discovered a new atomic particle, or a new species of flower; here we should not *expect* there to be existing words. But the position in education, or indeed the study of human beings generally, is not that we are already quite clear about distinctions made in ordinary language and can move on to new ground: it is rather that we are not clear — not, at least, consciously and explicitly clear — about the concepts and distinctions that we already have.

5. It is, I hope, by now clear enough that no question of 'value-judgements' arises here, and it ought also to be clear how far we need to bring in the notion of a 'consensus', or 'definition' reached by 'agreement'. Obviously in one sense we need 'agreement': that is, if six people (or sixty) are studying X, they must agree about what is to

count as X, otherwise they will be in a muddle and perhaps studying different things. But, equally obviously, 'agreement' or 'consensus' by itself is not enough. There might be, in some social group, a 'consensus' that X meant such-and-such, but the consensus might be *wrong*.

That it is possible to talk of a 'wrong' or 'mistaken' consensus here is apparent from what I have already said about the nature of the task. An example may clarify this and some previous points. Suppose we start with some such phrase as 'educated in religion'; 'we', let us suppose, are a study group in the UK or USA or some English speaking country. The points emerge as follows:

(1) If we ask what 'educated in religion' might mean — that is, if we ask for a paraphrase or translation — then there will be better and worse answers, the criterion being simply how these words, placed in conjunction as they are, function in English. Translations like 'being indoctrinated with Christian values', 'learning about our cultural heritage', etc. would be poor.

(2) If somebody says 'Well, what we want to do is to inculcate the Christian religion' one would naturally reply 'That may be good or bad, but then you must do it under a new research title: not now "education in religion", but (perhaps) "making people into Christians" — that is, if you are using words in their usual senses'. He may now say:

(a) 'Very well, I'll change the title', and that is legitimate, but leaves the original interest — whatever was covered by 'education in religion' — still to be researched:

(b) 'But what I and my group — the "consensus" of which I am part — are going to mean by "educated in religion" *is* "making people into Christians" ': and here we should say that, despite the 'consensus', that was still not what the words meant. Perhaps the members of the group had paid insufficient attention to (obvious) points, e.g. that 'religion' doesn't equal 'Christianity'. If the person or group still wishes to stick to what they 'are going to mean' by it, then we should say that what they are proposing is a special use of language, different from what is normal. This again is not particularly wicked; but, first, it seems cumbersome and unnecessary — if they want to make people into Christians they might as well say so, in so many words; and secondly, the substance of the original topic — whatever is actually meant by 'educated in religion' — remains untouched.

6. From this example, and from others in the main text of this book, it

seems plausible to say that the difficulties experienced with this procedure are largely of our own making. It is not that we undertake the procedure, but find it in itself very hard (though that may also sometimes be true): it is rather that we do not undertake it at all. There are various ways of opting out of it. One is just to act arbitrarily, by fiat, and say 'Well, without further ado, I (or my group) am going to mean such-and-such by X'. A second is to pick whatever meaning seems easiest to handle on other grounds: 'operational definitions' are like this, and fail unless they are also *adequate* definitions. A third is to *accept* some account of the meaning handed down by some authority — 'society', 'teachers', or some 'consensus' — uncritically: that is, without bothering to consider whether what is accepted is in fact correct.

This last option (and perhaps the other also), may be supported by the fantasy that 'there is no such thing as "correct" anyway — it all depends on your culture (society, etc.)'. This misses the whole notion of there being a certain kind of truth, connected indeed with the use of words but not just 'about words', which stands on its own feet: the kind of truth that Socrates was trying to get at in the Platonic dialogues. As I have said, we know quite well in our saner moments — if only by reflecting on extreme cases — that this is not so: that there is a real job here, which can be done well or badly: that not just *anything* can reasonably be counted as 'happy', 'intelligent', 'educated in religion', or whatever; in brief, that we have to know what we are talking about. The particular words or phrases which we may use for this procedure — 'making sense', 'defining terms', 'clarifying concepts', 'phenomenology', even perhaps 'philosophy' — do not matter. What matters is that we have a clear idea of the task, and of its necessity.

7. It seems clear that, in practice, people (or some people) find this difficult, not — or certainly not chiefly — because of any intellectual complexity, but for various psychological reasons which I do not claim to understand fully. To say this should not sound superior or patronizing: it applies, in various degrees, to other enterprises besides this one. Some people (I am one) find it difficult to adopt the right sort of *attitude* to the requirements of literary or artistic criticism: others may find difficulty with science, or history, or practically anything. This is not, or not only, because we are stupid, but because we are in some sense allergic. But at least we can avoid thinking that such enterprises are useless or 'irrelevant' just because we cannot understand them: as I, for instance, might be tempted to write off literary criticism as a waste of time, 'just playing with words', 'an invention of Leavis and his cronies', or whatever. In this case, images clustering round terms like 'Oxford philosophers', 'logical positivism', 'linguistic philosophy' and others hinder rather than help understanding. Perhaps only the kind of

trust, seriousness, and willingness to abandon vested interests of all sorts that I have tried to describe earlier in this book can improve matters.

Notes

1. PER *passim*.
2. Harré and Secord (1972).

REFERENCES

ARGYLE, M. (1967) *The Psychology of Interpersonal Behaviour* London: Penguin Books.

BERNE, E. (1966) *Games People Play*. London: Deutsch.

BLOOM, B.S. *et al.* (1956) *Taxonomy of Educational Objectives*. New York: McKay Co., Inc.

BRUNER, J.S. (1960) *The Process of Education* Cambridge, Mass.: Harvard University Press.

BRUNER, J.S. (1966) *Towards a Theory of Instruction*. Cambridge, Mass: Harvard University Press.

DEARDEN, R.F. (ed.) (1972) *Education and the Development of Reason*, London: Routledge.

DOWNIE, R.S. *et al.* (1974) *Education and Personal Relationships*. London: Methuen.

ENTWISTLE, N.J. *et al.* (1973) *The Nature of Educational Research*. Bletchley: Open University Press.

FODOR, J.A. (1968) *Psychological Explanation*. New York: Random House.

GOLDMAN, R. (1964) *Religious Thinking from Childhood to Adolescence*. London: Routledge.

HAMLYN, D.W. (1967) 'Logical and Psychological Aspects of Learning' In: *The Concept of Education*, PETERS, R.S. (ed.). London: Routledge.

HARRÉ, R. and SECORD, P.F. (1972) *The Explanation of Social Behaviour*. Oxford: Blackwell.

HIGHET, G. (1956) *The Art of Teaching*, London: Methuen.

HIRST, P.H. (1967) 'Logical and Psychological Aspects of Teaching a Subject'. In: PETERS, R.S. (ed.). *The Concept of Education* London: Routledge.

HIRST, P.H. (1972) 'The Nature of Educational Theory'. In: *Proceedings of the Philosophy of Education Society of Great Britain*, Vol. VI, No. 1, January. Oxford: Blackwell.

HIRST, P.H. (1974) *Knowledge and the Curriculum*. London: Routledge.

HIRST, P.H. and PETERS, R.S. (1970) *The Logic of Education*. London: Routledge.

HOLLINS, T. *et al.* (1973) *The Objectives of Teacher Education*. Slough: NFER.

LAMBERT, R. and MILLHAM, S. (1968) *The Hothouse Society*. London: Weidenfeld and Nicholson.

LOMAX, D.E. (ed.). (1973) *The Education of Teachers in Britain*. London: Wiley.

MCPHAIL, P. *et al.* (1972) *Moral Education in the Secondary School*. London: Longman.

MISCHEL, T. (ed.) (1971) *Cognitive Development and Epistemology.* New York: Academic Press.

MISCHEL, T. (ed.) (1974) *Understanding Other Persons.* Oxford: Blackwell.

MOORE, T.W. (1974) *Educational Theory: An Introduction.* London: Routledge.

O'CONNOR, D.J. (1972) 'The Nature of Educational Theory'. In: *Proceedings of the Philosophy of Education Society of Great Britain,* Vol. VI, No. 1, January, Oxford: Blackwell.

PETERS, R.S. (1958) *The Concept of Motivation.* London: Routledge.

PETERS, R.S. (1966) *Ethics and Education.* London: Allen and Unwin.

PETERS, R.S. (1968) 'Theory and Practice in Teacher Training'. In: *Trends in Education,* No. 9, January. London: HMSO.

PETERS, R.S. (ed.) (1973) *The Philosophy of Education.* Oxford: Oxford University Press.

RYAN, A. (ed.) (1973) *The Philosophy of Social Explanation.* Oxford: Oxford University Press.

SEABORNE, M.V.J. (1972) 'History of Education'. In: WOODS, R.G. (ed.). *Education and its Disciplines,* London: University of London Press.

SUGARMAN, B.N. (1973) *The School and Moral Development.* London: Croom Helm.

TAYLOR, W. (ed.) (1969) *Towards a Policy for the Education of Teachers.* London: Butterworth.

TIBBLE, J.W. (ed.) (1966) *The Study of Education.* London: Routledge.

TIBBLE, J.W. (ed.) (1971) *The Future of Teacher Education.* London: Routledge.

WARNOCK, G.J. (1971) *The Object of Morality.* London: Methuen.

WILSON, J. (1971) *Education in Religion and the Emotions.* London: Heinemann.

WILSON, J. (1972) *Practical Methods of Moral Education.* London: Heinemann.

WILSON J. (1973) *The Assessment of Morality.* Slough: NFER.

WINCH, P. (1958) *The Idea of a Social Science.* London: Routledge.

WINCH, P. (1959) 'Nature and Convention'. In: *Proceedings of the Aristotelian Society,* 1958/59.

YATES, A.J. (ed.) (1972) *Current Problems in Teacher Education.* Hamburg: UNESCO.

370.71
W 749

115 489

DATE

370.71
W 749
                                    115489

AUTHOR
Wilson, John

TITLE
Educational Theory...

DATE LOANED	BORROWER'S NAME		DATE RETURNED
MAR 8	Antoine Brisbon	Freshman	MAR 23 94
	247-617-9665		

DEMCO